GENDER

GENDER:

An Ethnomethodological Approach

SUZANNE J. KESSLER

WENDY McKENNA

THE UNIVERSITY OF CHICAGO PRESS
Chicago & London

The University of Chicago Press, Chicago 60637
The University of Chicago Press, Ltd., London

01 00 99 98 97 96 95 94 93 92   5 6 7 8 9 10

Library of Congress Cataloging in Publication Data

Kessler, Suzanne J., 1946–
    Gender: an ethnomethodological approach.

    Reprint. Originally published: New York : Wiley, c1978.
    Bibliography: p.
    Includes indexes.
    1. Sex role.   2. Attribution (Social psychology)
3. Sex change.   4. Ethnomethodology.   I. McKenna, Wendy,
1945–   . II. Title.
HQ1075.K47   1985   305.3   84-28139
ISBN 0-226-43206-8 (paper)

To Our Parents

Esther Luttan Balsam and Sidney Balsam

and

Emanuel Goldenberg

and to the Memory of

Mollie Ruben Goldenberg

PREFACE

It is self evident that man seeks to justify (explain metaphysically) or mythologize only those natural phenomena whose irreducible character he refuses to concede. Hence, the fact that mankind has always mythologized —most recently in scientific jargon—the existence of two sexes, is *prima facie* evidence that he refuses to accept this as an *irreducible* fact, whose understanding can only be impeded by the assumption that it is something to be "explained," i.e., to be justified metaphysically in the form of "Just So Stories" for college graduates. [Devereux, 1967, p. 178. Italics in original.]

Many people would agree with Devereux that the sexes do not need to be explained and that, in fact, trying to explain the existence of two sexes can get in the way of understanding. However, to take the sexes for granted, to treat the existence of two sexes as an irreducible fact, obscures each individual's responsibility for creating the world in which she/he lives. Our refusal to concede the "irreducible character" of "natural phenomena," rather than leading us to a "Just So Story," has resulted in an alternative theoretical framework which will give the reader a new way to understand the existence of two sexes. What does it mean to say that the existence of two sexes is an "irreducible fact"? In this book we will show that this "irreducible fact" is a product of social interaction in everyday life and that gender in everyday life provides the basis for all scientific work on gender and sex.

Our theoretical position is that gender is a social construction, that a world of two "sexes" is a result of the socially shared, taken-for-granted methods which members use to construct reality. This position is grounded in the ethnomethodological perspective (explained more fully in Chapter 1) which asserts that the "irreducible facts" in which members of a group believe are given their sense of objectivity and reality through the course of social interaction. Our position is contained in the book as a totality, rather than in our treatment of any particular topic. We believe that the book, as a whole, will make that perspective meaningful to readers. However, for those who do not find themselves compatible with phenomenologically based theories, this book can be read as a set of questions about gender which are amenable to traditional scientific methodologies.

Over the last 70 years there has accumulated a large body of research and theory on gender, dealing with such issues as how children develop a sense of themselves as either female or male, how they learn to generalize these labels to others, and how they are socialized to behave in accordance with the gender to which they have been assigned. However, regardless of the importance given to social factors, it has been generally taken for granted that *fundamentally* gender is a consequence of a biological blueprint.

Recently, an increasing number of studies have provided evidence that in atypical cases, where biological factors conflict with social and psychological ones (e.g., transsexualism), these influences override biology in determining gender identity and influencing gender role. It appears that the relative contributions of social/psychological and biological factors are similar in typical cases as well. Even for those who do treat gender as largely social, however, the question of how people are classified as male and female in the first place is not asked.

In our society, the decision that one makes as to whether someone is a woman or a man is probably necessary, and is certainly crucial for all future interactions and for giving meaning to the other person's behavior. For the most part, classifying people as women or men is a deceptively easy procedure. For this reason, all theoretical and empirical work in the area of gender has taken this process for granted. Occasionally, however, we do see people whose gender is not obvious (e.g., teenagers in "unisex" clothes). It is then that we begin to consciously look for gender cues as to what they "really" are. What do these cues consist of? In asking people how they tell men from women, their answer almost always includes "genitals." But, since in initial interactions genitals are rarely available for inspection, this clearly is not the evidence actually used (except by doctors or midwives assigning gender at birth).

In thinking about those nonobvious cases where gender cannot be taken for granted, it becomes possible to see that there is an ongoing process, certain procedures to follow (e.g., look for "male" cues) which result in a decision about the person's gender. From our perspective, what happens in exceptional cases is merely an example of what also happens in nonexceptional cases, a conclusion that follows from the ethnomethodologist's decision not to treat gender as an "irreducible fact." The process by which one classifies another as female or male we have called the "gender attribution process."

The general objective of this book is to review previous scientific work on gender, to demonstrate how scientific treatment of gender is grounded in the everyday gender attribution process, and to present some findings on gender attribution in everyday life. Our research, which we report in Chapters 4, 5, and 6, is not meant to "prove" anything. The use of statistical tests to determine the significance of data and to prove hypotheses is grounded in a belief that data reflects an objective reality, independent of members' methods for constructing that reality. In the ethnomethodological tradition, we offer our findings as demonstrations of the points we are talking about, suggesting that given our basic assumptions, there are new ways to collect and interpret information on what it means to be female or male.

For those concerned with theory and research on gender, the process of gender attribution has important implications. At a time when social scientists are beginning to reconsider their models of male and female functioning, it is crucial that attention be devoted to answering questions about the social uses of the terms "male" and "female" and what they reflect about the bases of traditional models as well as the more recent ones being developed.

Subjects in all research on human behavior are either females or males. For a psychologist to ask the question, "How are girls different from boys?" overlooks the fact that in order to ask the question, she or he must already know what girls and boys are. Before we can ask questions about gender differences, similarities, and development, gender must be attributed. Until now, the process of gender attribution has been taken for granted by most natural and social scientists, but scientists would not be able to talk about differences in the first place unless they knew how to classify the incumbents of the two categories which they are comparing. And we will never be able to say how this is done by making more and more detailed lists of differentiating factors (e.g., males are more competitive, females admit to a wider range of feelings), because in order to make these lists we must have already differentiated.

We are not in any way taking issue with the adequacy or inadequacy of this body of research. We do not expect social scientists to refrain from any further research on gender differences until we have explicated the gender attribution process for them. Nor are we saying that social scientists do not know how to attribute gender or have neglected to do so. On the contrary, gender as it is constructed by psychologists, sociologists, anthropologists, and biologists, is grounded in the everyday gender attribution process. What we *are* saying is that we can show how it is that they can do what they are doing. This will be the work of our book.

In addition, there are some specific issues of importance to both lay-persons and social scientists which, while not a major focus of this book, are related to it. One is the implications of the trend toward more overlapping gender roles. Does the gender attribution process give any clues as to whether blurring the distinctions between male and female roles will have consequences for the individual or society? We will deal with this issue in detail in the last chapter.

Another issue in which an increasing amount of popular and scientific interest has been shown over the last 10 years is transsexualism. The existence of a group of people who want their physical characteristics changed so that these may be congruent with the gender they believe themselves to be, has raised critical questions about what a man or a woman really is. Transsexualism suggests that being a (social) female or a (social) male is not dependent on one's original physical structure. Nor is it dependent on performing specific gender role behaviors, as indicated by recent reviews of research which conclude that there are few "sex" differences in behavior. What then is being a female or male dependent on? We have learned a great deal from transsexuals about what is important in gender attribution, since "passing" as a male or a female is a constant concern for them. The specifics of what we have learned from transsexuals are dealt with in Chapter 5. On a practical level, transsexuals who are concerned with learning what they can, and in some cases must, do in order to be taken by others as men or women might find this material useful.

An overview of the book will give the reader an idea of those areas on which we have chosen to focus.

Chapter 1, *The primacy of gender attribution*, introduces our framework for talking about gender. We offer definitions of gender-related terms, and discuss why gender attribution is primary to an understanding of what it means to be a woman or a man.

Chapter 2, *Cross-cultural perspectives on gender*, focuses on the implications of the lack of universal criteria for distinguishing males from females. The discussion is centered on the institution of the "berdache" in other cultures and what that suggests about the social construction of gender.

Chapter 3, *Biology and gender*, reviews the normal development of females and males from conception, and discusses the contribution of specific biological factors to the devolpment of the components of gender. This is followed by an analysis of the relationship between biology and gender as a social construction, demonstrating that it is the latter which provides the foundation for the former.

Chapter 4, *Developmental aspects of gender*, is a critique and review of what psychoanalytic, social learning, and cognitive-developmental theories have asserted about the development of gender identity and gender role. Our own research on gender attribution by children is reported in the context of a discussion of the development of gender attribution processes as children learn the "rules" (methods) for seeing a world of two genders.

Chapter 5, *Gender construction in everyday life: Transsexualism*, demonstrates that members of a group produce, in concrete situations, a sense of gender as objective fact through an examination of our own, as well as others', interviews with transsexuals, since transsexuals offer the richest source of information on gender as a social construction. The *Appendix* is a detailed illustration of one particular transsexual's construction of gender. We have excerpted material from letters she sent us during the period of her transition from male to female. Following the letters we comment on those features of her experience that correspond to points we make in Chapter 5.

The book concludes with Chapter 6, *Toward a theory of gender*. Here we present the results of a study on the relative contribution of physical gender characteristics to gender attribution, and offer a schema for understanding what it means to be female or male. We argue that the constitutive belief that there are two genders not only produces the idea of gender role, but also creates a sense that there is a physical dichotomy. We conclude with the implications for science and everyday life of seeing gender as a social construction.

Suzanne J. Kessler
Wendy McKenna

Bronxville, New York
Purchase, New York
October, 1977

ACKNOWLEDGMENTS

The ideas presented in this book began to take shape in our last years of graduate school and were developed more fully when, at the State University of New York, College at Purchase, we taught a course on the psychology of gender. We want to thank the students in that class for serving as sounding boards for our ideas, providing important feedback, and collecting some initial data.

Although they may not all be aware of how much they contributed to our intellectual commitment to ethnomethodology, there are four individuals to whom we are especially indebted: Peter McHugh, Stanley Milgram, Harold Garfinkel, and Lindsey Churchill.

Readers of drafts of chapters, including Sybil Barten, Florence Denmark, Mary Edwards, Nancy Foner, Peter Swerdloff, and some anonymous reviewers, made useful comments. Howard Ehrlichman, who offered valuable criticisms of the entire manuscript, as well as consistent encouragement, has our respect and affection.

Mary Honan, Molly Peter, Lori Schreiner, Jesse Solomon, Debbie Winston, and Kathy Gunst conscientiously collected the data reported in Chapters 4 and 6, and Darcie Boyd skillfully drew the overlays. Lauren Wood typed the final manuscript quickly and carefully.

The research reported in Chapters 4, 5, and 6 was partially supported by Faculty Research Grant #33–7110–A from the State University of New York Research Foundation.

Charles Ihlenfeld, June Reinisch, Naomi Smith, and Zelda Supplee kindly provided us with introductions to some of the transsexuals we interviewed. The transsexuals cannot, of course, be named, but we acknowledge their generous cooperation, especially Rachel, our friend, who consented to have her letters and comments appear in the Appendix.

We want to thank Rose and Herbert Rubin and Harold and Bonnie Klue for providing hospitable environments that minimized the pain of writing the final manuscript.

Bill McKenna has a unique place in these acknowledgments. Not only did he provide frequent insights into phenomonology, but he never ceased believing that, even though we were "only" psychologists, we could make a contribution to the study of gender.

This book is truly a collaboration. The order of authorship is alphabetical, and were it not for the constraints of linear reality, the authors would be listed and indexed circularly. Any attempt to determine which parts of the book should be attributed to which author would be futile.

S. J. K.
W. McK.

CONTENTS

GENDER

1

INTRODUCTION:
THE PRIMACY OF
GENDER ATTRIBUTION

As we go about our daily lives, we assume that every human being is either a male or a female. We make this assumption for everyone who ever lived and for every future human being. Most people would admit that the cultural trappings of males and females have varied over place and time, but that nevertheless, there is something essentially male and something essentially female. It is a fact that someone is a man or a woman, just as it is a fact that the result of a coin toss is either heads or tails, and we can easily decide the case by looking. Of course, the coin may be worn and we may have to inspect it very closely. Analogously, a person may not clearly be one gender or the other. But just as we assume that we can determine "heads" or "tails" by detailed inspection (rather than concluding that the coin has no heads or tails), we assume that we can do the same with a person's gender. Not even with biologically "mixed" individuals do we conclude that they are neither female nor male. Biologists may assert that a hermaphrodite's gender is not clear, but in everyday life ultimately some criteria can (and will) be found by which each one is placed in one of two mutually exclusive gender categories along with everyone else. Even the biologist would say that hermaphrodites are a combination of the two existing categories, rather than a third gender category.

If we ask by what criteria a person might classify someone as being either male or female, the answers appear to be so self-evident as to make the question trivial. But consider a list of items that differentiate females from males. There are none that *always and without exception* are true of only one gender. No behavioral characteristic (e.g., crying or physical aggression) is always present or never present for one gender. Neither can physical characteristics—either visible (e.g., beards), unexposed (e.g., genitals), or normally unexamined (e.g., gonads)—always differentiate the genders. According to Webster's dictionary (1973), males are those who beget young by performing the fertilization function in generation, and females are those who bear the young. Although this distinction may be useful for strictly biological considerations it is of little value in everyday encounters. The item "sperm-producer" may only appear on lists that describe men, but men are not always sperm-producers, and, in fact, not all sperm-producers are men. A male-to-female transsexual, prior to surgery, can be socially a woman, though still potentially (or actually) capable of spermatogenesis.

Substitute any item for "sperm-producer," and the statement will still be true. Penises, vaginas, beards, breasts, and so on in any combination are not *conclusive* evidence for categorizing someone as either a man or a woman in everyday life. Preoperative transsexuals can be men with vaginas or women with penises, and, of course, the bearded lady is still a lady.

We could make probability statements like most people with beards are men, or most people with breasts, high voices, vaginas, and long fingernails are women, but when we meet someone, the "decision"[1] that we make as to whether that person is a man or a woman is not stated in terms of probabilities. They are either one or the other, zero or 100 percent. We may modify our decision ("He is an effeminate man"), but we do not usually qualify it ("Maybe he is a man"). If we should have to qualify it, then we seek further information until the qualification is no longer necessary.

For example, we might look closely at the person's cheeks for signs of beard stubble, or we might even ask someone if they know the gender of the person in question. We make a *gender attribution*,[2] that is we decide whether someone is male or female, every time we see a new person. The way we decide has seemed so obvious that the process has been virtually ignored in theory and research. With the exception of two suggestive works, one by Garfinkel (1967) and one by Birdwhistell (1970), no one has overtly raised the possibility that gender attribution is more than a simple inspection process. In contrast, we assert that not only is gender attribution far from a simple inspection process, but *gender attribution forms the foundation for understanding other components of gender*, such as gender role (behaving like a female or male) and gender identity (feeling like a female or male).

This perspective forms the core of our book. In this chapter we lay the groundwork for this perspective by detailing the existence, importance, and primacy of the gender attribution process to both science and everyday life, and by raising questions about the inevitability of the gender *dichotomy*. Our final goal is not only to demonstrate that gender attribution is primary, but to delineate, as much as possible, both the necessary conditions for presenting oneself as female or male and the necessary rules for making sense out of such a presentation. Both of these are crucial in deciding a person's gender. We argue that the question of what it means to be a male or a female is merely another way of asking how one *decides* whether another is male or female.

Gender very clearly pervades everyday life. Not only *can* gender be attributed to most things,[3] but there are certain objects (i.e., people) to which gender apparently *must* be attributed. The immediate concern with doing this when we meet an ambiguous person illustrates the pervasive, taken-for-granted character of the gender attribution process. Over and over again, transsexuals who were in the process of changing from one gender to the other, emphasized how uneasy people seemed to be interacting with them, until some sort of decision had been made about whether they were male or female—a decision that was often reached by asking them, "What are you?" Contrary to our expectations when we began researching gender, there does not seem to be a prohibition against asking certain people what gender they are, especially if it is done in a joking manner. However, those who were asked reported feeling embarrassed and uncomfortable, indicating that something had gone wrong with the interaction, that a "violation" of unstated rules had occurred (Garfinkel, 1967).

Ambiguous cases make the dichotomous nature of the gender attribution process extremely salient. In our culture, a person is *either* male *or* female. The gender dichotomy raises many questions. If Leslie is not male, is Leslie then necessarily female? Do we decide what someone is, or what they are not? This suggests that an analysis of "conditions of failure" (see Wittgenstein, 1953) might be appropriate in describing the gender attribution process. In other words, it may be that a "female" attribution is made when it is impossible to see the other person as a male, and vice versa. Whether attributions are made on the basis of the presence or the absence of cues is something we pursue.

The essential question we are asking is: How is a social reality where there are two, and only two, genders constructed?[4] Is the process the same for everyone, regardless of the person's reason for making the attribution? That is, does the biologist (for example) in making a gender attribution do the same thing when in the laboratory as at a party? While it is important to understand scientific criteria for telling males from females, for the most part we will analyze gender attribution from the point of view of the "naive" person, that is, all of us when we are using our common sense understandings of everyday life. Even scientists must ultimately rely on their own common sense knowledge. In fact, ". . . any scientific understanding of human action . . . must begin with and be built upon an understanding of the everyday life of the members performing those actions" (Douglas, 1970, p. 11).

Our warrant for asking the question: How is a reality constructed where there are two genders? comes from the theoretical assumptions underlying the ethnomethodological approach. We can only present the briefest summary of these assumptions here, and in doing so we emphasize those that are most relevant to our particular interests in this book. [Readers are referred to Mehan and Wood (1975) for a comprehensive treatment of ethnomethodology.]

In our everyday lives and, for most of us, in our professional lives, we proceed on the basis of certain "unquestionable axioms" about the world which Mehan and Wood (1975) call "incorrigible propositions" and others (e.g., Garfinkel, 1967) call the "natural attitude." The most basic incorrigible proposition is the belief that the world exists independently of our presence, and that objects have an independent reality and a constant identity. For example, suppose you look out your window and see a rose in the garden, but when you go out to pick it, you cannot find it. You do not assume that there was a rose but now it has disappeared, nor do you assume that the rose turned into something else. You keep looking until you either find the rose or figure out what conditions existed to make you think there was a rose. Perhaps it was the configuration of shadows, or you might notice a butterfly which you mistook for a rose. By interpreting the results of your search in this way, you thereby verify the reality and constancy of objects like roses and butterflies, and validate that they exist independently of your interaction with them.

Not only the rose itself, but all its characteristics (color, fragrance, etc.) have this factual status. And what is true of roses is also true of people. In the natural attitude, there is reality and constancy to qualities like race, age, social class, and, of course, gender, which exist independently of any particular example of the quality. It is a fact that there are two genders; each person is a mere example of one of them; and the task of the scientist is to describe, as accurately as possible, the constant characteristics that define male and female, for all people and for all time. This is reality in Western society.

By holding these beliefs as incorrigible propositions, we view other ways of seeing the world, other sets of beliefs about what reality is, as "incorrect," "primitive," or "misinformed." We know, for a fact, that people do not turn into birds, and if a Yaqui shaman thinks that they do (Castanada, 1968), he is wrong. His belief probably stems from "distorted" perceptions which occur under the influence of drugs. The shaman thinks that some plants carry the power to make him into a bird. According to Western reality, the *real* truth is that the plants are hallucenogenic and cause a physiological reaction which results in a distorted perception of the world.

Ethnomethodologists challenge this interpretation of the shaman's behavior, not by asserting that we are wrong in seeing his actions in this way, but rather by contending that the shaman's interpretation is as real for him as ours is for us. Indeed, both realities are created in the same way—through methodical (i.e., orderly, systematic, and thus recoverable), interactional work which creates and sustains whatever reality one is living, be it that of the shaman, the "man in the street," the biologist, or any other reality one could name.

In order to see the world as the ethnomethodologist does, it is necessary to ask the following questions: Suppose that we treat our belief in constancy and independent existences as just that, beliefs. Then suppose that, for the purpose of discovering what happens, we temporarily suspend our belief in these propositions. How does the world look then? This technique, known as "bracketing," is a method suggested by phenomenologists (e.g., Husserl, 1931). If we bracket the natural attitude, the constancy and independent existence of objects disappears, and we are left only with particular, concrete situations.

From this perspective we can then assert that, somehow, in each situation, a sense of "objective facts" which transcend the situation is produced. Thus we have grounds for asking the ethnomethodological question: What are the methodological ways by which members of a group produce, in each particular situation, this sense of external, constant, objective facts which have their own independent existences, not contingent on any concrete interaction? Applied to our interests in this book, the question becomes: How, in any interaction, is a sense of the reality of a world of two, and only two, genders constructed? How do we "do" gender attributions? That is, what kinds of rules do we apply to what kinds of displays, such that in every concrete instance we produce a sense that there are *only* men and women, and that this is an objective fact, not dependent on the particular instance.

Gender attribution is a complex, interactive process involving the person making the attribution and the person she/he is making the attribution about. (This distinction between attributor and other should not obscure the fact that in most interactions participants are simultaneously being both.) The process results in the "obvious" fact of the other being either male or female. On the one hand, the other person presents her or himself in such a way as to convey the proper cues to the person making the attribution. The presentation, however, cannot be reduced to concrete items that one might list as differentiating women from men. Most of the cues people assume play a role in the attribution process are really *post hoc* constructions. One transsexual we talked with put it well when he[5] said, "Gender is an anchor, and once people decide what you are they interpret everything you do in light of that."

The second factor in the interaction are the rules (methods) that the person doing the attributing uses for assessing these cues. These rules are not as simple as learned probabilities, such as people with beards are usually men. They are rules that construct for us a world of two genders, such that to say, "I knew he was a man because he had a beard" makes sense in the first place. In other words, "because he had a beard" is understood as a reason because of our methods for constructing "male" and "female". In another reality, "I knew he was a man because he carried a bow and arrow" might be more sensible (see Chapter 2). Part of being a socialized member of a group is knowing the rules for giving acceptable evidence for categorizing. In our culture, physical evidence is the most acceptable reason. Giving a reason is not the same, though, as making the categorization in the first place. We will argue that the fact of seeing two physical genders is as much of a socially constructed dichotomy as everything else.

Much of our work in this book consists of examining the treatment of gender in the social and biological sciences, in light of our perspective that the reality of gender is a social construction. Because of the confusion in terminology which pervades the literature on gender and gender differences, we must define certain terms, which, while overlapping in many ways with previous definitions, are not necessarily identical to them. Where appropriate we indicate how our meanings differ from those of others. One of the major differences is that our definitions are mutually exclusive and consequently narrower than those in current usage.

GENDER AND SEX

The term "gender" has traditionally been used to designate psychological, social, and cultural aspects of maleness and femaleness. Stoller (1968), for example, defines gender as "the amount of masculinity or femininity found in a person" (p. 9). "Sex" generally designates the biological components of maleness and femaleness. Given this perspective, there are two sexes, male and female, and, correspondingly, two genders, masculine and feminine.

We will use gender, rather than sex, even when referring to those aspects of being a woman (girl) or man (boy) that have traditionally been viewed as biological. This will serve to emphasize our position that the element of social construction is primary in all aspects of being female or male, particularly when the term we use seems awkward (e.g., gender chromosomes). The word "sex" will be used only for references to reproductive and love-making activities and, at times, in reference to purely physical characteristics when explicating the position of someone else who uses this word.

The cultural/biological distinction traditionally associated with the usage of gender versus sex is a technical one, applicable to scientists in the laboratory and some textbooks, but little else. Gender is a word which, until very recently, was rarely used by people in everyday life, and even in technical writings the two terms are often used interchangeably and confusingly. For example, in a study reporting the treatment of young boys who exhibit feminine behavior, the authors use "cross-gender behavior" and "sex-role deviation" to describe the same phenomenon (Rekers and Lovaas, 1974). Another illustration of the lack of rigor in the use of terms is from Rosenberg and Sutton-Smith (1972): "By sex we mean the gender (male or female) with which the child is born" (p. 1). If "gender" and "sex" mean different things, then they ought not to be used interchangeably; if they mean the same thing, then the cultural/biological distinction may be open to question.

This brief discussion of terminology is important for what it reveals about the underlying ways of constructing our ideas of gender/sex. Although some social scientists are questioning the concepts of masculinity and femininity as mutually exclusive (e.g., Bem, 1974), gender, as the cultural expression of all that is feminine or masculine in a person, is still treated as dichotomous. It may be easier today to see that particular individuals have both masculine and feminine features, but we still generally treat gender as dichotomous and most certainly treat sex that way. Even those who study biologically "mixed" persons (e.g., someone born with XY chromosomes and a vagina) prefer to treat those persons as special cases of dichotomous sex. "There are, with few exceptions, two sexes, male and female," states Stoller (1968, p. 9), and although his and others' work is to a large extent based on these "few exceptions," he does not consider sex to be overlapping in the way gender may be.

Gender Assignment

Gender assignment is a special case of gender attribution which occurs only once—at birth. The cues for this special case are quite clear. The person making the assignment (doctor, midwife, etc.) inspects the genitals, categorizes them as vagina or penis, and announces the gender on the basis of that inspection. Vagina means the neonate is assigned the gender label "girl," and penis means the neonate is assigned the gender label "boy." Others have a right to check the assignment if they wish, but, again, genitals are all that is looked at. In cases where the genitals are ambiguous, assignment is withheld until other criteria are inspected. In our culture, these consist of the various biological components of gender discussed in Chapter 3. If there has been a "mistake," a reassignment can be, and often is, made. However, since reassignment involves so much more than mere genital inspection, and, in fact, the "proper" physical genitals may not be there, "reassignment" is a misleading term. Reassignment could imply that the child had been one gender and is now the other, when actually the child is seen by everyone as having been the "new" gender all along. "Gender reconstruction" would be a better term, since the child's history, as short as it may have been, must now be reinterpreted. For example, what was originally seen as an empty scrotum might later be seen as always having been misformed labia. This suggests that "gender assignment" and "gender construction" may be synonomous.

Gender Identity

Gender identity refers to an individual's own feeling of whether she or he is a woman or a man, or a girl or a boy. In essence gender identity is self-attribution of gender. Rules for self-attribution are not necessarily the same as rules for attributing gender to others, although it is as necessary to make a definite self-attribution as it is to make unqualified gender attributions about others. One young man who lived as a female for three years did not have a female gender identity. Even though successful at passing, he finally could not tolerate the conflict between his male gender identity and the female gender attributions which were consistently made to him. It was necessary to make a choice, and he decided to be a male. To him this meant not only living as a male in the eyes of others, but thinking of himself as a male without any doubts. This example not only points out the difficulty of trying to maintain a self-image without a clear gender identity, but it also shows how one's gender identity can be relatively independent of the gender attributions made by others.

The only way to ascertain someone's gender identity is to ask her/him. Clinicians may believe they can "get at" someone's gender identity by the use of projective tests, but they are probably measuring gender-role identity (see below). Of course, the person might lie and not reveal her/his true gender identity, but there is no other method of getting the answer besides asking. Another problem with asking is that the question, "Are you a boy/man or a girl/woman?" determines the nature of the answer. The question implicitly assumes that the respondent is either one or the other and there is no other category. Even if a less leading way of asking the question could be formulated [and all questions, to some extent, structure the desired answer (Churchill, 1969)], we still may not get accurate answers, either because the respondent knows that "I don't know" or "Neither" or "Both" are not acceptable answers or because she/he knows that the answer must be congruent with the evidence (e.g., physical characteristics) presented to the person who is asking. In any event, gender identity is what the person feels she/he is, regardless of the gender attribution other people would make about her/him, and regardless of the validity of our techniques for determining gender identity. To claim that your *gender* is what you feel yourself to be ignores the fact that people almost always attribute gender without asking one another. The equating of gender and gender identity is understandable, however, since the question, "Are you male or female?" can either be interpreted as, "What do you feel yourself to be?" or "How are you categorized by others?" The reason why most people do not have difficulty interpreting the question is that in the common-sense world there is no reason to distinguish gender identity from gender attribution. There is just gender.

The development of a gender identity appears to occur during a critical period. That is, there is a period of time in the young child's life before which she or he is too young to have a gender identity, and after which whatever gender identity has developed cannot be changed. There is only one reported case of a nonpsychotic person not developing either a male or female gender identity during childhood (Stoller, 1968), and even this case is not a clear one. Most of the evidence for the development of a gender identity during a critical period comes from cases where the initial assignment was deemed in error and an attempt was made to "correct" it by reassigning the child and making the necessary physical changes. Almost all attempts of this sort made after the age of about three are unsuccessful, in the sense that the individual either retains her/his original gender identity or becomes extremely confused and ambivalent. When the child *is* able to develop a new gender identity to go along with the reassignment, professionals conclude that the earlier gender identity had not been firmly entrenched. This circularity is a rather obvious example of the operation of incorrigible propositions. Given a belief in the permanence of gender identity after a critical period, the inability to reassign a child in some cases *and* the ability to do so in others serves as proof of the "truth" of the invariance of gender identity. Even though emphasis on a critical period makes the acquisition of a gender identity seem like an all-or-nothing event there is a developmental process involved in learning that you are either a girl or a boy, what it means to be one or the other, and that this is a permanent aspect of your life.

Instead of thinking in terms of "critical periods," a term that suggests innate biological mechanisms, it is possible to discuss gender identity from a different perspective. It may be that gender can be successfully reassigned up to the point when the child incorporates the rules which construct gender, specifically, the "fact" that gender is unchangeable (see Chapter 4).

Gender identity should not be confused with the similar-sounding concept of *gender-role identity*. This is often referred to in the literature as "sex-role identity" (e.g., Rosenberg and Sutton-Smith, 1972). Gender-role identity refers to how much a person approves of and participates in feelings and behaviors, which are seen as "appropriate" for his/her gender. Money and Ehrhardt (1972) have included gender-role identity as a part of gender identity, by defining the latter as "the persistence of one's individuality as a male, female, or ambivalent . . . especially as it is experienced in *self-awareness and behavior* . . ."(p. 4, italics ours). How you think you should behave and how you experience your behavior as female or male are related to what gender you feel yourself to be, but they ought to be recognized as separate issues. Failing to separate the two concepts leads many scientists (like Money and Ehrhardt) to conclude that someone with atypical feelings about how their maleness or femaleness should be expressed in behavior has a gender identity problem. This could lead one to assert that the lessening rigidity in gender behaviors will result in a large number of persons who do not know whether they are male or female. There is no evidence to support that assertion, although gender identity and gender-role identity might influence one another in various ways. For example, given rigid expectations, a boy could think that because he does not like "boy things" and does like "girl things" he might be a girl (Green, 1974). As expectations become more flexible, such gender identity conflicts may be less likely to occur.

Gender Role

A role, as the concept is used in sociology, is a set of prescriptions and proscriptions for behavior—expectations about what behaviors are appropriate for a person holding a particular position within a particular social context. A gender role, then, is a set of expectations about what behaviors are appropriate for people of one gender. People can be categorized as role occupants either through their own efforts ("achieved" roles, such as doctor, mother, student) or on the basis of attributes over which they are seen to have no control ("ascribed" roles, such as Black, infant, Italian). Obviously, gender roles in our society are treated as ascribed roles.

According to the traditional perspective, someone is "born into" the category "male" or "female," and by virtue of her or his birth becomes obligated to perform the male or female role. In other words, one is expected to behave in accordance with the prescriptions and proscriptions for one's gender. Most writers agree with this definition, although they sometimes call it "sex role" (e.g., Yorburg, 1974), thereby emphasizing the ascribed nature of the role.[6]

The obligatory nature of gender roles is so firm that when dictionaries attempt to define woman and man, they often do so by listing gender role behaviors. ("Man: one possessing a high degree of . . . courage, strength, and vigor" Webster's, 1973, p. 889). Even Stoller, who is so aware of the ambiguities surrounding gender, cites, as proof that an XO chromosome individual is as natural a woman as any XX woman, the fact that she likes to cook and sew (1968, p. 21).

Gender roles have many components, including interests, activities, dress, skills, and sexual partner choice. For each of these components, there are clear, and different, expectations for those who occupy the male role and the female role (cf. Yorburg, 1974). Because these role expectations are so pervasive, it is not necessary to list exactly what they are.

As with other roles, sanctions against violating various pre- and proscriptions vary. In fact, the sanctions, rather than the expectations, may be what is changing in contemporary society. Women are still expected, in general, to want a home and family, but deviance from that expectation is now more permissible. On the other hand, men still cannot wear skirts, if they want to be taken seriously.

A *stereotype* is a set of beliefs about the characteristics of the occupants of a role, not necessarily based on fact or personal experience, but applied to each role occupant regardless of particular circumstances. In addition, stereotypes are conceived of as having an evaluative component. That is, they are not merely descriptive of expected behaviors, but these expected behaviors are evaluated as good, bad, desirable, and so on. For example, the stereotyped female role in our society consists of such low-valued behaviors and traits as passivity and helplessness and such high-valued ones as "very tactful" (Broverman et al., 1972). In this book we are not particularly concerned with stereotypes, *per se*, because, by definition, stereotypes are not assumed to be "objective" in the way gender role, in which stereotypes are grounded, is seen to be.

Because gender is an ascribed role, certain gender role expectations are seen as being an expression of the biological (i.e., unchangeable) foundations of gender. Some writers (e.g., Hutt, 1972) have given most gender differences a biological basis, while others (e.g., Maccoby and Jacklin, 1974) have limited their ascriptions to expectations such as aggressiveness, even though there is still scientific debate about whether these behaviors in humans have a primarily biological foundation. Theories of gender role development (i.e., how children learn the proper behavior associated with their gender) vary in the emphasis which they place on biological and environmental factors. All the major theories, however, make the assumption that dichotomous roles are a natural (and hence proper) expression of the dichotomous nature of gender. This assumption is being increasingly reexamined, but the grounds for questioning existing dichotomous gender roles do not question the existence of two genders. It is only by questioning dichotomous criteria for gender attributions that the dichotomous nature of gender, itself, becomes problematic.

THE PRIMACY OF
GENDER ATTRIBUTION

Having provided definitions of gender assignment, gender identity, and gender role, we now explore how these components form the foundation for some gender-based categories which our society has for describing people: transsexual/nontranssexual; transvestite/nontransvestite; homosexual/heterosexual. What we demonstrate through this discussion is that knowing someone's gender assignment, identity, or role, or knowing that they belong in one of the gender-based categories, or even knowing *all* of this will give a great deal of information about a person but will not inform the person's gender because there will never be sufficient information for a definite gender attribution to be made. However, once a gender attribution has been made, the meaning of gender-related information for any particular individual can be interpreted.

Transsexual

"Transsexualism is the conviction in a biologically normal person of being a member of the opposite sex. This belief is these days accompanied by requests for surgical and endocrinological procedures that change anatomical appearance to that of the opposite sex" (Stoller, 1968, pp. 89–90). By opposite sex, Stoller means opposite from that which one was assigned. (Note how the use of the word "opposite" serves to underscore the dichotomous sense of gender.)

If you know that an individual's gender identity and gender assignment conflict then you know that the person is a transsexual. This certainly gives you important information about someone, but it does not tell you whether he/she is female or male. We are not asking about biological criteria for being male or female, nor are we concerned with value judgments about "real" men and "real" women. Our interest is in the everyday process of gender attribution, a process that even members of the medical team engage in when evaluating transsexuals according to medical criteria (see Chapter 5). Even when transsexuals are in transitional stages, they still receive definite gender attributions. For example, genetic males at the initial stages of estrogen treatment may look like "feminine" men, and at some later stage may look like "masculine" *women*. No matter what stage of "transformation" transsexuals we have met were in, in each and every case it has been possible, necessary, and relatively easy for us to make a gender attribution.

Once a gender attribution has been made the "transsexual" label becomes clarified. For example, if you attribute "man" to a person who is a male (assignment) to female (identity) transsexual, you know that he has not begun to "pass"[7] or is not "passing" well. On the other hand, if you make the gender attribution "female" to this person, you know that she is credible as a woman in every way. Gender attribution gives meaning to the gender-based category.

Transvestite

Clinically, a transvestite is someone whose gender identity corresponds to her/his assignment, but who obtains erotic pleasure by dressing ("dress" includes hairstyle and accessories) as the other gender. Only when the gender of the individual's dress is in conflict with *both* assignment and identity is that individual labeled "transvestite."[8] (We recognize that the female/male dichotomization of dress is forced because it ignores the fact that some individuals dress androgynously and that most transvestites cross-dress only on occasion.)

There is some question as to whether "transvestite," in the preceding sense, is an appropriate category for an individual with a female assignment and a female identity who dresses as a male, since there is no evidence that dressing in male clothing (e.g., jockey shorts) is erotic for someone with a female identity. Nevertheless, there are women who dress as the male gender role dictates. Therefore, we will talk about "cross-dressing," a more neutral term which does not imply eroticism.

Knowing that someone is a cross-dresser does not tell you if they are a woman or a man. Knowing that they are a woman or a man, on the other hand, allows you to make an interpretation of their cross-dressing. The clinical usage of "transvestite" contrasts with the everyday usage of the term. A transvestite, for most people, is someone who is *known* to be one gender but who dresses as the other, for example, a man who wears female clothes. Some transvestites are called "drag queens." Such individuals are often assumed to be mimicking the members of the other gender or trying to be like them rather than responding to a fetish (see Newton, 1972). This may be especially true in regard to females who cross-dress. The term "butch" implies imitation rather than eroticism. People categorize a person as a transvestite based on the gender attribution they have made about that person and their conclusion that this gender attribution conflicts with the way the person is dressed. In everyday life we rarely if ever, have any knowledge of another's gender identity or gender assignment. The fact that the attribution comes first, suggests that neither knowing how people dress, nor their gender identity, nor their gender assignment is necessary in order to make a gender attribution.

Heterosexual/Homosexual

People are classified as heterosexual or homosexual on the basis of their gender and the gender of their sexual partner(s). When the partner's gender is the same as the individual's, then the person is categorized as homosexual. When the partner's gender is other than the individual's, then the label "heterosexual" is applied.[9] (The label "lesbian" is dependent on a definite prior gender attribution, i.e., that both partners are female.) This homosexual/heterosexual distinction is as forced as the others, since clearly there are degrees of preference in sexual partner choice.

This gender-based categorization makes the primacy of gender attribution particularly salient. Knowing that someone is homosexual or heterosexual tells you something about the person, but it does not tell you if they are male or female. In fact, attaching one of these gender-based labels to someone first of all depends on the gender attributions made about *both* partners (e.g., that one is male and the other is female). The gender attribution determines the label "homosexual" or "heterosexual" but the label itself does not lead to a gender attribution.

Feminine/Masculine

We have discussed how the way one dresses and the inferences made regarding the motivation to dress in a particular way, whom one chooses as a sexual partner, and whether one's identity is in accord with one's gender assignment, determine whether one is placed in a particular gender-based category with its own name, etiology, and prognosis. One's interests, activities, and personality traits, on the other hand, do not have this status. Although people rarely exhibit only male or only female interests, and so on, an individual who has predominantly male interests, as defined by the particular culture, is "masculine," and an individual with predominantly female interests is "feminine." ("Effeminate" describes men who caricature stereotypical feminine behavior. Obviously, in order to use this adjective, a gender attribution must already have been made.) Interests, activities, and personality traits give no information about the type of gender attribution that would be made, but knowing the person's gender would give meaning to their "masculinity" or "femininity."

There are no separate nouns in the English language to refer to people with stereotypical male or female interests. The slang terms "pansy" or "bulldyke" refer more to expressive style, in conjunction with choosing a sexual partner of the same gender, than they do to interests, activities, and personality traits. The fact that we have nouns for style but only adjectives for interests is important, because style may be a cue for gender attribution, whereas interests may not.

CONCLUSION

Knowing the relationship among the gender components is, as we have shown, not sufficient for making a gender attribution. What is the gender of a masculine, homosexual, transsexual who cross-dresses? Not even having concrete information about these components is sufficient. Consider the following: (1) Lee was assigned the gender "male" at birth. (2) Ronnie has a female gender identity. (3) Chris wears female clothing and hair styles. (4) Sandy chooses men as sexual partners. (5) Leslie has feminine interests and engages in feminine activities. Do any of these pieces of information tell you whether Lee, Ronnie, Chris, Sandy, or Leslie are men or women? For example, Lee might be a man, or, on the other hand, Lee could have had one of the syndromes to be discussed in Chapter 3 and have been born with an enlarged clitoris that was mistaken for a penis. If this were discovered early enough, a "reassignment" could have been made and Lee might be a woman. Or, Lee might be a postoperative transsexual, and therefore a woman in just about any sense of the word.

This same type of exercise could be done for the rest of the examples. It becomes clear that no one piece of information about a component of gender is sufficient for making a gender attribution.

Not only are we not able to make gender attributions from only one piece of information, but the knowledge itself is relatively meaningless without a prior gender attribution. For example, if you already know Sandy is a man, the fact that Sandy chooses men as sexual partners conveys very different information than it does if you know that Sandy is a woman.

Even information about *all* the components is insufficient. Is a person with a male gender assignment, a female gender identity, male interests, male sexual partners, and female clothing, a male or a female?

There is no way to answer this question in the absence of concrete interaction with the individual described. No amount of descriptive information we could give you about the person would allow you to attribute gender with absolute certainty, short of our making the attribution for you. Information about secondary gender characteristics might enable you to make a more educated guess than knowledge about gender components or gender-based categories alone. You might be right most of the time in guessing that a feminine heterosexual with facial hair, a deep voice, and broad shoulders was someone to whom you would make a "male" gender attribution were you to interact with the person. However, the person could turn out to be a woman, and your tentative gender attribution would just be a guess. Gender attributions are not guesses. In our everyday world people are either male or female, not probably one or the other.

Even knowledge about what many consider the ultimate criteria for telling woman from men, namely genitals, is not the answer. Attributions are almost always made in the absence of information about genitals, and most people do not change their gender attributions even if they discover that someone does not have the "appropriate" genitals. On occasion, friends of ours have interacted with persons whom they later accidentally discovered were preoperative transsexuals. In other words, they found out that someone about whom they had made a gender attribution did not have the "right" genitals. In no case did they change their gender attribution in light of this knowledge, although there may have been changes in other attributions made about the person. Secondary gender characteristics and genitals are important cues, but they are never sufficient for making a gender attribution. Whether someone is a man or a woman is determined in the course of interacting. How this is done is one of the concerns of the final chapters.

The primacy of gender attribution becomes obvious when we recognize that assignment and identity can be seen as special cases of attribution, and, even more importantly, that in order to meaningfully interpret someone's assignment, identity, and role, and the relationship among them, one must first attribute gender. Identity, role, and assignment are not the same as attribution, but they can only be interpreted when placed in context by the gender attribution process.

The gender attribution process is the method by which we construct our world of two genders. As we mentioned earlier, a defining feature of reality construction is to see our world as being the only possible one. One way to investigate the possibility of other worlds is to see how gender is conceived of in other cultures. A review of the anthropological literature can raise important questions about the gender attribution process, and this is the work of the next chapter.

NOTES

1. The use of the term "decision" does not necessarily imply that people consciously deliberate or choose, nor that they could verbalize the "decision"-making process. The term is used in the ethnomethodological sense (see Zimmerman and West, 1975) to refer to the rule-guided, socially shared activity of gender attribution, the character of which is explicated as the theme of this book develops. In no way do we mean to suggest that people have any trouble making these decisions, nor are we suggesting that unless they became aware of how they are deciding they might be making mistakes.

2. We have chosen to use the word "attribution" because it implies an active process, based on information received, and involving implicit rules for assigning characteristics. Our theory of gender attribution should not be confused with attribution theory in social psychology (e.g., Jones, Kanouse, Kelley, Nisbett, Valins, and Weiner, 1971). In the first place, attribution theory has been developed within a positivist framework and does not concern itself with the deep structure of social interaction. It is concerned with the conditions under which people assign motives, traits, characteristics, etc. to others on the basis of limited information which they have about the other. Attribution theory has not been concerned with the gender attribution process, although gender, itself, has been studied as a determining factor in explaining behavior. For example, Deaux and Enswiller (1973) found that a woman's success was attributed to luck, while a man's success was more likely to be attributed to his skill. In discovering what different motives and traits are attributed to males and females who behave in the same way, we can learn about the circumstances under which gender is used as an explanatory factor. In these cases, though, the question of "How do you know if the person is male or female in the first place?" is still glossed. "Gloss" is used here in a technical, ethnomethodological sense (see Garfinkel and Sacks, 1970). To gloss is to let the meaning of something become clear as the process of interaction proceeds, without explicitly stating (and without being able to state) what

it is that is meant. Glosses are pervasive in science as well as everyday life. Our purpose is to explicate one gloss in particular—saying that someone is female or male.

3. People readily categorize as "male" or "female" such things as colors and numbers, as indicated, for example, in a study carried out by Diane Gertz, a student at the State University of New York, College at Purchase. Whether there is agreement about the proper gender of "25" is interesting, but of more importance in this context is the fact that all of her thirty subjects gave a gender label to "25" and that many were able to support their "attribution" with "good" reasons.

4. Our use of the terms "construction" and "social construction" reflects our theoretical position that the sense of an objective world is accomplished by persons engaged in concrete day-to-day activities. (See the discussion which follows in the text.) This accomplishment or construction is social because those engaged in the activity are members; that is, they share a common method for producing the sense of objective facts like gender. We are indebted to Garfinkel (1967) for our position. However, we make no claim to be faithful to Garfinkel's particular intentions.

5. Throughout this book, the gender pronoun we use for an informant (whether the informant is a professional, an "everyday" person, a transsexual, or anything else) refers to the attribution that we made in interacting with the person.

6. Recently, several sociologists (Thorne, 1976; Lopata, 1976) have questioned the whole concept of gender "role." Since a person's gender affects expectations about *all* behaviors in many different role settings (e.g., "a female doctor" versus "a male doctor"), gender may be too pervasive and permanent to be considered a role and may be better thought of as a status or an identity. We continue to use "gender role" for the sake of clarity, but we agree with the preceding criticism of the concept and mean "role" in its broadest sense.

7. The term "passing" commonly refers to being taken for something one is really not. For example, a Black person who is light-skinned might attempt to be taken for a white person. In this sense she/he is passing as white. Our usage, on the other hand, carries no implication that a person is *really* not what she/he appears to be (see Garfinkel, 1967 and Chapter 5). In the sense that we mean passing, everyone is passing, i.e., doing something in order to be taken as she/he intends.

8. If there is any question as to what the individual's gender identity "really" is, the term transvestite cannot be applied. Only if an assigned male considers himself to be a male is his cross-dressing as a woman considered clinically to be transvestism. On the other hand, transsexuals who dress in accordance with their assignment, but other than their identity, may consider themselves to be cross-dressers but would not be

considered so by naive persons. There are at least two reasons why transsexuals may not have begun to dress in accordance with their gender identity. They may not have enough of the secondary gender characteristics that correspond to their gender identity to pass; there may be economic reasons such as continuing to hold a job that is dependent on their being seen as the gender that was originally assigned. It would be inappropriate to clinically refer to the cross-dressing transsexual as a transvestite, since he/she does not cross-dress for erotic reasons. There have been no reports of transsexuals who, after living in their new gender, return to their original way of dressing for erotic reasons.

9. A transsexual who is not yet living in accord with her/his gender identity and is forced by circumstances, or chooses, to relate sexually to an individual whose gender category is the same as the transsexual's gender identity, may be considered heterosexual by others. The transsexual would consider that relationship to be homosexual.

2

CROSS-CULTURAL
PERSPECTIVES ON GENDER

Imagine a family that has several daughters but no sons. The father needs a son to help hunt for the family, since in this society females do not hunt. Finally, another child is born, but it is another daughter. Because of their need for a hunter, the parents decide to make the child a son. When the child is five years old they tie the dried ovaries of a bear to the child's inner belt in order to prevent the child from ever conceiving. The child is dressed as a boy, taught male skills, and eventually develops great strength and becomes an excellent hunter.

Imagine another family in which there is a son. The child shows an interest in female tasks and shuns male tasks, so the parents decide to test him. They put their son in a small enclosure with a bow and arrow and some basket weaving material. Then they set fire to the enclosure and watch to see what he grabs as he runs out. The child grabs the basketry material and from that point in time the child becomes their daughter.

These events are described in anthropological reports as having occurred about 100 years ago among various American Indian societies (Honigmann, 1954; Crawley, 1960; Hill, 1938).

The stories raise many questions. What does it mean that the first child was made the son and the second child became a daughter? If it means nothing more than *made like a son* or *treated like a daughter,* then the events described become less "exotic." Even in our culture we know that there are children who are treated like other gender—cross-dressed, given other-gender names, perhaps in unusual cases even referred to as the other gender. But unless the parents are psychotic, they know that by treating the child as though she/he were the other gender, they have not turned their child into the other gender. In our society that would necessitate an alteration of the genitals.

What if, however, the two cases presented previously are examples, as far as the Indians were concerned, of transforming the child into the other (or even a third) gender. What would that mean about those societies' concept of gender? What criteria would need to be met in order for us to decide that, for the members of these cultural groups, it was not just a matter of cross-gender role behavior?

Cross-cultural findings can be easily incorporated into the positivist framework. There are two genders (male and female) with no overlap, and two gender roles (masculine and feminine) with some degree of overlap. There are even some individuals in certain (maybe all) cultures who perform *all* of the other gender's role behaviors. The positivist interpretation of the introductory examples is that the children were performing the other gender's role behaviors. This perspective is illustrated by statements like, "In Madagascar there are certain boys who live like women" (Westermarck, 1917, p. 461). Kroeber (1940) writes, ". . . born a male he became a woman, socially," indicating, with the word "socially," that the person was only treated as a woman.

In contrast, consider the possibility that the children had *become* the other gender. This would mean that members of one gender category may become members of another gender category through certain practices that may seem invalid to us, and that there may indeed be more than two gender categories for some cultures. Our purpose in this chapter is not to prove, in a positivist sense, that this is true. Rather, we show that by viewing gender as a social construction, it is possible to see descriptions of other cultures as evidence for alternative but equally real conceptions of what it means to be a woman or a man.

Just as transsexualism in our society is informative because it raises the possibility that gender is an accomplishment, studying gender categories in other cultures also makes gender problematic, that is, uncovers our taken-for-granted belief in the facticity of gender which prevents us from seeing gender as a social accomplishment. A cross-cultural comparison can show that it is possible to construct the world in many ways. The kinds of questions that arise from studying gender in other cultures would be less likely to arise if we focused only on our own society, for membership in a culture blinds us to the constructed nature of that culture's reality.

Edgerton's (1964) analysis of intersexuality among the Potok of East Africa illustrates the difference between the kind of questions we are interested in asking and those typically raised in anthropological work. Edgerton's aim was to discover how intersexuality (the condition of having both male and female genitals, sometimes referred to as hermaphroditism) is responded to in a society where economic, social, and scientific concerns are different from Western culture's. He takes it for granted that the assumption of only two biological sexes, men and women, is universal. He cites the cases of two individuals, each born with male and female genitals. Both were stigmatized but one individual assumed more of a female role and the other more of a male role. Edgerton does not discuss how it was decided which gender role should be assumed. We can speculate that it was either the relative sizes and clarity of the male or female genitals, or the familial need for a daughter or son. Whatever the initial reason, it seems clear from Edgerton's description that there were individuals in Potok society who were categorized as neither male nor female. This is the kind of suggestive data that forces us to consider whether gender is as objective a reality as we normally treat it. Granted, intersexed individuals are exceptions in a world where most people are "biologically normal," but it is by studying how exceptions are accommodated that we can best understand the nonexceptional cases. Edgerton does this by relating the treatment of these individuals to the economic and social concerns of the culture. In contrast, we are asking (1) Is there evidence that the individual's maleness or femaleness is decided irrespective of biological considerations? and (2) Is there evidence that these individuals were seen as neither male nor female but rather as members of a third gender category? If either are true, then the Potok construction of gender differs from Western society's.

Martin and Voorhies (1975) asked similar questions about gender categorization in other cultures, and concluded that certain societies recognize more than two "gender statuses" and may recognize more than two categories of "physical sex." In addition, "gender statuses" are not necessarily assigned on the basis of genitals. (By "gender status," Martin and Voorhies appear to mean what we have been calling "gender role.") Their work provides additional evidence for our interpretation of the literature. However, they do not offer an analysis of how their conclusions relate to concepts of gender in Western cultures.

The questions we are asking differ from those typically raised by cross-cultural studies of gender role. What do we know if we have evidence that in cultures other than ours women and men may perform gender roles that are different from our own? Mead (1935,

1961) has made perhaps the largest contribution to the cross-cultural study of gender roles, specifically in support of the argument that individuals are born with the potential to develop whatever gender role the society dictates. Although some people may still argue for innate gender roles (e.g., Hutt, 1972), cultural relativity has by and large been accepted, and is now an orthodox position. Mead (1935) observed that among the Mundugumor both males and females are expected to behave in what we think of as stereotypically masculine ways—aggressive and nonemotional. In contrast, the Arapesh expect both males and females to behave in what we think of as stereotypically feminine ways—co-operative and maternal. Mead's third comparison tribe was the Tchambuli whose gender-roles are the reverse of ours—men are regarded as inherently delicate and emotional and women as active and managerial.

We are not concerned with providing an exhaustive review of the literature on cross-cultural gender role behaviors. (Reviews and analyses are provided by Yorburg, 1974; Rosenburg and Sutton-Smith, 1974; D'Andrade, 1966; Millet, 1970.) We are touching on this literature primarily to point out that Mead's work and the work of others illustrates that men and women can engage in behaviors that are different from ours and still be men and women.

What we are asking is: What does "still be men and women" mean? Implicit in this is the idea that doing gender-specific tasks is not the same as being a gender. All of the gender-role research rests on the assumption that there are two genders. It does not question that dichotomy, tell us what the criteria are for gender category membership, or tell us whether one can (and how one does) transfer from one category to another. What would we accept as evidence that gender for a particular group of people was not dichotomous, that instead it was trichotomous, or that it was fluid, or that as a classification it had no meaning?

THE BERDACHE

In order to gather evidence bearing on these questions, we focus on reports about a special category of people—the berdache. The children in our introductory illustrations were berdache. According to the traditional, positivistic perspective, the berdache were those people in aboriginal North America who received social sanction to assume the gender role opposite to that which they were originally assigned. According to our perspective, they were those people in aboriginal North America who received social sanction to become a gender other than that to which they were originally assigned.

Much of the early literature on the berdache is descriptions of the berdache role (cf. Skinner, 1924). Most of the current analyses of the berdache phenomenon focus on the function of the berdache institution in various kinds of societies (cf. Forgey, 1975). Although the term berdache is technically reserved for members of American Indian societies, berdache-like people have been found in Alaska, Siberia, Central and South Asia, Oceania, Australia, Sudan, and the Amazon region. Most berdache were reported to be males who became females,[1] but instances of females who became males have been cited (e.g., Borgoras, 1907).

In researching the ethnographic literature, one cannot help but notice the lack of consistency in terms and definitions used in describing the berdache. Both Karlen (1971) and Rosenberg and Sutton-Smith (1972) treat "berdache" and "transvestite" synonymously. "Bravery is a determining point among the Plains Indians, and thus a timid male may be assigned the role of the transvestite." (Rosenberg and Sutton-Smith, 1972, p. 71). "Transvestite" and "homosexual" are used interchangeably by Devereux (1937) to describe the Mohave berdache and by Hassrick (1964) to describe the Sioux "Winkte," or berdache. Other ethnographers discuss berdache and hermaphrodites as though they were essentially the same, even though the groups they are discussing (e.g., the Navaho, Hill, 1935) make a distinction. Although some berdache were homosexual, and some homosexuals were transvestic, and some transvestites were hermaphroditic, to treat these gender-based categories as identical is to obsure crucial distinctions. Not all berdache were homosexual; not all cross-dressed; and there is no evidence that the berdache were biologically ambiguous. (It is probably important in terms of our perspective that many ethnographers assumed that there was a physiological component to the berdache phenomenon.)

Forgey's (1975) and Angelino and Shedd's (1955) analyses are notable in their recognition of the complexity of the berdache phenomenon. Angelino and Shedd state that before such questions as "Are there certain types of social organizations which are correlated with the presence or absence of berdache?" (p. 121) can be answered, there must be general agreement on what the berdache were. They trace the word "berdache" from its original usage by French explorers to describe passive homosexual North American Indians, to its eventful usage as synonymous with transvestism and effeminacy among the Indians. We do not know whether the first explorers to use the term berdache were mistaken in their appraisal of these people or whether they recognized the limitation of their translation, but had no other word that seemed appropriate.

The term "berdache" is said to be "derived from the French word 'bardash,' which derived from the Italian term 'berdascia,' which derived from the Arabic 'bardaji,' which derived from the Persian 'barah,'" (Forgey, 1975, p. 2). Barah meant "slave, kept-boy or male prostitute." The original meaning emphasized homosexuality and prostitution, but this meaning was altered in America by the additional consideration of cross-dressing.

Angelino and Shedd (1955) differentiate the berdache from (1) the hermaphrodite whose status has a physiological root and who is often considered to belong to a special category from birth (Edgerton, 1964), (2) the homosexual who does not necessarily cross-dress, (3) the transvestite who does not necessarily take on the social role of the other gender, and (4) the individual who has a slight interest in activities of the other gender. These distinctions are useful, but Angelino and Shedd's solution to the problem of definition is inadequate. By defining the berdache as "an individual of a definite physiological sex (male or female) who assumes the role and status of the opposite sex, and who is viewed by the community as being of one sex physiologically but as having assumed the role and status of the opposite sex" (p. 125), Angelino and Shedd have differentiated the berdache from other gender-based categories, but have provided no answer to the question: What gender were the berdache?

As far as we can tell, the berdache, like the transsexuals in our society, were "biologically normal" but underwent some type of gender transformation. It is specifically because of this that members of both categories are of such interest. Heiman and Cao Van Lê (1975) differentiate the berdache from the transsexual in contemporary Vietnam. They conclude that the berdache was a clearly defined role, while transsexual is not. In some societies (e.g., Siberian Chuckee), the berdache role was institutionalized. There was a ceremonial role with prescribed privileges and responsibilities; there was nearly always a person to fill this role, and it was considered a high status position. Other societies (e.g., Zuni) did not institutionalize the "role-reversal," but did provide an acceptable role for individuals who had "gender-identity problems." Berdache in these societies were more likely to be low status and treated with toleration. The contemporary transsexual, on the other hand, does not have a visible role; she/he merges into the general culture as indistinguishable from "normals" (except for some celebrity exceptions).

Heiman and Cao Van Lê's analysis is interesting, but it may say more about the differences between societies than the differences between berdache and transsexuals. Using some common criteria for defining a transsexual (e.g., a gender identity different from the gender assignment, childhood memories of having been seen as the "wrong" gender, a long history of cross-dressing, a preference for nonhomosexual partners, an abhorence of their own genitals), there is almost no data of this kind on the berdache, and therefore, it would be premature either to equate or definitively differentiate the two groups. Granted, the role a society provides an individual gives some clue as to what that individual "really is," but it is only part of the evidence.

As we discuss in Chapter 5, the transsexual phenomenon does not undermine the dichotomy of gender; it reinforces it. The berdache, in contrast, may not have been considered a special type of man or woman (one who had crossed over categories) but rather a third type of person. The word "transsexual" can either be used as a noun to refer to any person whose gender identity conflicts with her/his gender assignment, or it can be used as an adjective, for example, "transsexual male" with the emphasis either on the fact that (a) the transsexual who is being referred to is of the male-to-female type, or (b) the male who is being referred to has a particular kind of history—that of a female.

The term "berdache," however, is used as a noun and not to modify a person's maleness or femaleness. This suggests that it is treated by ethnographers (and perhaps by the cultures where berdache were found) as a distinct category. It is as though once persons were revealed to be a berdache, they were then considered to be outside the male/female framework. Transsexualism is a term implying transition from one state to another. Berdache may not have had that meaning.

Descriptions of the berdache institution have been used to support a number of different arguments. Karlen (1971) reviewed the material in order to show how some societies institutionalized various forms of homosexuality; Benjamin (1966) cites berdache data to point out that transsexualism has existed in other cultures. We are taking some of the same data and using it to explore the possibility that gender is not constituted in universal ways. Before making an analysis of the berdache phenomenon in light of our interest, we will summarize some ethnographic reports about berdache. Even though there have been so many varying (and seemingly inconsistent) reports about the berdache, most writers state their findings as though the particular berdache they encountered were perfect examples of some generally agreed upon category called "berdache." This is clearly not so.

Some berdache were exclusively "homosexual," (that is, their sexual activities were with people who had the same genitals as they did), while some were only occasionally so, and others not at all. Of course, the term homosexual only makes sense here if we assume that the berdache were only acting like the other gender. If we assume that berdache became the other gender, or were members of a third category, then what may have seemed homosexual to the ethnographer, would actually be heterosexual and vice versa. The categorizing of berdache as homosexual or heterosexual by ethnographers does not imply that the berdache's culture considered this distinction meaningful.

Some berdache performed the new gender role completely, including cross-dressing, mannerisms, work tasks, and obeyance of gender-specific taboos, while some performed only aspects of it. Parsons (1916) describes a six-year old that she saw: He (Parson's attribution) was dressed like a boy in trousers and a shirt, but the shirt was longer than the other boys' and not tucked into his trousers. He wore a bead necklace that was not worn by either boys or girls and had delicate features uncharacteristic of either gender. His hair was cut like the other boys', but he used verbal expressions that the girls used. He played with girls.

Reichard (1928) reports hearing about one adult berdache who did women's work, spoke with a woman's voice, had a beard and wore men's clothing; and another berdache who performed female tasks, attended women's dances, wore male attire and spoke like a man. One of Devereux's (1937) informants describes a berdache who was dressed like a woman, but was married to other women.

What conclusions are we to draw from these reports? We do not have enough evidence to say that the berdache adopted only those aspects of the gender role which their particular society deemed important. In order to talk sensibly about what determined how much of the gender role the berdache adopted, we need to know what the established gender roles consisted of. Since anthropologists used their own culture's gender role dichotomy as criteria for evaluating the berdache, it is often difficult to interpret their reports. For example, Devereux's (1937) belief in rigidly dichotomized gender role categories kept him from making sense out of a berdache role that was not synonymous with either the male or female gender role. "Curiously enough, it was said that some women became 'hwame' (berdache) after having borne a child" (p. 508). Martin and Voorhies (1975) provide convincing evidence that there was a berdache gender role separate from the traditional masculine and feminine ones in the berdache cultures. Given the existence of a third gender role, this opens the possibility of a third gender category, separate from male and female.

It is possible to understand more about the berdache gender phenomenon by looking at the attitudes of the people toward the berdache. Attitudes toward the berdache apparently varied. The Zuni seemed to tolerate the berdache, but regarded them with some embarrassment (Bennedict, 1934; Parsons, 1916; Stevenson, 1901); the Amhara pitied them (Karlen, 1971); the Mohave accepted them but joked behind their backs (Devereux, 1937); the Aleuts considered it fortunate to have one in the home (Crawley, 1960); the Choctow despised them (Karlen, 1971); the Sioux held ambivalent attitudes toward them—respect, fear, and disdain (Hassrich, 1964); the Cheyenne held them in high esteem (Hoebel, 1960); the Chuckhee were afraid of them (Bogoras, 1907). Not only is there variation between cultures, but reports of treatment of the berdache within a culture vary from writer to writer and also from individual berdache to individual berdache. After reviewing all the ethnographies, it is tempting to conclude that treatment of any particular berdache varied with the specific personality characteristics of that berdache.

Cultural attitudes can be traced, in part, to the culture's theory of why someone became a berdache and are reflected, in part, in the rights and privilages accorded to the berdache. A society that believed that an individual was selected by a hermaphrodite god to become a berdache (e.g., Bellacoola people, McIlwraith, 1948) would look more favorably (or at least with greater awe) on that individual than a society which assumed that the behavior was a matter of choice (e.g., Zuni people, Parsons, 1916) or was congenital (e.g., Crow people, Denig, 1961). These ethnotheories had consequence in the obligations of the berdache to the society: Some were healers, storytellers to war parties, go-betweens in love affairs; some seem to have been nonexceptional members of the society.

Problems of Interpretation

We have been careful to qualify much of the description of the berdache by deliberately using phrases such as "seem to be," or "were apparently considered." The nature of the data on which our conclusions are based is in many ways suspect and in need of examination. In fact, some of the problems inherent in collecting and interpreting the data may limit how much we can really know about gender construction in other cultures.

Some problems are common to any anthropological investigation: making contact with reliable informants; learning to differentiate serious reports from jokes, myths, and lies; and getting people to discuss personal aspects of their lives. (See Pelto, 1970, for a complete discussion of methodological issues in anthropology.)

Other problems are specific to the study of the berdache and make any findings difficult to interpret.

(1) Much of the data was collected by missionaries and explorers who were not committed to objective scientific procedures. Westermark's (1917) review of the berdache (complete through 1908) is referenced by many contemporary writers, but is comprised almost entirely of reports by nonanthropologists. It should not be assumed that anthropologists have always been successful in achieving value-free reports, but at least they are intellectually committed to achieving them and (more recently) are examining the difficulty/impossibility of this task.

(2) Since the berdache were in existence primarily in the nineteenth century, those who wrote about them in this century may only have met one or two members of this dying institution, or more likely, may only have heard about them from other tribal members who might not have had firsthand contact with them. Reichard (1928) states that several berdache were mentioned in the geneologies, but she never saw one. She then proceeds to describe them. The development of interest in gender issues in the middle of the twentieth century has resulted in the publication of some reviews of the literature on the berdache. So, for example, we have Karlen, a writer in 1971, summarizing and interpreting the work of anthropologist Devereux, who, in 1937, reported a biography of a "lesbian transvestite" which he (Devereux) constructed based on retrospective reports by members of the Mohave community, most of whom never knew this berdache.

(3) Because there were not a large number of berdache and because of the problem of secondhand reporting we just discussed, many of the generalizations about the berdache institution are based on only a handful of cases. Hill (1943), for example, gives hearsay evidence about five berdache and recounts his own acquaintance

with one. Hill is cited widely in reviews of the berdache among the Navaho. This particular problem makes it difficult to assess the representativeness of any one incident and similarly makes it easy to see why there may be so little concensus in discussing the berdache.

(4) We have no way of assessing the extent to which the image of the berdache given to the ethnographer by the villagers was influenced by the villager's asumptions about the ethnographer's attitudes. Lurie (1953) suggests that the Winnebago people were reluctant to discuss their berdache honestly with white men because the Winnebago could tell that the white men regarded the institution negatively. Reluctance could stem not only from embarrassment at revealing behavior that was being judged by outsiders as immoral, but also from beliefs in the sacredness of the institution and an unwillingness to share this aspect of the culture. If we take these possibilities seriously, then there are some problems in interpretation. How do we interpret the culture's real attitude toward the berdache? Specifically we must account for some reports that find the berdache to be held in disdain. And how do we account for reports that find the berdache to be a "gender-role disorder"? If the informants sensed that the ethnographer considered homosexuality and cross-dressing sinful, then they may have presented their attitude toward the berdache as corresponding to the ethnographer's. If the informants sensed that the ethnographer considered nondichotomous gender as nonsensical, then they may have presented their definition of the berdache phenomenon as corresponding to the ethnographer's definition.

(5) Anthropologists as positivists collect data about other cultures and then interpret it by reference to their own organizing concepts. In terms of gender, they know there are two genders with different gender roles and they look to see how these gender roles are filled in another culture. "The task of anthropology is to chart the range of human variation, both biological and cultural, and to discover the factors making for and controlling this variability" (Kluckhohn, 1948, p. 88). The anthropologists' interest has not been to question the universality of their organizing concepts, but rather to apply them to new data.[2] The anthropologists are interpreters of events: "The villager does this; the villager says that; thus the villager means . . ." We read these accounts and must then either accept or reject the interpretation of the accounts. In addition, according to the ethnomethodological perspective, the anthropologists have not only constructed the interpretations for the reader, but they have

also constructed the accounts. That is, even before the anthropologists construct interpretations based on informants' accounts, they have methodologically structured the informants' behavior to transform it into a sensible (for the anthropologists) account.

For example, Opler, an anthropologist, asked a member of the Ute Indians of Colorado whether or not any members of that society indulged in homosexuality (Opler, 1965). Opler says that the question yielded amusement, disbelief, and counterquestioning on American urban culture, and he concludes that the Ute found that a ridiculous question and that homosexuality is not practiced among adult Ute. What we must ask ourselves is not only whether the conclusion follows (i.e., that homosexuality is not practiced by the Ute) but whether in fact, the description "yielded amusement, disbelief, . . ." is an objective report or an interpretation/coding of behaviors such as positioned mouth in what looked like our smiles, gave out noises that sounded like our laughter, opened eyes wide as we do when we seem not to believe something, and phrased the kind of sentences that we do when we want to know something. The data, then, are sounds from the mouth of an individual. The interpretation that follows is that the sound meant laughter, the laughter meant amusement, and the amusement meant "no." There are two problems here: whether the anthropologist's report is an accurate objective description of what was really happening according to positivistic criteria, and whether the report is a reasonable reconstruction of what the Ute were doing according to ethnomethodological criteria. Although these are problems common to any anthropological issue, in studying the berdache the problem is compounded because of the string of constructions. Using our earlier example of secondhand reporting, we see that Karlen's conclusions are a reconstruction of Devereux's reconstruction of tribal members' reconstructions.

Problems of Gender Attribution

Let us suppose that some Europeans come to an early twentieth-century Indian village for the first time. They have no idea that there are such people as berdache in this village. How would they find out? One possibility is that an informant would say: "We have someone here who was born a male, but who is living as a female." Even if the informant said: "We have someone here who was born a male, but who has *become* a female," this may have been interpreted as "living as." Another possibility is that the observers notice someone who seems to belong to one gender but looks like or is seen doing the tasks of the other gender. Sverdrup (1938) described a "well-dressed woman . . . who looked so different from the other women that we noticed her at once. She was unusually tall with a thin Indian face . . . She had to cut her whiskers and . . . occasionally her voice was very deep" (p. 125). Our point is that coming to a village with the concept of two genders, the observer sees two genders and understands the berdache phenomenon in those terms. The observers look for signs that fit their own criteria for the genders. Bogaras (1907) writes that a person was dressèd like a woman, but had a stubby black beard; "there could be no misunderstanding about the sex to which he really belonged" (p. 450). West (1967) notes that "they [the berdache] have a pretence to femininity" (p. 19). One problem with almost all ethnographic reports is that the ethnographer fails to state how she/he came to know that a particular person was a berdache. What is clear is that the anthropologist invariably made a gender attribution (either male or female) and assumed that the tribe had done so also. We could assume that the pronoun that the anthropologists use to describe the berdache reflects the gender attribution that they make. If so, then we must conclude that most anthropologists considered the berdache to be *really* the gender that was assigned at birth, since they generally referred to the berdache with the pronoun of their gender assignment. (Sverdrup's preceding description is an exception to that general finding.)

Although Devereux's (1937) Mohave informants often refer to berdache who were assigned male and became female as "she," Devereux is careful to show his "objectivity" by placing the female pronoun in italics or quotation marks. The same is true of his presentation of masculine pronouns. Rather than seeing the informant's choice of pronoun as informative of the berdache's gender, Devereux instead saw it as evidence of "the highly institutionalized character of this cultural complex" (p. 511).

If the anthropologists' use of pronouns is a direct translation from the culture, then these pronouns would be signs of the gender attributions made by the culture members. However, it is not always easy to tell what gender attribution the members have made. Zuni people, in pointing to a berdache, explained to an anthropologist that "she is a man." The anthropologist concluded that this was "certainly misleading to one not familiar with Indian thought" (Stevenson, 1901, p. 37). Presumably, one familiar with Indian thought would know whether the "she" was the defining gender label or the "man" was.

The difficulty in differentiating the gender attribution of the berdache as made by the anthropologist from that made by tribal members is illustrated in the following anthropological report: A long-time tribal friend of Stevenson (an anthropologist) had died. "So carefully was *his* sex concealed that for years the writer believed *him* to be a woman" (Stevenson, 1901, p. 310, emphasis ours). Stevenson had regarded her friend as a woman, since the friend was always referred to as she. Even after Stevenson "found out," she could not think of her as a man. From this report we see that even though Stevenson's initial gender attribution was so strong as to be almost impervious to change, she believed that the friend was really a man who successfully passed as a woman. The difficulty she had in changing the initial gender attribution in no way caused her to question the validity of the second attribution. But we do not know whether the tribal members had thought of the friend as:

1. A woman who had been assigned as a female and had always been a woman (i.e., they, too, were "fooled" by her passing).
2. A woman who had been assigned as a male, but who had transferred to the female gender and was accepted as such (somewhat analogous to the transsexual).
3. A man who was pretending to be (or thought he was) a woman; they humored him or showed respect for him by referring to him as a she.
4. A berdache who was not classifiable in terms of male or female.

If we assume that the pronouns used to address a person correspond to the gender the person is considered to be, then evidence points to the berdache having been considered by their society as belonging to the gender they "adopted" not the one they were assigned at birth. Hill (1935) states that he was told that polite persons always call the berdache by the kinship terms used for a woman of their relationship and age to the speaker, and that most uncles or nephews call her "mother." There are many other accounts of berdache whose initial gender assignment was "male" being referred to as female (e.g., Sverdrup, 1938; Parsons, 1916). An alternative interpretation is that the people were humoring[3] or honoring the berdache by using the pronouns that the berdache wanted used.

To further complicate the analysis, there is not always a correspondence between the pronouns used to *address* individuals and the pronouns used to *refer* to them. A particular hermaphrodite, whom Edgerton (1964) observed, was usually referred to as a woman but was addressed as "sererr" which means "male and female yet neither male nor female." This is analogous, according to Edgerton, to our concept of neuter and was a perjorative when addressed to a "normal" person. His analogy is, we think, a forced one, since the translation clearly goes beyond our concept of neuter. "Neuter" means no gender and we assign this only to nonhuman objects. The translation of "sererr" implies a concept for which we have no term. This introduces the seemingly insurmountable problem of concept translation through language translation.

Because we do not have berdache in our society, we have no English word for them other than "berdache." We have already discussed how some writers have substituted the terms transvestite, homosexual, or hermaphrodite for berdache, and we have explained the confusion resulting from their doing so. Some ethnographers, rather than assigning one of the gender-based labels to the berdache, have tried to solve the labeling problem by giving a literal translation to the tribal culture's label for the berdache. Examples of these translations are: "men–women" (Parsons, 1916; Lowie, 1935), "pretend to be 'nadle' (hermaphrodite)" (Hill, 1935), "homosexual of the ridge pool" (refers to being in the house doing female chores) (Karlen, 1971), "soft man" (Bogarus, 1907), "similar to woman" (Bogarus, 1907), "half man–half woman" (Hoebel, 1960), "neuter" (Denig, 1961), "human it" (Muensterberger, 1965), "not man–not woman" (Crawley, 1960). Occasionally the berdache is referred to with the same term that the society uses for referring to other types of people, for example, "cowards" (Karlen, 1971), "sterile people" (Karlen, 1971), "circumcised" (Crawley, 1960). Clearly, a number of these terms (e.g., "half man–half woman") could be seen as indicating the presence of other gender realities.

That there may not always be agreement among tribal members as to what their name for the berdache means, is illustrated by Lurie's (1953) interviews with the Winnebago. Their word "siange" was variously interpreted for her as meaning "a no good," "a eunuch," or an "unmanly man." Clearly, each person who provided Lurie with a definition held a different conception of the berdache. Any translation is dependent, in part, on the meanings for the person interviewed and on the interpretation of the translater. In trying to come to terms with other cultures' concepts of gender, it makes a difference whether the people thought of the berdache as neither male nor female, half male *and* half female, or definitely male or definitely female but with some characteristics of the other. The answer may lie in the language of the people, but if anthropologists interpret that language according to their own concepts, then the language analysis is inevitably limited. If anthropologists held the notion of two and only two genders, they would have to translate the culture's term for berdache according to that organizing principle. In other words, the berdache would *have* to be some variation of a man or a woman. The word chosen for translation necessarily structures our thinking about the berdache. Davenport, an anthropologist who lived among the Malanesians, asked them if there were men in the tribe who enjoyed men but did not enjoy women (1965). They could not understand his question since, as Davenport explained, they have no concept, and consequently no word, for exclusive homosexuality. To make our own analysis of their perplexity: If there were an individual in that society with a penis who desired men and not women, that individual might not be considered to be a man. The confusion with Davenport's question may have been because there were no exclusively homosexual males and yet there may have been individuals with penises who enjoyed other individuals with penises. Similarly, because we do not have berdache living in our society, we may not be able to understand the meaning of the names used to describe them in the way that members of the culture understood them.

CONCLUSIONS

What are we to conclude from this? We have shown how anthropologists as nonmembers may not know the meaning of events in other everyday worlds, and hence use their own construction of gender to construct gender in other societies. Within this serious limitation, we now attempt to construct evidence about the status of the gender components in other cultures, using the anthropologists' accounts as our resource.

Gender Assignment

Assigning people at birth to categories based on some concept of gender appears to be universal and, as far as we know, is always through a genital inspection. This is even true of the intersexed individual. While in our society intersexuality is usually resolved by choosing the gender (male or female) that the genitals most clearly approximate or by consulting other biological criteria, in societies, such as Potok, without access to surgical procedures or biological "facts" the intersexed child seems to be assigned neither a male nor a female gender, but a third gender—"intersexed." The fact that the Potok seem not to be confused about the gender of an intersexed child at birth, and that for them the child is neither female nor male, suggests the possibility of a third gender category.

Available data on the berdache do not inform this issue, since individuals did not become berdache until childhood, well after they had been assigned a definite male or female gender.

We make all statements about cross-cultural gender assignment with caution. Given the fact that anthropological accounts are produced by persons who take gender and gender assignment for granted, we can not know if there exist particular cultures which do not do this.

Gender Identity

This is the most difficult of the constructs to validate for a number of reasons. There are no visible signs of gender identity and it must be inferred from such evidence as self-referents. In addition, the concept of gender identity is a relatively recent one and consequently was not used by any of the ethnographers who studied the berdache directly.

What we can conclude from the accounts is that the berdache did not have to argue that their gender identity was discordent with their gender assignment or that they knew they were the "wrong" gender all along. We do not know whether they claimed to have felt themselves to be berdache all along or whether they felt clearly male or female at one point in time and then later felt clearly berdache.

Presumably if we asked all people who ever lived what their gender identity was, they might be able to respond to that question with a gender-related answer. There is no reason to believe, however, that the answer would inevitably be "male" or "female." It might me "man–woman" or "intersexed." There has never been a report of a culture with no gender categories. To say that gender identity is universal is probably true in the sense that all people know what category they belong to, but may be incorrect if we mean knowing whether they are male or female.

Gender Role

It is obvious that even if the male/female dichotomy is universal, how one is supposed to behave as a member of one of these categories has varied. Not only has male/female gender role varied, but the role behavior that someone must engage in in order to be seen as a berdache has varied from society to society. Accepting the nonuniversality of gender role does not necessitate a radical reinterpretation of gender. As we suggested earlier, it can be incorporated quite easily within a traditional positivist framework. What we suggest in the next section, though, does require a fundamentally different perspective for understanding gender role.

Gender Attribution

We cannot say that in all cultures people have always attributed gender according to the male/female dichotomy, although it is clear that all ethnographers have taken that for granted.

Based on some of the evidence we have cited in this chapter, we propose that there is a strong probability that in some nonindustrial cultures *gender role* is seen as the basis of gender attribution just as in our culture genitals are seen as the basis. In some cultures, as far as members were concerned, the invariant criteria for being seen as male or female (i.e., attributing a male or a female gender to someone) was the role one performed. Thus, a person with a vagina who performed tasks that persons with penises were assigned at birth (e.g., going to war) would be cognitively grouped with those persons with penises and seen to be of the same gender. The genital would have no importance in the gender attribution.

For example, the Navaho Indians of the nineteenth century were addressed by male or female kinship terms according to the type of clothing they wore (Reichard, 1928). On the Peleu Islands "the man dressed as a woman was regarded and treated as a woman" (Crawley, 1960). Devereux (1967) reports that tribal members sometimes made the "wrong" gender attribution to fieldworkers because of the fieldworkers' dress and behavior. For example, unless Catholic missionaries grew beards, they would often be seen as women because of their robes. Positivists see the person and the treatment of the person as necessarily separate phenomenon. They would see these as cases of persons being regarded and treated in terms of their dress, irrespective of their gender (which is a biological fact for the positivist). We, on the other hand, maintain that a person's gender is what they are regarded and treated as, that is, the gender of someone is the same as the gender attribution which is made about them. Gender is, in the first place, a social fact.

In the cases just cited, the person's gender corresponds to his/ her dress; in other cases (e.g., contemporary America) a person's gender might correspond to his/her genitals. In both cases the corresponding factors (dress or genitals) are not the same as the gender, but rather are essential signs that others use to support gender attributions. They are equally real signs. What is interesting is that while members of our culture can see that dress is not essential, and that people who think that are "wrong"/"primitive"/"misinformed," they have difficulty seeing that this is equally true of genitals.

Although genitals were not the defining feature of gender, they were important insignia in the same way dress is for us. Chuckee shamen who were transformed from men into women were "said to acquire the organs of a woman in time" (Bogoras, 1907). The Mohave berdache reportedly demanded that people call their penis a clitoris, their testicles "labia majora," and their anus "vagina" (Devereux, 1937). In describing the people's attitude toward a particular berdache, Devereux quotes their jeer, "the Hwame is proud now! She thinks perhaps she got a penis"[4] (p. 524). Karlen, who draws most of his conclusions from Devereux's data, provides us with a clear statement of the Western view of gender and interpretations of the berdache. "The sex-role reversal has a social reality to everyone (the Mohave). But they joked at times about the real hidden genitals, which hadn't changed along with the role" (Karlen, 1971, p. 470). In his view, the "real" genitals define the "real" gender. Although these societies may have recognized that the berdache's genitals were discordant with the berdache's role, there is no evidence that the genitals were in any way more real than the role in defining gender. The jokes might be similar to our jokes about female impersonators, but in reverse. We joke about their clothes, knowing they are "really" men. The Mohave may have joked about the berdache's penises, knowing that they were "really" berdache.

There is no mention of the berdache (unlike today's transsexuals) wanting to, or needing to, or trying to change their genitals in order to be seen as the appropriate gender; and there is no reason to believe that if surgery had been available they would have requested it. The ceremony that marked the berdache's movement from one gender to another included being given the clothing of the other gender to wear. The final stage in a transsexual's treatment is genital reconstruction. In both cases, the persons receive, in a culturally institutionalized manner, the essential insignia of their "new" gender. These signs are essential in the sense that without them the gender transformation cannot be taken seriously. Neither the ceremony nor the operation is seen as *causing* the transformation (in fact, in the case of transsexuals, there is no transformation [see Chapter 5]).

Not only were the genitals no more real than the role, but the genitals could apparently be ignored as a nondefining feature, while the role could not. To say "Robin is a man" may be equivalent in some societies to "Robin is a hunter," just as it is seen to be equivalent in our society to "Robin has a penis" or "Robin has a Y chromosome." We suggested in the preceding Gender Identity section that we should not expect that the answers to "What are you?" would necessarily be "male" or "female." It might be "man–woman." It might also be "hunter" or "story teller" or "potter." What we consider a correlate of gender may be seen by others as its defining feature. Similarly, what we consider the defining feature of gender may be seen by others as merely a correlate.

To accept as evidence of someone's gender whether a child grabs a bow and arrow or basket material as he/she runs outside of a burning enclosure, is no less legitimate than accepting as evidence whether a child has a penis or vagina or XY or XX chromosomes. It would be wrong to say that if only the "primitive" cultures knew about biology they would define male and female in the correct way (i.e., our way), since as we argue in Chapter 3, people do not make gender attributions on the basis of knowing about biological criteria. The ways in which a group constructs gender, in turn, determine the correlates cited for evidence of gender. For other groups to share our everyday reasons (i.e., biology) for attributing gender it would be necessary for them to share our construction of the world. It is this construction that results in our seeing our way as right, not any absolute standard. Being members of a certain sociocultural group, and having to rely on secondhand reports, we are not in the position to describe how people in other cultures make/made gender attributions. We have, however, shown how it is possible that the way we construct gender is not necessarily universal over time and place. We live in a world of two biological genders. But that may not be the only world.

NOTES

1. We generally refer to the berdache as "becoming the other gender" rather than "assuming the other gender role," because from our perspective, that appears to be a more accurate description of their treatment by members of their own culture. It is also possible that in some cultures the berdache became a *third* gender. In either case, "became" is the appropriate verb.

2. This would particularly be true of the earlier anthropologists. More recently, anthropologists (e.g., Dimen-Schein, 1977) have begun to consider how they apply their concepts to other cultures. Our primary data on the berdache were provided, however, by anthropologists prior to this contemporary consideration.

3. In our culture, examples of this include referring to a male-to-female transsexual as "she" even if the speaker does not believe in transsexualism or does not believe that the person is a transsexual. Male homosexuals in certain subcultures jestingly refer to one another as "she" with full awareness that they are all male (Newton, 1972).

4. Although female-to-male berdache were said to use dildoes, this was acknowledged as a mechanical device in order to satisfy their partners; it does not appear that it was considered a real phallus by anyone, including the berdache.

3
BIOLOGY
AND GENDER

As in every scientific discipline, the biological sciences make certain assumptions about the nature of reality. Biology,[1] however, has a unique role. Biological factors tend to be seen as the most basic and primary of causes. The emphasis on biological versus environmental causation has changed over time, at least partly because "biological" has been interpreted as synonymous for "unchangeable" and "natural" (in a religious or moral sense). Social historians have demonstrated how biological explanations have been used by both scientists and interpreters of science to justify the continued exploitation of certain groups. For example, if the scarcity of women in positions of power is seen as "biologically" caused, then, depending on how this type of causation is interpreted, it might be concluded that nothing can (or should) be done about it (Ehrenreich and English, 1973). The reaction of some scientists to this use of biology has been to search for environmental explanations for the same behaviors. If we view science as a way of constructing the world, then the question: Is gender totally biological or totally environmental? can be seen in a new way. As Ounstead and Taylor (1972) state, that is like asking if a coin is "really" heads or tails. Gender is at once totally environmental *and* totally biological. In other words, depending on the methods and assumptions that are applied to whatever is being observed, gender is whatever we make of it. In seeing the biological sciences as the foundation for all behaviors, we tend to overlook the fact that this is only one of an infinite number of ways of seeing the world. This does not mean, of course, that reality should or should not be constructed in this way; it only means that it is important to be aware that it is constructed.

In seeing biological facts as dictating the range of human possibilities, another point is also often overlooked, which is that biological facts change with time. It is easier to see the change that has already occurred than it is to see present facts as part of a process which will continue to change in the future. In everyday life, our tendency is to view what we know now as the final truth, and to forget that the truth undergoes constant change as new scientific discoveries are made. For example, we now know that many diseases are caused by microorganisms rather than moral weakness. We can see how a theory of disease based on the latter cause would lead to very different types of research and treatment than what we have now. However, because of the way realities are constructed, because of the "incorrigible propositions" which we hold (see Chapter 1), we say that earlier theories were "wrong" for various reasons, and that we now know the "true facts" about disease. What we tend to forget is that this is a continuing process. New discoveries, technologies, and interpretations force biologists to change some of their basic assumptions (although probably not all of their "incorrigible propositions") and, as a result, there will continue to be changes in the "facts" (see, e.g., Kuhn, 1970; Toulmin, 1961).

One of the most important contemporary examples of the points we have been making is the concern with the scientific definition of death. This is especially relevant to our study of gender, because until very recently life and death were seen as clearly dichotomous. An individual was either one or the other, and there was little debate about which state a person was in. As technology and instrumentation became more and more refined, however, the presence or absence of certain criteria for life became less clear. Was a person whose heart continued to beat only because she/he was attached to a respirator dead or alive? The need for "live" organs for organ transplants brought this question to the fore. A new, dichotomous, criterion was needed for making a "death attribution." Since biologists had come to see the brain, rather than the heart, as the source of life functions, and since a way of making brain function visible had been developed (EEG's), examining the indicators of brain activity seemed to be a way of answering the question of whether someone was still alive. However, except for totally flat recordings, which are not common, EEG's are not yet dichotomous criteria. They still must be interpreted by people.

An excellent illustration of how the "signs" of life and death receive their meaning only through their connection to more basic assumptions, is a study reported in *The New York Times* (Rensberger, 1976). Dr. Adrian Upton connected a blob of jello to an EEG machine set up in a hospital ward. The recordings, according to Upton, could have been interpreted as showing signs of life. "The neurologist said that similar electrical artifacts interfering with a real EEG test could confuse doctors into believing that a person's brain was still living while, in fact, it might be as lifeless as a blob of Jello" (p. 50). Life cannot be defined merely by a recording on a piece of paper. At the very least, the object from which the recording was taken must be one to which a "life attribution" could be made. Life is not defined by EEG's but by basic assumptions about what life is in the first place.

Legal actions have brought the question of the scientific definition of death into the public arena for debate, and it is becoming clearer that some group or groups, probably physicians, are going to have to *decide* what death is. The criteria may be scientific and they may be dichotomous (e.g., the presence or absence of a certain type of brain rhythm for a certain length of time), but that decision will show how the life/death dichotomy, and determinations regarding specific individuals, are socially constructed. Finally, it is even conceivable that evidence acceptable to scientists about what happens after "death," may one day bring the whole life/death dichotomy itself into question.

Our argument in this book is that what we have been saying about the life/death dichotomy is as true of the male/female dichotomy. Just as the EEG is one criterion for death, and just as EEG's are taken as a sign of life only when more basic assumptions are met, we will see how various biological criteria may be taken as a sign of gender only in certain circumstances. We begin by presenting the biological facts about gender and what they suggest about the biological foundations of gender identity, role, and attribution, within a biological framework. This is followed by a critical analysis of biologists' views of gender as they reflect the process of a socially constructed gender dichotomy.

BIOLOGICAL FOUNDATIONS OF GENDER[2]

For the biologist, both the concept of gender[3] and the gender of a particular individual is grounded in reproductive processes. All living organisms reproduce themselves, and there are two ways by which this can be done. Some plants and animals reproduce through a process of fission; part of the organism breaks off from the original, forming a new individual. Amoebae reproduce this way, as do strawberries, among others. In this type of reproduction, known as asexual reproduction, the genetic material of the new individual is identical to that of the original organism.

The second type of reproduction occurs when a new individual is formed from genetic material contributed by two separate members of the species. This process, sexual reproduction, has the advantage of allowing for greater variability and evolution among the members of the species. In order for the two sets of genetic material to fuse and form a new individual, there must be a way for the cell containing one set of genetic material to reach and merge with the cell containing the other set. There must also be provision for the nourishment of the developing structure until it has become a viable organism. These functions are accomplished by one reproductive cell having the potential to provide nourishment (the egg cell), and the other reproductive cell (the sperm cell) having the potential to reach and penetrate the cell wall of the first cell.[4]

In biological terminology, individuals who produce sperm cells are classified as "male" and individuals who produce egg cells are classified as "female." How are egg and sperm cell carriers designed to promote the success of this type of reproduction? How does this process of reproduction result in new individuals who carry either sperm or egg cells, but not both?[5]

The answers to these questions come from the study of biological factors in the normal development of females (egg cell carriers) and males (sperm cell carriers). The ways in which females and males function to promote the success of sexual reproduction depends on the species. For plants, and some animals, sexual reproduction is merely a matter of the random combination of a sperm cell and an egg cell. For example, a female sea urchin may deposit a large number of eggs in the surrounding water which may or may not be fertilized by sperm cells ejaculated by a male sea urchin in the immediate environment.

However, in other species, including *homo sapiens*, the process of selective combinations takes over. The male and female select one another as individuals for the purpose of engaging in at least one reproductive act. Selection makes it more likely that in any given case the reproductive cells will merge, and, thus, a much smaller number of egg cells needs to be produced. Selection necessitates that sperm and egg cell carriers be able to distinguish one another as such, and also be able to distinguish the other as being different from all members of the same reproductive category. Thus some type of gender dimorphism is necessary from a biological perspective. Nevertheless, "(e)ven granted dimorphism, sexual reproduction does not require a particular form for either sex, nor that the sexes should be clearly recognizable between species. Nor need the dimorphism be permanent throughout the life span. Nor indeed need the behaviors which bring the gametes [sperm and egg cells] together necessarily be permanent or similar within classes or species" (Ounstead and Taylor, 1972, p. 243). In other words, what has to be dimorphic is not so obvious.

It is at this point in the discussion of the reproductive process that biologists and those who interpret their work often make assumptions that may not be warranted, often construct dichotomies that may not exist. For example, Ounstead and Taylor, the authors we have just quoted, go on to state, "For man,[6] success in sexual reproduction *requires* . . . suitable behavior for the sex in training for the adult role . . . (and) suitable secondary sex characteristics" (Ounstead and Taylor, 1972, p. 243, emphasis ours). Why these should be required, and what "suitable" means, is left unstated. Perhaps the authors assume that we all know; and perhaps we do on some level. That is, we are able to tell if another person is female or male, and most of us present ourselves as members of our biological gender (i.e., as egg or sperm cell carriers).

However, the meanings of the terms "male" and "female" in everyday life, and in much biological writing, are quite different from the purely reproductive sense, especially when human beings are the subject of the writing. Females and males must distinguish each other for the purpose of reproduction, but (a) not all people can, or wish to, reproduce; (b) new technologies, such as artificial insemination and embryo transplants, may change methods of human reproduction; and (c) it is difficult to see how certain "suitable behaviors" (e.g., being cooperative vs. being competitive) are necessary in order for people to tell females from males. Nevertheless, despite the fact that the biological study of gender often goes far beyond its foundations, it should be remembered that the foundation of biological studies of gender is in the process of reproduction.

The second question we posed was how sexual reproduction results in new individuals who are either sperm or egg cell carriers, but not both. To answer this we present a brief review of biological factors in normal human gender development, which is followed by a discussion of the contribution of biological factors to gender identity, role, and attribution. In making this assessment, one of the most important sources of the information we have comes from the study of individuals who are born with various gender-related biological abnormalities. Since for ethical reasons scientists cannot study such factors as the effects of prenatal hormones on human behavior by controlling hormones during prenatal life, the only information we have about these effects in human beings is from those who were exposed, either inadvertently or because of other abnormalities, to abnormal levels of prenatal hormones. For the sake of clarity, each type of abnormality is discussed as it relates to particular biological factors.

THE BIOLOGICAL DEVELOPMENT OF FEMALES AND MALES

In human beings, the basic genetic coding is carried on 23 pairs of chromosomes. Every cell in the human body contains these 46 chromosomes except for the reproductive cells which, after they are fully mature, contain half of the necessary genetic material, that is, 23 chromosomes. The twenty-third pair of chromosomes are known as the "sex" chromosomes, because they determine what type of reproductive cell the mature individual will produce. Normally, the twenty-third chromosome of the egg cell is fairly large and shaped like the letter "X". The twenty-third chromosome of the sperm cell may be either "X" shaped, or smaller and shaped more like the letter "Y". When a sperm cell successfully penetrates an egg cell, and the 23 chromosomes from each reproductive cell pair to form the nucleus of the cell which will develop into the fetus, the result is one of two possible combinations for the twenty-third pair —either XX or XY. Since reproductive cells will contain only one of the individual's two gender chromosomes, XX individuals will only produce reproductive cells with X chromosomes while XY individuals will produce some reproductive cells with X chromosomes and others with Y chromosomes.

The gender chromosomes begin to affect the development of the embryo about six weeks after conception. At that time, the genetic coding on the Y chromosome, if there is one, causes the medulla, or inner layer, of the gonads (glands which have developed in the abdominal cavity) to develop into testes which, at puberty, will produce sperm. If there is a second X chromosome, rather than a Y, the cortex, or outer layer, of the gonads develop (sometimes as late as twelve weeks after conception) into ovaries which contain all the egg cells which will be released, beginning at puberty. Thus, the development of the gonads is directly influenced by the gender chromosomes.[7]

Soon after the testes have developed, at about eight weeks, they begin to produce a hormone, androgen, and a second substance, whose nature is not known, which is referred to as Mullerian inhibiting substance. During the third fetal month (8–12 weeks), the androgens cause a set of ducts, the Wolffian, to develop into seminal vesicles, ejaculatory ducts, and the vas deferens, while the Mullerian inhibiting substances causes a second set of ducts, the Mullerian, to atrophy. In the absence of androgen and Mullerian inhibiting substance, as when the gonads have become ovaries, the Wolffian ducts degenerate and the Mullerian ducts develop into fallopian tubes, a uterus, and the upper vagina. In the adult, only vestiges remain of the ducts and layers of the gonads which did not develop prenatally.

Other effects that androgens secreted by the fetal testes may have are not totally understood. It is known that they affect the genitals of the fetus, so that in the third month of fetal life, the genital tubercle develops into a penis, the urethral folds close, and the labialscrotal swellings fuse to form the scrotum into which the testes descend from the abdomen shortly before birth. It is also known that in the absence of androgens, the tubercle develops into a clitoris, the folds into labia minorae, and the swellings into labia majorae. By about 16 weeks, then, the development of the fetus into a potential sperm producer is complete, and by about 20 weeks the development of the fetus into a potential egg producer is complete, at least in terms of the physical apparatus (both internal and external) necessary to accomplish the individual's reproductive role. Other possible effects of the presence or absence of prenatal androgens are just beginning to be explored, particularly for human beings. We deal with this in later sections.

At birth, and until the beginning of puberty, the child produces low, steady, levels of both androgens and estrogens. When puberty begins (triggered by some unknown mechanism, perhaps a critical body weight [Frisch and McArthur, 1974]), the hypothalamus stimulates the pituitary gland to produce large amounts of follicle stimulating hormone (FSH). FSH stimulates the gonads to begin production of much higher levels of hormones than had been produced in childhood. Androgens and estrogens are produced by *both* testes *and* ovaries, but the ovaries produce more estrogen and progesterone than androgen (thus estrogen is the "female" hormone) and the testes produce greater amounts of androgens relative to the amount of estrogen and progresterone (thus androgen is the "male" hormone). These hormones are also produced by the cortex of the adrenal glands in both genders, in about equal proportions.

As is the case with prenatal hormones, the physical effects of pubertal hormones are clear. Androgens facilitate the development and growth of bones and muscles, affect the larynx so that it enlarges (deepening the voice and resulting in an "adam's apple"), cause hair to grow on the face and body, enlarge the genitals, set off the process that leads to sperm production and ejaculatory capacity, increase libido, and lead to the growth of pubic and axillary hair. Many of these effects occur in both genders, especially the last two. Estrogens cause breasts to develop, facilitate fatty deposits (especially around the hips and buttocks), decrease the serum cholesterol level, slow down growth of bones, and begin the process of ovulation and menstruation. Beyond the physical effects, however, it is important to know what, if any, are the psychological and behavioral effects of pubertal hormones. As in the case of prenatal hormones, this is an extremely difficult question to answer and will be temporarily postponed. Assessing the effects of various biological factors on gender identity, role, and attribution can best be done by taking these factors one at a time and reviewing the relevant scientific literature on their contribution to the components of gender.

Chromosomes and Gender

Chromosomes and Gender Identity. Most people have either XX or XY chromosomes. However, a significant number of possible combinations exist.[8] In fact, almost every combination of gender chromosomes has been found in human beings, with one exception. It appears that there must be at least one X chromosome in order for a fetus to be viable. This is probably because vital genes are carried on the X chromosome, while the smaller Y chromosome carries a minimal amount of genetic coding.

All the scientific evidence indicates that chromosomes have little or no direct effect on whether persons feel that they are female or male. One of the most compelling examples of this are people with complete androgen insensitivity. This is a genetic (but not gender chromosome linked) inability of the cells in the body to respond to androgens. Because the fetus cannot respond to prenatal androgens

secreted by the fetal testes in an XY fetus, persons with total androgen insensitivity develop normal female genitals and are assigned
the gender "female" at birth. At puberty, the testes produce enough
estrogen to "feminize" the body, and the condition is only discovered when failure to menstruate motivates a medical consultation.
There has been no report of affected individuals developing anything other than normal female gender identities.

Another example is transsexualism. A male-to-female transsexual,
for example, has XY chromosomes but a female gender identity. A
third example is studies of individuals with gender chromosome
abnormalities. People with only one gender chromosome or with
extra chromosomes may be affected in various ways (e.g., ability to
reproduce, development of secondary gender characteristics at
puberty, retardation), but none of the evidence indicates that they
develop anything other than typical gender identities. Their gender
identities are based on their gender assignments at birth (cf. Money
and Ehrhardt, 1972).

Chromosomes and Gender Role. There is no evidence linking gender
chromosomes to any *specific* behavior. However, there are two
hypotheses about the relationship between gender chromosomes and
gender differences in general. The Lyon hypothesis (Lyon, 1962) states
that in females one of the two X chromosomes in each cell becomes
inactive early in fetal life. This process protects genetic females
from many recessive gender-linked disorders. For example, hemophilia is a disorder carried by a gene on the X chromosome. When
only one of the two X chromosomes carries this gene, not all cells in
the person's body will contain this chromosome as the active one.
Both X chromosomes must have the hemophilia gene in order for the
disease to express itself in the XX individual. Since this would
occur very rarely, the second X chromosome in effect "protects"
the individual from the disease. When there is only one X chromosome, however, as in the case of genetically normal males, there is
no "protection" from the hemophilia gene, and all males with this
gene on the X chromosome will have the disease. Thus, there is a
much higher incidence of X-linked (sometimes referred to as "sex-
linked") diseases in chromosomal males than in chromosomal females. However, in terms of the everyday meaning of gender role,
susceptibility to, or incidence of, disease is usually not included as
a component.

The second hypothesis about gender chromosomes and gender
differences has been postulated by Ounstead and Taylor, (1972). They

assert that the Y chromosome causes slower development in those who have one, which enables such individuals (i.e., males) to gain more from each developmental stage. Their analogy is to a staircase, where the boy spends more time than the girl on each step. She gets to the top sooner, but he gets more information from each step, so that his development occurs in more depth. This effect of the Y chromosome could be either advantageous, as Ounstead and Taylor assert is the case with such traits as spatial ability, or it could be deleterious, as when there is more time to "transcribe" information from a mutant (e.g., hemophiliac) X chromosome. This hypothesis, according to them, can account for many gender differences in behavior. Ounstead and Taylor's hypothesis has not yet found a wide degree of acceptance in this country. It still does not answer questions about the extent (if any) of the genetic contribution to gender roles, nor does it explain causal mechanisms (if any) in genetic contributions to *specific* components of gender role, such as aptitudes or preferences.

Gender chromosomes do not appear to directly affect the specifics of gender role. Studies of individuals with chromosome abnormalities (Money and Ehrhardt, 1972), indicate that XXX individuals are not more "feminine" (on traditional measures of femininity) than XX individuals, nor are XO individuals less "feminine." XXY persons are not less "masculine" in their interests and behaviors than XY persons, nor are XYY individuals more so. Of course, physical abnormalities associated with genetic abnormalities may affect others' treatment and thus influence the affected individual's behavior. For example, some XYY persons may be taller than average and be treated as more "manly," or some XXY individuals may be retarded in pubertal development and thus be treated by others as younger than their chronological age. Such treatment, however, is not a direct effect of chromosomes on behavior. Rather it is an effect of chromosomes on physique; treatment differences based on physique are social, not genetic. There is no evidence that chromosomes themselves have any direct effect on gender role.

Chromosomes and Gender Attribution. We doubt that anyone would argue that chromosomes are relevant criteria by which we decide whether someone is female or male in everyday life. We usually are not even positive about what our own chromosomes are, much less someone else's. In fact, many people who make gender attributions with no trouble whatsoever, have never even heard of X and Y chromosomes. For biologists, however, chromosomes are an important criteria for attributing gender. If there is at least one Y chromosome the individual is male, and if there are no Y chromosomes the individual is female. This is, in fact, the most basic biological criterion for attributing gender, and is also the most clearly dichotomous. There is no question, genetically, whether an individual is female or male. And yet even this dichotomy is not always so clear. There do exist individuals who are genetic mosaics. For example, they may have some cells with XO chromosomes and other cells with XXY chromosomes. What is their genetic gender? As in the case of the scientific definition of death and life, such examples make obvious that attribution of gender, even in science, is sometimes a matter of making a decision.

There is also one everyday situation where chromosomes are the ultimate criteria for making gender attributions. In athletic competitions, particularly international games, the criteria are the biologists'—an individual with a Y chromosome may not play in the women's games. It is interesting to review the history of gender attribution in sports, for it illuminates how gender dichotomies are constructed and how important it is in modern society that the dichotomy not be challenged and that it be supported by scientific facts.

In ancient Greece's Olympic games, women were barred from competition. The ancient Greeks coped with the potential problem of female participants by having athletes compete unclothed. That this was an adequate "test" of gender is indicated by the fact that when a woman was discovered "passing" as a male trainer in 404 B.C. (women were also barred from watching the games), trainers were thereafter required to be naked also. Since then, however, there has been little concern with discovering whether male participants are "real" males. The reason given is that "there is little or no advantage [for women to compete as men]" (Hanley, 1976), since the superior strength of men makes them generally better than women in many athletic activities. In fact, there are no recorded cases of male competitors who were later "unmasked" as having been women.[9]

The presumed superior strength and ability of men would, however, give them an unfair advantage over women, were they to compete in women's games. It is not important if this assertion is supported by actual gender differences, nor, if it is, whether the reasons for the differences in athletic ability are biological or environmental. Given the acceptance of differences as a "fact," once women began to compete in the modern Olympics and other international competitions, the question of making "correct" gender attributions was raised, especially after it became known that some female athletes had turned out to be men.

How, then, could the governing committees of the competitions insure that the women were really women? Clearly, given past experience, everyday gender attribution processes were not enough. It would be too easy for a competitor to "pass." Thus prior to 1968[10] each country was required to provide certification of the genuineness of their female athletes' genders. Charges were made, though, that some of these certificates were fraudulent, and that some competing countries were not being truthful, or objective, in their certification procedures.

The result was that, beginning in 1968, a physical examination was required of each female athlete, which was carried out by an international, unbiased medical team at the site of the competition. In effect, this was reinstituting what the Greeks had done, and, indeed, some "women" withdrew from competition before the examination. This "test," too, was eventually challenged. It was alleged that physical characteristics were not enough evidence on which to make an absolutely certain attribution. It may have been felt that the availability of surgical and hormonal procedures to make a "male" body look like a "female" one, invalidated a physical examination.

At this point, the emphasis seems to have turned from insuring that there was no unfair competition to finding an unfailingly dichotomous definition of "female." The most clearly dichotomous criterion for attributing gender is the biologists' criterion of gender chromosomes. Therefore, in 1972, the "sex chromosome" test for determining if an athlete is "really" a woman was instituted.

The lining of the cheek is scraped, and the cells are stained and microscopically examined for Barr bodies. The number of Barr bodies in a cell (probably the nuclei of the inactivated X chromosomes) is one less than the number of X chromosomes in the cell. For example, if the chromosomes are XX, there would be one Barr body. No Barr bodies would mean either XO or at least one Y. If there are less than 10 percent Barr bodies, then further testing is done to determine the exact gender chromosome makeup. The criterion is dichotomous—any Y chromosomes and the person is declared *not female* and ineligible to compete in the women's games. (The person is not declared to be a male, and we wonder what would happen if an individual, after "failing" the test, insisted on entering the men's competition, even if she had breasts and a vagina.)

Only one case of "failing" the test has been publicized. Eva

Klobukowska, who passed the physical examination in 1964, and won several medals in the women's games at the 1964 Olympics, "failed" the chromosome test at the 1967 European Track and Field competitions. It is likely that she had some XO cells and some XXY cells. She was declared ineligible to compete as a female, and her Olympic medals were declared invalid. She had entered the games as a woman, and despite the decree of the International Amateur Athletic Federation that she is not, she continues to live, in her own eyes and others', as a woman. The actions of the IAAF underscore the fact that the biologists' criteria for gender become nonsensical when, in an attempt to be "fair," they are applied to everyday life.

There continue to be incidents which, while not as drastic as the case of Eva Klobukowska, illustrate the relationship between biological criteria for gender and social criteria for gender, and how the former can be constructed to support the latter. In countries where not as much value is placed on physical "femininity" as in the United States, and where athletes are able to devote most of their time, from early childhood, to intensive training in their sport, the bodies and movements of female athletes often appear "masculine" from an American point of view. In 1976, at the summer Olympics, the American women's swimming team was badly beaten, for the first time, by the East German women's swim team. One way for some members of the American team (not just the swimmers) to explain this loss, was to make comments which, by implication, cast doubt on the "real" femaleness of the East German female atheletes [e.g., "If they turn around, the only way you can tell it's a woman is by their bust" (Amdur, 1976)]. Of course, the East German women had to pass the "sex test" in order to compete, but if enough influential competitors begin to feel that chromosomes are no longer an appropriate criteria to avoid "unfair competition," then there will be an attempt to include other "biologically valid" criteria into procedures for deciding who is "really" a woman. The original reason for instituting "sex tests" was to eliminate "unnaturally" strong "women." Now it is becoming increasingly clear that strength is not gender dichotomous. This does not eliminate the possibility that someday there might be a test to decide how much muscle a "real" woman is allowed to have, and anything more would mean she either was not a woman or she had been taking "male" hormones.

A final example is the case of Renee Richards, who, as Richard

Raskind, competed in, and won, several men's tennis tournaments. As a postoperative transsexual, Dr. Richards attempted to compete in women's tennis. As a result, the Women's Tennis Association requested that chromosome "sex tests" be instituted for female players. It must be a chromosome test, because Dr. Richards (and others like her) would "pass" a physical examination but undoubtedly "fail" a chromosome test, since she has XY chromosomes. Why has there been such concern with eliminating her from playing women's tennis? The Association's contention is that men have an unfair advantage over women because of their strength. (Thus, in their eyes, she is still a man.) However, she weighs much less than she did when she played as Dr. Raskind, and the fact that she now produces less androgen and has more circulating estrogen, probably means that she has little, if any, "unfair advantage" in strength. The problem is not so much "unfairness," but lies more in Dr. Richards' challenge to the reality of the gender dichotomy. To maintain the dichotomy there has to be proof that she did not change genders, and her chromosomes are that "proof"—no matter how impossible it might be to see her as anything but a woman in every other way and in any possible circumstance.

As more is discovered about genetics, and new techniques are developed for examining the structure of chromosomes, it is likely that chromosomes will be "discovered" to be less dichotomous than they are now thought to be (Stoller, 1974). As a result, "more exact" criteria will be "discovered" for attributing chromosomal gender. The "ultimate" criteria for determining gender will continue to change as the scientists' facts change. Nevertheless, it is doubtful that the incorrigible proposition that there are two genders will change, and this, in itself, will help determine what the "facts," for scientists as well as athletes, will be.

Internal Reproductive Organs and Gender

Gender Identity. The presence or absence of gonads and internal reproductive structures (e.g., uterus, sperm ducts) has little effect on gender identity. Although the normal development of these structures is interfered with in several clinical syndromes (including Turner's (XO) syndrome, and some forms of hermaphroditism), there is no evidence that the gender identity of affected persons is influenced (Money and Ehrhardt, 1972). The absence of these organs, in fact, may not be discovered until signs of puberty fail to appear, motivating a visit to a physician. By this time, however, the child has developed a secure, stable gender identity.

It is also possible for individuals to develop a gender identity in conflict with the biological gender of their internal reproductive organs. This occurs in transsexualism, and in cases of complete androgen insensitivity where, as described earlier, an XY fetus develops testes and other "male" internal reproductive organs, but is insensitive to the effects of androgens, and has a vagina and clitoris. Such individuals develop a normal female gender identity.

Gender Role. The same syndromes discussed previously provide evidence that, except insofar as they enable individuals to differentially participate in the reproductive process, gonads and internal organs *per se* do not affect how someone dresses, expresses her/himself, or otherwise exhibits interests and behaviors "appropriate" to her/his gender (Money and Ehrhardt, 1972). However, since reproduction and gender are mutually dependent in biology, those who cannot reproduce cannot perform their (biologically defined) gender role. Gender role in everyday life and the social sciences obviously includes much more than reproductive behavior. However, much of the writing on the negative effects of blurred gender roles (cf. Winick, 1968) can be traced back to this basic biological principle.

Gender Attribution. Although internal organs are important *biological* criteria for the attribution of gender (the individual who can produce and ejaculate sperm is male, the individual who can produce an egg and nourish a fetus is female), in everyday life it is obvious that we do not decide whether someone is female or male by determining whether they have ovaries or testes, a uterus or sperm ducts. We assume, once we make a gender attribution, that a person has the appropriate internal organs, but should we find out that they do not (e.g., we might discover that someone has had a hysterectomy), we do not change our attribution. Even if we discover that someone has the "wrong" internal organs (e.g., if we find out that a male friend has a uterus), once we have made an attribution, we will see the organs as being a mistake of some sort, not the attribution as having been mistaken. Attributions, once made, are extremely resistant to change, and information about the person is fitted to the attribution, rather than vice versa. We discuss this in more detail in Chapter 5.

Chronologically, the next step in the sequence of biological factors in the development of gender is the presence or absence of prenatal horomones. However, for the sake of clarity, that discussion will be postponed and combined with a discussion on the effects of pubertal hormones and gender.

External Reproductive Organs and Gender

External Reproductive Organs and Gender Identity. The possession of a vagina, labia, and clitoris, or a penis and scrotum is neither a necessary nor sufficient condition for developing a female or male gender identity, respectively. Although most people with penises have male gender identities, and most people with clitorises have female gender identities, there are important exceptions. Preoperative transsexuals have the "wrong" genitals for their gender identity (and, indeed, that is why they seek surgery). Children who are born with ambiguous genitals, not yet "corrected" surgically, almost always develop unambiguous gender identities, as do children and adults with uncorrectable genital defects, like micropenises (Money and Ehrhardt, 1972). Although genitals are a crucial aspect of our construction of gender, it is not in terms of the *direct* role which they play in the development and maintenance of gender identity. Rather, as we shall see, they serve as a sign of gender.

External Reproductive Organs and Gender Role. Freud notwithstanding, the possession of a particular set of genitals is not a direct causal factor in how masculine or feminine one's interests and behaviors are. Nor do one's genitals necessarily determine one's choice of a sexual partner. We decide on a potential sexual partner on the basis of a gender attribution, not a genital inspection. Even though one definition of heterosexuality is sexual activities with a partner whose genitals are different from one's own, a heterosexual person who has a vagina, for example, does not look for a person who has a penis. "She" looks for a "he," assuming that when a "he" is found, and sexual contact takes place, the (assumed) penis will actually be there.

We are not saying that one's genitals have no effect on behavior. It is quite possible that having a vagina and clitoris may lead to very different experiences in life than having a penis. Certainly those who have vaginas and who menstruate have experiences that those who have penises and who ejaculate cannot have, and vice versa. On the other hand, one's whole body affects the experiences one has. Height, weight, skin color, and physical attractiveness (see, e.g., Waters & Denmark, 1974) are also crucial factors in how one is treated and in the way one experiences the world. We maintain that whatever the effects of having a particular set of genitals are on one's life experiences, they do not necessarily lead to any particular gender role behaviors. Having a scrotum and penis does not make a person strong and aggressive, nor does having labia and a clitoris make a person weak and passive, or vice versa. Even those who stress biological factors in gender differences no longer claim that genitals are the causal factor. Prenatal horomones, of which genitals are a correlate, are asserted to be the cause of such differences, as we will explain in the section on hormones and gender role.

Genitals and Gender Attribution. The relationship between this biological factor and this component of gender is unequivocal in at least one instance. Penises and vaginas are *the* criteria by which gender is assigned at birth. Penis means "male" and labia and vagina means "female," and that, except in the most ambiguous cases, is all that is necessary to determine the neonate's gender. There is some question as to whether the formula is really labia and vagina=female, or whether it is instead no penis=female, since at birth there is no search (i.e., internal examination) for a vagina or clitoris. (We report additional evidence for this formula in the last chapter.)

On the other hand, and despite the fact that plastic surgeons cannot yet create a fully functional penis where there is none, in ambiguous cases the medical profession has historically tended to assign the gender "male" when the infant was capable of functioning as a male in the reproductive sense (i.e., when there were functioning testes), regardless of the adequacy of the penis (Money and Ehrhardt, 1972). This practice suggests that the biological, reproductive, definition of gender is, in circumscribed cases, the primary basis on which gender attributions are made. For example, in a case where a mother amputated the penis of her 15-month-old son, the medical team made the decision to keep him "male," despite the fact that he no longer had a penis (Westman and Zarwell, 1975). The medical basis of this decision seems to have been that reassigning him as female, and performing the necessary surgery, would have necessitated castration and thus rendered this individual sterile. A fertile male without a penis was seen as preferable to a sterile female with a vagina.[11]

In ambiguous or difficult cases such as the one just described, criteria other than genitals are examined, and the ultimate decision is often made on biological grounds only, rather than by considering the fact that the individual will not be living in a biological framework. In nonambiguous cases, however, external reproductive organs are crucial for gender assignment.

Except for the moment of gender assignment, genitals play little role in gender attribution. This is largely because in our society genitals are almost always concealed. We expect, for example, that all men have penises under their clothes, but we cannot see them. The actual physical genitals play little role in gender attribution. The role of the expected genitals, however, is important, and is discussed at the end of this chapter and in Chapter 6.

Hormones and Gender

Today few biologists would argue that reproductive organs or chromosomes *per se* affect gender identity or gender role. (Gender attribution is not of interest in the literature.) In everyday life, some persons might state that some of these factors are crucial to being a woman or a man (e.g., "you're not a 'real' man if you're sterile"), but their statements would be considered naive from a scientific point of view. Hormones, however, are another matter. While nonscientists tend to ignore hormones because they are not visible, and hormonal mechanisms are complex and difficult to understand, there are vast amounts of time and money being spent on research to determine the effects of the gonadal hormones in both human and nonhuman animals. What is known and what questions are still unanswered? Are the effects of prenatal hormones different from the effects of the hormones secreted once the individual reaches puberty? Before discussing specific research that relates to these questions, we want to make certain general criticisms of, and comments about, the numerous studies on the relationship between gender hormones and the components of gender, particularly gender role.

In the first place, many of the studies, particularly those using human beings as subjects, are correlational. That is, various levels of hormones are found to be associated with various types and levels of behavior. Frequently, however, the direction of the relationship is assumed to be "hormones cause behavior" despite the fact that "behavior causes hormones" is in many cases as plausible. This is true in studies of homosexuality, aggression, intelligence, activity level, spatial ability, and a myriad of other behaviors which have been said to be influenced by the level of gonadal hormones. It could be, for example, that high androgen levels cause aggressive behavior, but alternatively, high levels of aggressive behavior could lead to higher amounts of androgen production. In fact, Rose et al. (1972) found support for this in colonies of rhesus monkeys. When a more aggressive monkey was introduced into the colony, thus changing the dominance hierarchy, the levels of androgens secreted by the other monkeys, who were now forced to be less aggressive, decreased.

We are not asserting that the direction is always "behavior leads to hormones." Both directions may be correct in different cases, but too often the explanation emphasizes the causal factor of hormones rather than behavior. Correlations can also be due to the influence of a third factor, associated with both gonadal hormones and behavior. For example, Vande Wiele points out that in the adrenogenital syndrome (a condition that results in the overproduction of prenatal adrenal androgen), many hormones and hormonal relationships are out of balance, not just androgens (Friedman et al., 1974). To assume that "tomboyishness" or higher intelligence in affected girls is due to abnormally high levels of prenatal androgen as some have done (e.g., Money and Ehrhardt, 1972) may be unwarranted.

Besides unexamined hormonal relationships, other biological factors may play a part in such a correlation. If intelligence is genetically linked, then there is the possibility of selective sampling. The more intelligent parents may bring their daughters for treatment and/or may be more likely to agree to participate in scientific studies. Their daughters, then, would tend to have above average intelligence scores also. (Of course selective sampling could be a factor even if the genetic component in intelligence is minimal.)

A second problem is that the nature of the two groups from which the bulk of data comes present difficulties in interpreting the research on hormones and behavior. The two groups are: persons with various sorts of clinical syndromes, and animals. A factor often overlooked in studying the former group is the effects of knowledge of the abnormality on the behavior of the individual and those close to the individual. The role that this awareness might have on the results of the studies has tended to be downplayed, despite the large body of literature on demand characteristics and experimenter effects, which seems particularly relevant here (cf. Rosenthal, 1966; Orne, 1962). For example, if there is a relationship between prenatal exposure to androgens and intelligence (Money and Lewis, 1966), how much of the relationship is due to at least some of the parents knowing that their daughters were prenatally exposed to higher than normal levels of "male" hormones? Such parents might have encouraged, or not discouraged, "masculine" play behavior, which may be related to scores on certain tests of intelligence (Sherman, 1967). How many of these parents reported more "masculine" behavior in their daughters at least partly because they had an idea that that was what the researcher was looking for? Even in cases where normal hormonal levels are presumed to affect behavior (e.g., the premenstrual syndrome—see below), one factor that is often overlooked is that people are aware of some biological cycles and expect these cycles to have certain effects on behavior. These expectations may be an important factor in how behavior is interpreted as well as in what behaviors actually occur.

One of the major advantages of animal studies is that these types of "bias" can be eliminated, and controlled experiments that would be unethical using humans can be conducted. On the other hand, there are difficulties in generalizing from the results of research on animals to human beings. The majority of studies with rats, mice, and guinea pigs take as their dependent variable adult sexual and reproductive behavior. Other "gender" differences that have been studied include activity level and structural differences in the brain (Reinisch, 1974). Those who study animal behavior are aware of certain difficulties in the interpretation of their studies. For example, the effects of hormones may be indirect. Hormones change body structures which change behavior. Androgens administered to female animals greatly enlarge the size of the clitoris. This morphological change rather than direct hormonal effects may be the critical factor in the increase in mounting and thrusting behavior seen in such animals (Money and Ehrhardt, 1972).

In addition, animal sexual behavior is not gender role behavior. Even if we accept traditional definitions of gender role, these definitions clearly go beyond the instinctual responses of animals. To compare lordosis and mounting with the range of human sexual activities and relationships is absurd. To what are we to compare lordosis? A naked woman lying on her back with her legs open? Is the wearing of lipstick really analogous to the "sex swelling" of primates, as some have implied (Morris, 1967)? Should we compare estrous cycles (where the female animal exhibits clear physical signs of sexual arousal at the time of ovulation) to human menstrual cycles (where there are no clear signs of arousal, where the timing is not during fertile periods, and around which a complex social mythology has developed)? What is the subhuman analog of the alleged social sensitivity and illogical thought processes of women or of the alleged insensitive, logical behavior of men? Traditionally, scientists have dealt with this problem by conceiving of human behavior as more fluid and more under environmental control. Nevertheless, they maintain that the basics of all behavior, the biological foundations, can be understood through the study of animal behavior.

It is noteworthy that even the rigid dichotomization of animal sexual behavior is beginning to be questioned by some biologists (Goy and Goldfoot, 1975). This new assertion is that the dichotomy is not absolute. Animals of both genders *in all species* exhibit both types of sexual behaviors. It is the ratio of behaviors which varies within genders, between genders, and between species. Such "new" findings illustrate the social construction of science. Are animals getting more androgynous? It seems more likely that, as society in general constructs new ways of seeing the world, scientists are looking for, and therefore finding, "new" behaviors in their animals. Facts depend on what the scientist brings with her/himself to the lab. (See Herschberger, 1970, Chapter 2, for an excellent illustration of this in regard to primate studies.)

If we think about each of the three components of gender, the relevance of animal studies to understanding gender in humans becomes very tenuous. Rats and other animals do not have gender roles or gender identities. In fact, animals do not have genders at all—merely sexes.

Another way of stating this is that when a person sees an animal and makes a gender attribution on the basis of other than strictly biological criteria (like genitals or coloring, which, not coincidentally, is known as "sexing" an animal), and uses instead criteria like behavior, size, or softness, the person is said to be anthropomorphizing. For some people, cats are "she" and dogs are "he" because the animals are perceived as having gender stereotyped characteristics; but most people are well aware of the anthropomorphizing they do about animals' "genders." One of the rules for differentiating between human and nonhuman animals is that humans are said to have self-consciousness and an awareness of the past and future, as well as the present. Without these attributes, it is senseless to talk of something "having" an identity or "playing" a role, and thus senseless to attribute a gender to them. If animals do not have genders, then how far can we extrapolate from animal research to the study of gender in humans? The argument that animal biologists study animals' sex, a purely biological concept, and not gender, a social concept, does not solve the problem. Not only are the two terms used synonymously (see Chapter 1), but, more importantly, the ways in which gender is constructed necessitates that any interpretation of animal "sex" behavior applied to human beings transforms "sex" into "gender."

It is not our intention to present an exhaustive review of gender hormones and behavior. Many excellent reviews exist, including Money and Ehrhardt (1972); Friedman, et al. (1974), and Reinisch (1974, 1977). Rather, we will briefly summarize the research as it relates to the components of gender, and as it illustrates the social construction of gender by biology.

Prenatal Hormones and Gender Identity. Since we cannot ascertain whether animals think of themselves as female or male, evidence for any relationship between prenatal hormones and gender identity must come from research on human beings. There are two questions we can ask: When XX fetuses are exposed prenatally to high levels of androgen are they more likely to develop male gender identities? When XY fetuses are exposed prenatally to low levels of androgen are they more likely to develop female gender identities?[12]

The answers to these two questions appear to be "no," although the evidence is not based on a large number of cases, and all of these cases involve clinical syndromes. The evidence for the answer to the first question comes mainly from the study of genetic females with the adrenogenital syndrome or progestin induced hermaphroditism. Although the individuals were exposed to abnormally high levels of prenatal androgens, the gender identities that developed were a function of gender assignments at birth (Money and Ehrhardt, 1972; Lev-Ran, 1974).

Evidence for the effects of low levels of prenatal androgens on the gender identity of genetic males comes from studying those born with partial androgen insensitivity (Money and Ogunro, 1974). In this syndrome there is some sensitivity to the effects of prenatal androgens, so that the genitals are more "male" than "female" at birth. The gender identities of these boys were, as in the case of the genetic females, a function of gender assignments at birth. In other words, hormones affect the genitals which affect gender assignment which affects gender identity. As yet we have little knowledge about the effects of variations in prenatal hormonal levels that have not affected reproductive organs but which might, nevertheless, affect the components of gender. Research in progress[13] may help answer this question.

The answers could have important implications. For example, many scientists are concerned with whether prenatal hormones are an important factor in the etiology of transsexualism. Money and Brennan (1968) have hypothesized that there may be a "gender identity center" located in the hypothalamus and limbic system of the brain. Pauly (1968) hypothesizes that the location of this "center" is the temporal lobes. In any case, the hypothesized mechanism is that prenatal androgens, during critical periods of fetal life, organize specific brain structures so that the individual is predisposed to develop a gender identity as male. In the absence of androgens, the hypothesized brain structure develops in a "female" direction. This is the same mechanism by which the reproductive structures develop.

Hypothesizing human gender differences in brain structures is based on research on the effects of prenatal hormones on animal brains. This research has shown that there are structural and chemical differences, depending on the level of prenatal androgens (Reinisch, 1974). For example, in female rats, early exposure to androgens affects the hypothalamus, resulting at puberty in a failure of ovarian hormones to be released cyclically. How generalizable is this and other findings to human beings?

In human females whose andrenogenital syndromes are untreated, not only is there exposure to high levels of prenatal androgens, but there continues to be secretion of steady high levels of androgen. As a result, cyclical release of gonadal hormones (estrogen and progesterone) is suppressed, and there are no menstrual cycles. If the prenatal androgens have affected brain structures, then one would expect that there could never be normal menstrual cycles. However, once these women are treated for the syndrome, the normal female pattern of cyclic hypothalamic function is restored (Lev-Ran, 1974). The restoration is independent of the morphology of the woman's body. Even if she has a penile urethra (i.e., urinates through a "penis"), she will eventually begin to menstruate through this structure.

There are several possible explanations for this, and other, differences between rats and women (or men). Some do not challenge the biological framework. For example, the adrenogenital syndrome may begin after the critical period for the development of brain structures. Thus there is no reason why normal hypothalamic functioning and normal menstrual cycles should not occur once treatment is instituted. Another possible explanation comes from a framework that sees biology as only one way of constructing the world. If concepts of gender identity and gender role are social constructions, then their origins should be sought in rules for seeing the world rather than in brain structures. The first type of explanation will eventually be supported or discarded through more research and experimentation. The second, however, can be answered only through a totally different paradigm, the one we are presenting in this book.

Pubertal Hormones and Gender Identity. By the time a person reaches puberty, her/his gender identity has already been established. The effects of pubertal hormones, namely the development of secondary gender characteristics and the development of sexual interest in others (probably due to androgen in *both* genders), is to reinforce gender identity, to reassure the person that she/he is "really" a female or a male, as indicated by the physical signs. In cases where development at puberty is contrary to what is expected (e.g., development of breasts in a male or appearance of a beard in a female), the effect is not to make the individual feel that she or he is the other gender. Unless there is some prior history of gender identity problems, the individual and her/his family react with concern about what is wrong and seek medical help and advice about "correcting" the problem. The fact that treatment is "corrective" indicates that the gender is seen as already having been there long before puberty, regardless of what the physical signs at puberty turn out to be. There is no intrinsic reason why this is so—it is merely the way in which we construct gender. We could conceive of an alternate construction where gender did not exist until puberty and then was attributed solely on the basis of the development of secondary gender characteristics.[14]

Prenatal Hormones and Gender Role. Ever since the discovery of "male" and "female" hormones at the beginning of the twentieth century, the gender hormones have been claimed to be the biological factor which accounts for the "obvious" behavioral differences between females and males. Supposedly, androgens contribute to making a person aggressive, strong, outer-directed, achievement oriented, sexual; estrogens make a person weak, passive, maternal, and asexual. This is really an unfair oversimplification of most serious, contemporary scientific writing. However, such oversimplifications often appear in popular treatments of "sex differences" (e.g., Lang, 1973) as well as in earlier scientific works (e.g., Frank, 1929).[15]

The same mechanism presumably responsible for the effects of prenatal hormones on gender identity is hypothesized for the development of gender role. Brain structures are influenced by prenatal androgens, such that thresholds for certain behaviors later in life are affected (Money and Ehrhardt, 1972). For example, prenatal exposure to a particular level of androgen at a particular critical period may predispose an individual to be sexually attracted to women at puberty, although ultimate sexual partner choice is a function of many other factors (Money and Ehrhardt, 1972). Again, there is little that biologists are absolutely sure about in the relationship between hormones and behavior in human beings. The types of behaviors that are most studied in terms of possible prenatal hormonal antecedents include aggression, sexual partner choice, and intellectual and cognitive abilities (see the reviews cited on p. 63 for specific studies).

Pubertal Hormones and Gender Role. The effects which androgen and estrogen secreted at puberty have on behavior are not totally clear either. Money and Ehrhardt (1972), among others, assert that, as with animals, the effects of pubertal hormones depend on what happened, hormonally, during the prenatal period. Few, if any, behaviors, with the possible exception of sexual arousal, have been shown to be caused by pubertal hormones. The extent to which pubertal hormones contribute to behavioral differences, even if they do play some role, has not been demonstrated to be very large and a great deal more research is needed.

Unlike prenatally, when estrogens are believed not to have an effect on the fetus, pubertal estrogens are thought by some (e.g., Bardwick, 1971) to have a significant effect on female behavior. It is part of the folklore of our culture that a menstruating woman is good for nothing, and, perhaps, even dangerous. She is thought to be irritable, moody, unreliable, anxious, unpredictable, irrational, and difficult to live with. These beliefs have been part of our culture for much longer than the time period in which scientists have known about endocrinological functioning (cf. Weideger, 1976). Thus, it seemed logical, when estrogen and progesterone were discovered, to search for biological explanations of these emotional changes by attributing them to the effects of "female" hormones on behavior.

Before the discovery of these hormones, physicians claimed that female behavioral "problems" like hypersexuality and aggressiveness could be cured by the removal of the "female" organ, including, at times, the clitoris (cf. Barker-Benfield, 1972). Then, with the discovery of the gender hormones, the particular causal substance was thought to have been located. Finally, when the mechanisms underlying the cyclical release of ovarian hormones were discovered, the premenstrual and menstrual parts of the menstrual cycle were seen as the "dangerous" times, because these were the periods when the levels of the "female" hormones were at their lowest.

Recently, the supposed lability of women has been attributed not to hormones *per se*, but rather to the "raging hormonal influences," the "drastic" changes in levels of estrogen and progesterone which occur during each menstrual cycle. Scientific effort has been devoted to understanding the complex hormonal feedback loops that cause ovulation and menstruation, and to finding biochemical causes for the changes in affect and performance associated with the menstrual cycle (cf. Dalton, 1964). There has been a search for other factors, such as enzymes, related to hormonal levels, which might account not just for cyclical changes in female behavior, but also for the differences between the behavior of women and the behavior of men (Broverman et al., 1968). This research takes it for granted that there are two genders, that there are differences between them, and that the cause of these differences can be found in biology. It is also taken for granted that females are affected by the changes in the level of their ovarian hormones.

With few exceptions (e.g., Hollingworth, 1914), it was not until this decade that serious investigation of whether or not there really were affect and performance changes associated with the menstrual cycle began to be carried out. In brief, recent studies indicate that although women *report* affect and behavioral changes during their menstrual cycles, when affect is measured on a daily basis throughout the cycle, or when performance is tested, there is little evidence to support the women's (and scientists') assertions, especially with regard to performance (McKenna, 1974).

The most current research has been devoted to discovering how beliefs and expectations about the menstrual cycle and behavior can affect both self-report of behavior and others' perceptions of women's behavior during the menstrual cycle (Koeske and Koeske, 1975; Koeske, 1975; Paige, 1973). These studies show that, although there is little evidence that cyclical changes in hormone levels have a strong influence on behavior, knowledge of these changes (e.g., being aware that one is premenstrual) may have a significant effect. Whatever the effect of cyclicity *per se*, it is becoming clearer that there are many types of physiological cycles, in both women and men, many of which might affect behavior, and most of which are not gender specific (cf. Parlee, 1976).

What can account for the fact that the direction of research on the menstrual cycle and behavior has been changing to include more "social" factors? One of the most important reasons is that as ways of seeing gender change (especially ways of seeing the role of women), it becomes "obvious" that certain factors, which in the past have been ignored, should be investigated.

Prenatal Hormones and Gender Attribution. The relationship between prenatal hormones and the gender attribution process is indirect, at best. Since the level of prenatal androgens is responsible for the development of the genitals into a penis and scrotum or (by its absence) into a clitoris and labia, it is indirectly responsible for the singular cue on which gender assignment is based. Prenatal hormones in and of themselves play no role in gender attribution.

Pubertal Hormones and Gender Attribution. Pubertal hormones also play an indirect role in gender attribution. That is, secondary gender characteristics like beards and breasts, which may be cues for attributing gender, develop as a result of the gender hormones secreted at puberty. The hormones themselves, though, are not crucial to the attribution process. Beards, breasts and other gender characteristics can be bought in a store.

BIOLOGY AND GENDER

A summary of the relationship between biological factors in the development of gender and the components of gender can be found in Table 3.1. There are two significant points to be noted in an inspection of the table: (1) What is known about the contribution of biology to gender components varies widely, depending on the factor and the component. Within a positivist framework, there are still important unanswered questions about the relationship between biology and gender. (2) The ways in which biologists tell females from males is very different from the gender attribution process which occurs in everyday life. Nevertheless (and this is not obvious from the table), biologists' criteria for gender are grounded in everyday gender attributions.

In the remainder of this chapter we first present an overview and critique of biology and gender from a positivist perspective and then conclude with a discussion of gender and biology as a social construction.

Table 3.1 Relationship between Biological Factors in the Development of Gender and the Components of Gender

Biologists' Criteria for Determining Gender	Gender Identity		Gender Role		Gender Attribution in Everyday Life	
	Relationship	Evidence*	Relationship	Evidence*	Relationship	Evidence*
Chromosomes	no	androgen insensitivity syndrome	unknown but possible	gender-linked diseases (no specific role relationship yet demonstrated)	no, except for sports	transsexuals
Gonads	no	Turner's syndrome	no	Turner's syndrome	no	transsexuals
Internal reproductive organs	no	Turner's syndrome	no	Turner's syndrome	no	transsexuals
Prenatal hormones	possible	no conclusive evidence	possible	no conclusive evidence	no	transsexuals
External reproductive organs	no	transsexuals	no	transsexuals	Yes, at time of gender assignment and early childhood; rarely thereafter	gender assignment procedures; transsexuals
Pubertal hormones	no	adrenogenital syndrome, assigned as males at birth	unlikely	effects on muscular development may be minor factor in certain "sex differences" (e.g., playing tennis)	indirectly, if certain cues are emphasized	if deliberately searching for and/or growing facial hair

(* Examples only)

69

Biology and Gender from a Positivist Perspective

Research clearly indicates that there are no causal links between gender identity or gender role and gonads, internal reproductive organs, or genitals. The relationship between gender role and pubertal hormones or genetic factors is still very much open to question. A relationship between prenatal hormones and gender identity and gender role, probably mediated by the effect of prenatal hormones on brain structures, is one that has received the most support in the scientific community.

In 1955, Money, Hampson, and Hampson published an article based on studies of matched pairs of hermaphrodites, discordant only in the gender which they were assigned and reared (e.g., one member of a pair with identical gender chromosomes and equally "masculinized" genitals was assigned and raised as a girl and developed a female gender identity and role; the other was assigned and raised as a boy and developed a male gender identity and role). The authors of this article asserted that there was complete psychosexual neutrality at birth, that is, no predisposition to develop a particular gender identity. Although Money no longer holds a totally environmental position on the question of gender identity (Money and Ehrhardt, 1972), he continues to believe that whatever predispositions toward a particular gender identity exist due to prenatal hormonal influences can be overcome before the age of 3 or 4.

Critics of the theory of basic psychosexual neutrality offer various arguments against it: (1) The number of individuals with biological gender abnormalities is extremely small relative to normal cases. This is true, but the number of "experimental" subjects (e.g., rats prenatally exposed to androgens in a lab) is always "relatively small." Nevertheless, results of such studies are taken very seriously by scientists. (2) The normal process might not be the same as the abnormal process. This may be, but the answer awaits further research. (3) The third criticism is based on the assumption that genital appearance is highly correlated with "masculinization" or "feminization" of brain centers. If the genitals have been "masculinized" by prenatal exposure to androgens, or "feminized" by the absence of prenatal androgens, then the brain has probably been similarly affected. The gender identity that eventually develops is due then to the influence of brain structures. The gender assignment–gender identity relationship is merely correlational. This criticism is the weakest of the three since as Lev-Ran (1974) has pointed out, the matched pairs of hermaphrodites studied by Money, Hampson, and

Hampson (1955) were *identical* genitally, gonadally, and genetically (in terms of their gender chromosomes). This would indicate that the members of a pair were exposed to very similar, if not identical, levels of prenatal androgens. Nevertheless, the members of the pairs were assigned *"opposite"* genders and developed gender identities in accordance with their assignments.

These three criticisms of the theory of psychosexual neutrality at birth come directly from a biological framework without challenging any basic assumptions about gender. Further biological research will indicate their validity.

The scientific evidence seems to point to prenatal hormonal influences which exert an effect relatively easily overcome by assignment and rearing. If a boy with partial androgen insensitivity, who has been exposed to minimal amounts of prenatal androgens, has to overcome difficulties that other boys do not have to face (e.g., that he may not be able to function in the male role during intercourse because of a micropenis), he nevertheless does learn and develop a male gender identity (Money and Orgunro, 1974). Even today, with the possibility of requesting reassignment following surgical and hormonal treatment, most people do not choose reassignment, indicating that they probably do not feel "misassigned." This contradicts the view of some scientists (cf. Zugar, 1975) who see these people as being forced to fit into a mold against which their biology dictates.

Prenatal hormones (which sometimes seem to be the *deus ex machina* of the 1970s) may also be important in the development of gender role. We have already discussed in detail our criticisms of the research. It is clear that it is, and will continue to be, difficult to assess the contribution of biological factors to gender role behaviors. This is partly because the concept of gender role involves so many behaviors, and each of the behaviors is so varied in its expression and in the emphasis placed on its appropriateness for one gender or the other.

Few scientists would maintain that biological factors determine what type of clothes a person wears, but other behaviors are not so clearly socially determined. Is there, as Money and Ehrhardt (1972) have suggested, a prenatal organization of brain functioning which later results in greater sexual arousal to visual material in those exposed to higher prenatal androgen levels? Is this hypothesized "sex difference" a critical part of gender role? How would such a mechanism work? What are the implications? What is the relationship between actual differences in the ways women and men behave and the differential expectations which we have for their behavior (i.e., our concepts of gender role)? If the questions that can be raised about one specific response to one specific stimulus are so complex, it is easy to see how complicated the issues are when the behaviors are even more general (e.g., aggression, emotionality).

Any serious research on biological contributions to gender differences in behavior must first establish beyond doubt that there *are* actual behavioral differences. Recent reviews of the literature on "sex differences" (e.g., Maccoby and Jacklin, 1974) have concluded that there are relatively few reliable differences. This conclusion should help make researchers more careful and less likely to take differences for granted.[16]

Much of our critique of research on the menstrual cycle and behavior can be applied to studies of the effects of gender hormones on gender role behavior in general. Intragender differences in behavior are, for the most part, as variable as intergender differences, and hormone levels may or may not play a role in the variability of behavior. (See Maccoby and Jacklin, 1974; Lewis, 1975). Even if hormones are important, however, dichotomizing both the hormones and the behaviors as gender-specific is not dictated by the data, but rather by our construction of the world.

We believe that the most fruitful direction for research to take would be to investigate biological factors separate from the gender categories in which they have been placed. Biologists could then study how different levels of the factor affect behavior.

Comparisons between persons who are matched on all important biological factors except for the level of a particular hormone they produce, to see if there are differences in certain behaviors, would mean concentrating on intragender comparisons, since intergender comparisons are confounded by other biological factors like chromosomes and genitals. Efforts should be directed away from studying biological factors in "sex differences" and toward studying biological factors in behavioral differences. Relevant to this type of research is the question of the relationship among the components of gender. If, for example, prenatal hormones are a factor in the development of gender identity, does this imply that they are a factor in either gender role or gender attribution? It is clear that the components are related, but are the factors which contribute to the components necessarily related?

Referring to Table 3.1, the only column in which we have placed a definite "yes" is in the gender attribution column. From our point of view, the "yes" appears because of the visibility of genitals and secondary gender characteristics and the role they play in the gender attribution process. It is conceivable, though, that if the concept of gender attribution became integrated into positivist approaches to gender, there might eventually be a search for biological mechanisms which contribute to presenting onself in order to be taken as female or male and perhaps for mechanisms important in knowing how to interpret these presentations—a biological radar system.

Such research could include a search for brain structures, affected by levels of prenatal hormones, which result in a tendency to move and present oneself in a certain way, or which result in a greater ability to learn certain ways of acting, speaking, and so on rather than others. There might be an examination of the role of pheromones (cf. McClintock, 1971) in the gender attribution process. Perhaps we know (in a biological sense) which gender someone is by our reaction to chemicals transmitted through odor. Certainly these are all answerable questions which can be pursued through scientific inquiry.

Biology and Gender as a Social Construction

The question of how prenatal and/or pubertal hormones influence gender role behaviors ("sex differences") does not call into question either the existence of two genders or whether, indeed, there are any differences.

There is no a priori reason for attributing gender to hormones, the individuals being studied, or the behaviors that result, in order to ask questions about the effects of prenatal hormones on the brain and behavior. Just as we might ask questions about the effects of insulin on the brain and behavior, so we might ask about the effects of androgen (or estrogen) on the brain—anyone's brain. The reason research is not based on this question is that even scientists are constrained by living in a world of only two genders.

The discovery of the "sex hormones" in the nineteenth century was, at first, thought to be the end of the search for the biological criteria that differentiated the genders. When it became clear that males and females alike produce estrogen, androgen, and progesterone, the presence or absence of hormones could no longer be used as criteria to attribute gender, although the relative proportion of hormones was still considered to be a viable test for the degree of "maleness" or "femaleness" of an individual. However, as more is discovered about human endocrinology, the idea of "male" versus "female" hormones has become somewhat questionable (cf. Dworkin, 1974). Some of what we now know about the gender hormones makes it clear that talk about "hormone dimorphism" is a construction. In the first place, the three gender hormones, estrogen, androgen, and progesterone, are chemically very similar and often difficult to measure. For example, a urine specimen cannot be "sex-typed" on the basis of a hormone assay (Botella Llusia, 1973). Secondly, not only are all three hormones produced by both genders, but, at times, they are produced in comparable amounts. Vande Wiele makes the point that, except for the time around ovulation, males and females produce the same amount of progesterone and to call progesterone a "female" hormone is misleading (Friedman et al., 1974). Finally, estrogenic substances, if administered during pregnancy, can, under certain circumstances, "masculinize" a fetus (Money and Ehrhardt, 1972).

If hormones do not always (or even almost never) differentiate women from men, then what does? The confirmation of the existence of "sex chromosomes" in the early part of the twentieth century was a second important discovery in the search for the factor which defined "female" and "male." As we stated earlier, chromosome composition is not always clearly dichotomous, but it still seems to be the best criterion at the moment. No matter what the criteria, though, and no matter how contradictory or confusing the results of research have been, at no time have biologists challenged the basic incorrigible proposition which they hold, not as biologists but as members of everyday society, that there are two genders. No matter how much scientific knowledge is increased, the fact of two genders is not challenged, and there continues to be a search for dichotomous differentiating criteria.

In 1932, Lillie, a biologist, wrote that "there is no such biological entity as sex. What exists in nature is a dimorphism within species into male and female individuals, which differ with respect to contrasting characters. . . . Sex . . . is merely a name for our total impression of the differences" (Lillie, 1932, p. 3). In 1959, a psychologist wrote: "Persons do not exist; there are only male persons and female persons . . . biologically, sociologically, and psychologically" (Colley, 1959). In 1972, this statement was termed "perspicacious" by a British psychologist (Hutt, 1972). What these three scientists make clear through their statements is that the primary fact is the existence of two genders. This fact is not to be challenged by any data, but rather all data is to be fitted into this framework.

Although the scientists we have just quoted take a strong biological determinist position on gender, we are not arguing for or
against biological contributions to gender differences or similarities.
It is simply that these statements make overt what lies behind all
scientific work on gender, even the work of those who argue for
minimal biological differences. This is the belief in two genders.
One side of the determinist fence states that estrogens account for
female variability, and lack of certain skills, and that androgens
account for male intelligence, and aggressiveness (cf. Hutt, 1972),
while the other side argues that whatever differences exist are due
to environmental factors (cf. Oakley, 1972), and that the only real
biological differences are that women menstruate, gestate, and
lactate, while men impregnate. Our point is that neither side of the
argument calls into question the fact that there are females and
males, even if the differences between them are minimal. By what
criteria, then, do they determine if someone is female or male?

The answer is: in the same way everyone else does. Although
scientists have devised lists of biological criteria which differentiate
women from men (chromosomes, gonads, etc.), they always begin
by being able to tell females from males in the first place, without
any information about these criteria. Although it seems as if the
biological facts have an existence independent of gender labels (i.e.,
there are XY chromosomes, etc., and all these together are labeled
"male sex"), the process is actually the reverse. Concepts of gender
lead to the discovery of "differentiating facts." For example, in order
to know if women and men differ in brain structures, we would
need to get a group of women and a group of men, label the brains
according to the donor's gender, and then examine the brains for
differences. The way the original group would be gotten would be
through the everyday gender attribution process. The scientists
would not ask for XX brains from the morgue; they would ask for
brains from female corpses. The biologists' activities are grounded
in the everyday gender attribution process.

The concept of gender identity is an excellent example of the
social construction of gender and how it grounds biological facts.
One of the criticisms of the theory of psychosexual neutrality is that
asking people about their gender identity necessitates a definite
answer in our society. "How many . . . patients in a freer society
would question their imposed sex, especially if not reinforced in
their given sex by surgery and hormones?" (Zuger, 1975, p. 580).
This criticism is worth examining in some detail. Zuger, himself, in
making this criticism does not challenge the concept of gender

identity. Presumably he believes that everyone has a gender identity which is largely biologically determined. It is not clear whether the "reinforcement" he refers to is limited to biological factors. That is, is the reinforcement only biological, in the sense that hormonal treatment affects gender identity, or is it social, in the sense that the individual knows, for example, that someone with a vagina and an insensitivity to androgens can be nothing but a (social) woman, despite such person's doubts about whether that is really what they are?

It is true that the only way to determine gender identity is to ask, and, as we stated in Chapter 1, the answers are in part determined by the questions. However, in a society where gender is constructed differently (see Chapter 2), gender identity might no longer be a useful concept. Its usefulness for biology is that it supports the dichotomy of gender. Gender identity remains the one psychobiological concept which is fixed and dichotomous.

Biology and the Process of Gender Attribution

The only physical characteristics that can play a role in gender attribution in everyday life are those that are visible. Hormones, chromosomes, internal reproductive organs, and, for adults, genitals are unimportant in the process of classifying someone as female or male in everyday life. This is obvious, but it is worth taking note of because of its implications. In the first place, if we (socially) define a person's gender as that gender which others attribute to them, then most biological criteria are irrelevant. A women, for example, in a social sense, is not the one who produces egg cells. Rather, once a person attributes "woman" that person also attributes the ability to produce egg cells to the individual. Whether or not any particular woman actually has the capacity to conceive and gestate is not important. It is assumed that she can unless proven otherwise, in which case, if a "good" reason is given, the "woman" attribution is not called into question. (We discuss "good" reasons further in Chapters 4 and 5.) The biologists' criteria are neither a necessary nor sufficient condition for being female or male in everyday life.

The ultimate biological criterion for defining gender is the individual's role in reproduction, which is dependent on whether or not there is at least one Y chromosome. These criteria are abstractions, not members' methods for attributing gender. All human beings, no matter what their degree of scientific sophistication, attribute gender. Children attribute gender (see Chapter 4) long before they learn about even the most simple biological criteria for being male or female.

Nevertheless, the role of biology in the gender attribution process is to provide "signs" for us. Signs are not gender, but they serve as "good reasons" for our attributions in a world where biological facts are seen as the ultimate reasons. Genitals are the sole criteria for attribution at the time of gender assignment. After that point, if people are asked for their reasons for making an attribution the answers are most often in terms of physical characteristics. These answers are seen as good reasons (e.g., "He had a beard, so I knew he was a man"), but the signs that we use as good reasons are not necessarily universal, as we have seen in Chapter 2. The use of physical signs indicates how much of our construction of gender is grounded in the belief that biological criteria are the ultimate criteria.

Gender is not the only constructed classification that is grounded in biology. The family is another. In our society the defining criterion for being a relative is either marriage into a family or the biological linkage of "blood." Schneider (1968) has shown how "relatives" are defined in American culture on the basis of these criteria; but the criteria are not universal. We construct the closest links between people in terms of how much "blood" (i.e., biological inheritance) they share, so that siblings are seen as more closely related than cousins; in other cultures, other criteria are important, so that mother's brother may be seen as a much closer relative than father's brother. In our society they would be equally related.

The process of gender attribution, like the concept of "relation," may be universal, but the grounds given for making a certain classification are not.[17] They depend on the various "incorrigible propositions" defining various realities. In our culture, physical and biological reality is the ultimate reality, and biological facts give grounds for and support the facticity of two genders. At the same time biology itself is grounded in, and gets its support from, the basic assumption that there are only two genders.

In this chapter we have summarized what scientific research has discovered about what it means to be male or female and how people get to be one or the other. We have discussed how biologists' gender attributions are based on abstractions but grounded in the everyday gender attribution process. If we accept the rules that constitute biology as a form of life, then there is much of interest to help us understand gender and pointing to directions that further research should take. If we view biology as a construction, then we can see how a study of the gender attribution process is basic to an understanding of how it is that biologists can study gender in the first place.

NOTES

1. Our use of "biology" and "biologists" includes all the biological sciences and those whose work is within those sciences. This would include physiology, endocrinology, genetics, etc.

2. For a more detailed discussion of reproductive processes and human gender development, see Beck et al., 1973.

3. Biologists almost always use the word "sex" rather than "gender," leaving the latter term to refer to social aspects of being male or female. However, there is confusion in the use of the two terms (see Chapter 1).

4. In some species (e.g., honeybees) the egg cell is capable of developing by itself, without a sperm cell, into a new individual. This is known as parthenogenesis, and is considered to be an asexual means of reproduction.

5. Certain species, particularly the Australian wrasse, a coral reef fish, exhibit what is known as "sequential hermaphroditism." In such species, egg cell carriers may become sperm cell carriers under certain conditions. In addition, there are organisms that have the capacity to produce both types of reproductive cells (e.g., earthworms).

6. We assume that they mean to include woman, too.

7. Recent research (Wachtel et al., 1976) indicates that the development of testes is due to a single gene on the Y chromosome. Occasionally, this gene transfers to an X chromosome in gamete formation and the individual develops into an XX male, with testes and other "male" organs.

8. Frequent genetic abnormalities include XXX, XO or Turner's syndrome, XXY or Klinefelter's syndrome, and XYY. The different abnormalities vary in the extent to which individuals are affected by them. XXX individuals usually have no known concomitant abnormality, whereas individuals with severe cases of Turner's and Klinefelter's syndromes often have severe abnormalities, such as mental retardation. Based on data from Ounstead and Taylor (1972) and Walzer and Gerard (1975), about 15 of 5000 births involve an abnormality of the gender chromosomes. This is about twice the rate of Trisomy-21 (Down's syndrome), which is 7.4 per 5000 births (Walzer and Gerard, 1975). Although the incidence of each abnormality is fairly low, taken together chromosome abnormalities are not as rare as most people think.

9. This lack of concern reflects not only an interest in fairness, but also

the cultural orientation that there is something less "wrong," in any circumstance, with women passing as men, or engaging in "male" activities, than vice versa. We guess that if a man did turn out to be a woman, she would be banned from the competition and her medals would be taken away, but that tests for male athletes would not be instituted. If nothing else, it might be too embarrassing for men to admit that they have to "watch out" for female competitors.

10. The dates in the text refer to the Olympics. The International Amateur Athletic Federation instituted physical examinations in 1966 and chromosome tests in 1967.

11. Fortunately, decisions such as this one are relatively rare. A reading of the presentation of the case leads one to conclude that the major concern of the staff was avoiding legal suits.

12. Although it is true that estrogens, in dosages thousands of times the normal level for pregnancy, can "masculinize" animal fetuses (Reinisch, 1974), this condition does not occur in human beings or animals, outside the laboratory. Mammalian fetuses under normal circumstances appear to be relatively immune to the effects of estrogen, probably to insure that the fetus is protected from the high levels of estrogen circulating in the mother's blood during pregnancy (Sherfey, 1972).

13. C. Jacklin, personal communication, December 6, 1976.

14. Initial reports describing a group of individuals living in the Dominican Republic seemed to indicate that this has occurred in certain cultures. These people, called *Guevedoces* ("balls at twelve") by the villagers, are born with ambiguous genitals, raised as girls, but at puberty develop masculinized secondary gender characteristics. According to the original report (Imperato-McGinley et al., 1974), at this point they are able to change their genders and develop an "unequivocal male psychosexual orientation" (p. 1213). The report challenges some basic "facts" about gender.

Money (1975) and Sagarin (1975) have asserted that the parents of these children, and other villagers, knew about or suspected the later virilization. Consequently they defined the genitals as a penis from birth and did not rear their children as girls. Perhaps they reared them *like* girls, but with the expectation that at puberty they would become males.

It is impossible to know how accurate the initial report was, although there is no reason *not to* believe that the villagers constructed gender in the way described. At this point, of course, future treatment of *Guevedoces* will be influenced by the villagers' contact with "science." The counter arguments are important, however, because they indicate not only an alternative description of how the villagers might have constructed gender, but they also indicate how scientists interpret data to support their facts which, in turn, support the socially shared construction of a world of two invariable genders.

15. The explanation of these oversimplifications, from the point of view of traditional positivism, is that these authors were either unaware of the "true" facts and/or they did not have enough information to interpret the facts "correctly." From our point of view, "oversimplification" is the wrong word. The "facts" known to earlier scientists were as true or false as the present facts. To say that they were wrong is to misunderstand the nature of science (see Kuhn, 1970). As for popularized treatments of science, what we asserted in Chapter 2 about how early anthropologists' accounts of gender "among the natives" were constructions of constructions is also relevant here. Most scientists, at least sometimes, are aware of how tentative, conditional, and open to question their findings are. The publication of findings filters out some of this tentativeness, and the reading of publications by those whose concerns are different from the scientists' often leads to statements of clear-cut truths which, if traced back to their source, are not really that clear. A good example of how scientific and popular treatments of the same subject matter differ radically in their presentations is a comparison between Money and Ehrhardt (1972) and the popular version of this book (Money and Tucker, 1975).

16. It is interesting that researchers should now be "discovering" that there are few "sex differences" in behavior. How much of this discovery is a result of changing ways of seeing gender?

17. Among the Nuer people, a father is "the person in whose name cattle bridewealth is given for the mother. Thus, a woman can be married to another woman, and be husband to the wife and father of her children, despite the fact that she is not the inseminator" (Rubin, 1975, p. 169). This implies not only a different construction of "relation" but, perhaps, a different construction of gender.

4

DEVELOPMENTAL
ASPECTS OF GENDER

Jesse (six years old) was asked to draw a picture of a boy and a picture of a girl. When questioned by an interviewer: "What makes her a girl?", he answered, "Because there is a sun and girls go out on sunny days." "What makes this other drawing a picture of a boy?" "Because I colored it and the man is out tonight. He has to work at night. The moon and he is outside."

Loren (4½ years old) explained that his drawing of a boy differed from his drawing of a girl "because it (the boy) has no long hair; cause the eyes are different they are rounder; because he is bigger than a girl. She (the girl) has long hair; and she has little curlies in her hair; and she has ears; and because she is smaller."

Jesse and Loren can also answer the question: "Are you a girl or a boy?" accurately. They know that they are boys. A child of Loren's age, however, may not be sure whether he will be a man or a woman when he grows up, while Jesse's peers know they will be men if they are now boys. Both Jesse and Loren can list many differences between boys and girls (boys are rougher, girls wear dresses) and were we to observe their choice of toys, ask about their preferred activities, and study some of their behaviors, we would probably conclude that there are definite differences between them and their female peers, differences more evident among the six year olds than the four year olds.

If we thought of children as nothing but little adults, physically weaker and less experienced but essentially miniature replicas, we might be forced to conclude that Jesse and Loren were mentally defective, or, at least, intellectually slow. Not only are some of their answers to questions about their pictures peculiar, but the reasons they give do not correspond to the actual pictures they drew. Jesse's picture of a boy also has a sun in it; Loren's girl has round eyes and his boy has ears too. (See Figures 4.1–4.4.)

Of course, in the twentieth century we do not consider children

Figure 4.1 Jesse's drawing of a boy.

to be miniature adults. We accept the reality of development from child into adult as a process of transformations through stages, each moving closer and closer to mature behavior and thought processes. We do not expect young children to be rational and responsible, and these expectations are reflected in law, in childrearing practices, and in the scientific study of human development. (See. DeMause, 1975, for an historical review of the concept of "childhood.") Children do not experience the world the way adults do. They differ from adults not merely in terms of having less experience and knowing less, but also in terms of the way the conceptualize reality, including the reality of gender.

What accounts for the development of gender role behavior as children grow towards adulthood? How do children learn they are either boys or girls? Is there a learning process in being able to accurately tell girls from boys and women from men?

Unless we assume that the components of gender are completely biological and merely unfold in the course of maturation, it is necessary to seek environmental factors which, at least, interact

Figure 4.2 Jesse's drawing of a girl.

with biological factors and lead to the acquisition of gender identity, gender role, and gender attribution processes. This has been, and continues to be, the task of psychology, particularly developmental psychology. As a positivist science, like biology, psychology accepts the reality of gender and its components, particularly gender identity and gender role. The "fact" of masculinity and femininity (adherence to a particular gender role) is as real and objective for psychology as hormones are for biology, and is theoretically as amenable to measurement, quantification, and study. Even the current interest in androgyny (e.g., Bem, 1978) is grounded in the assumption that there are real masculine and feminine traits which can be combined (cf. Rebecca et al., 1976).

There are three main theoretical perspectives in the study of human psychological development: psychoanalytic, social learning, and cognitive developmental. In this chapter we present a general overview of the three theories and discuss their contributions to an understanding of the development of gender identity, role, and attribution. We do not intend this to be an exhaustive critique of the

Figure 4.3 Loren's drawing of a boy.

theories.[1] We evaluate, from a traditional perspective, what the theories assert about how children learn there are two genders, how they learn what their own gender is, how they learn what gender others are, and how they learn the behaviors "appropriate" to their gender. However, as with our discussion of biology, our main interest is in presenting psychology as a way of seeing gender.

PSYCHOANALYTIC THEORY

Freud did not write about "gender role," "gender identity," or "gender attribution." He wrote about "Some psychical consequences of the anatomical distinctions between the sexes" (Freud, 1925). His theory is grounded in the premise that people are born with one of two possible anatomies, and he spent a large portion of his intellectual life investigating how these two anatomically distinct groups develop different kinds of mental lives and have different kinds of experiences. There was no question that these psychical and behavioral differences existed. The question was "why?"

Figure 4.4 Loren's drawing of a girl.

According to Freud, around the age of five, children become aware that they either possess a penis or do not possess a penis. This recognition leads them to develop a particular fantasy involving their genitals (or lack of) and their parents. Out of that fantasy comes a resolution of feelings about the genitals and the parents. This resolution entails identifying with one of the parents and, consequently, internalizing the values of that parent, and eventually exhibiting the same behaviors as that parent. Since the parents' behaviors are (presumably) gender-typed, the child's will be also.

The recognition that one has or does not have a particular set of genitals is, for Freud, tantamount to recognizing that one is a particular gender. "I have a penis" means "I am a boy" and "I do not have a penis" means "I am a girl." In this system gender identity is genital identity. If the child fails to accept the reality of her/his genitals (or lack of), then the child has not accepted that she/he is female or male. Freud saw gender identity as so intrinsically tied to genitals that he did not even consider it necessary to provide the theoretical underpinnings of that connection. Nor does he explain how children learn to see *genitals* as the dichotomizing feature by which they distinguish all people and categorize themselves. Why not size, or hair length, or other more public differences?

Recent research draws Freud's equation of genital discovery and gender identity into question. There are children who have male gender identities even though they do not have penises and children who have female gender identities even though they do have penises (Money and Ehrhardt, 1972). We do not know how Freud would have dealt with evidence from these cases. Children appear to have fixed gender identities by age three (Money and Ehrhardt, 1972), earlier than Freud asserted, and before they show awareness of genital and/or anatomical gender differences (Kohlberg, 1966). How would Freud have explained the fact that blind children develop stable gender identities with no apparent difficulty and share cultural ideas about gender (Person, 1974), even though they cannot see genital differences? Most of the evidence indicates that awareness of genital differences is not paramount in the development of gender identity.

Freud believed that the recognition that one has a penis or does not have a penis was not sufficient for behaving in a way that is appropriate for people who have penises or do not have penises. Unconscious and semiconscious fantasy is the process that links gender identity to gender role. When children with penises masturbate, they imagine that adults have negative feelings about their masturbation, especially the masturbatory fantasies they have about their mothers, who are their first love objects. They perceive their fathers as rivals for their mother's affections and consequently resent their fathers and would like to get rid of them. They imagine that their fathers would be angered by these feelings and would retaliate in kind with aggression. Specifically, the children fantasize that their fathers will castrate them. Since the children identify with their genitals, this would essentially mean total destruction. The fantasy of castration is given some support when the children with penises notice children without penises and think that those children must have been castrated.

Castration anxiety is unbearable and the only way to resolve it is to relinquish, through repression, all desires for the mother and to identify with the father. In psychoanalytic terms, "object choice" (wanting someone) is replaced by "object identity" (wanting to be like someone). By identifying with their fathers they obtain their mothers vicariously. Through identification they assume the values and role behaviors of their fathers. Although the children with penises resolve their castration anxiety by identifying with their fathers, there is typically some identification with both parents, since their first identification has been with their mothers. The amount of identification with each parent, and consequently the amount of male or female gender role behavior the children display, is, in part, dependent on the relative strength of their masculine and feminine constitutional makeup, a factor that Freud did not explicate in great detail. Nevertheless, by virtue of having a penis, an active sexual organ, the children who successfully resolve their Oedipal desires and castration anxiety will develop gender role behaviors that are characterized by activity.

Children without penises[2] undergo a different set of fantasy experiences. At around the age of five they become aware of the fact that they do not have penises. Presumably this comes from seeing children with penises and making comparisons. The clitoris, which had been the focus of sexual feeling until this point, and which had been valued for the erotic pleasure it produced, becomes devalued and is now viewed as an inadequate penis. Masturbatory activity is relinquished. According to Freud (1925), penises are valued by children who lack them because penises are ". . . strikingly visible and of large proportions, at once recognize(d) as the superior counterpart of their own small and inconspicuous organ . . ." (p. 252).

The mothers, who had been valued for the needs they satisfied, now become devalued because they, too, lack penises and because they are blamed for the children's deficiency. The children may believe that they had penises but lost them as a form of punishment. Because the fathers have penises, they take on greater value and become the children's object choice.

The children without penises, then, are in the same position vis-à-vis their fathers as the children with penises are vis-à-vis their mothers. The children without penises must relinquish their fathers and identify with their mothers. Through identification with their mothers, they incorporate ideal female values and the appropriate role behaviors for the female gender. They come to accept their vaginas, rather than their clitorises, as their true genital. Although children without penises are also constitutionally bisexual, and will identify to some extent with both parents, by virtue of having vaginas, passive sexual organs, those children who successfully resolve their Oedipal desires will develop gender role behaviors that are characterized by passivity.

Because there is no strong motivation to resolve their Oedipal conflict (analogous to castration anxiety in the children with penises), these conflicts are never fully resolved. This results in a number of unfortunate consequences. They will have weaker consciences and will never fully give up their desire to have penises, although there will be some ways that that desire can be symbolically fulfilled (e.g., giving birth to sons).

In Table 4.1, the development of gender role, according to psychoanalytic theory, is shown arising out of the initial recognition of one's own genitals. For Freud, the study of gender was essentially the study of gender roles. The problem was not how children learn that there exist two genders, or even how they learn that they are a particular gender, but rather (in contemporary terms) how do children develop the appropriate gender role—how and why do boys become masculine and girls become feminine? In the normal course of development, a child would know what genital she or he had, would develop the appropriate fantasy, and would incorporate the values and behaviors appropriate to her/his gender.

It should be clear that gender attribution was not an issue for Freud. Although there is no doubt that, for him, gender equaled genitals, he did not see gender attribution as problematic. Any intrapsychic conflict had to be between gender identity and gender role, rather than gender identity and gender attribution. It is difficult to incorporate, within an orthodox psychoanalytic framework, persons with penises, seen as male by others, who conceive of themselves as really being female, unless this is seen as psychosis or other severe pathology. Presumably, Freud would have considered trans-

Table 4.1 Theories of Gender Development

Freudian psychoanalytic:	own awareness of genitals (implicit: gender identity)	→ fantasy	→ identification	→ gender role
Social learning:	others' awareness of genitals	→ differential reinforcement	identification (modeling) ↗ ↓ → gender role	→ gender identity
Cognitive developmental:	others' awareness of genitals	→ labeling	→ gender identity	→ gender role → identification

sexuals people who, because of an unresolved Oedipal conflict, would not accept their own genitals and consequently their own gender. Transsexualism would have been seen as an extreme form of homosexuality, with a masochistic component, accompanied by such severe guilt feelings that the individual could not accept the homosexuality.

Freud's developmental theory has been criticized for several reasons besides his equation of genital awareness with gender identity. It does not take into account the fact that in non-Western cultures children with different genitals may not perform very different role behaviors or may exhibit role behaviors that are the reverse of our own culture's (Mead, 1935). In addition, the fantasy that Freud described may be inappropriate in cultures where the child's father is not the authority figure (Malinowski, 1932).

The theory is also based on a biological assumption, accurate when Freud was writing but now known to be false, that fetuses were "constitutionally bisexual," that is, that they had the potential for developing into either gender; one potential was expressed, while the other was suppressed. The contemporary facts are that fetuses develop in a "female" direction unless something (e.g., prenatal androgens) is added. This knowledge, combined with the belief that boys have to change their identification from their mothers to their fathers, while girls do not have to make any changes, is used to support the contention (contrary to Freud's) that gender development is more difficult for boys than for girls (Person, 1974). (Freud concentrated on the idea that boys were the ones who did not have to change the gender of their love object.)

An additional criticism of Freudian theory is that gender development does not end with the resolution of the Oedipal phase. Children continue to learn gender roles throughout childhood, and preadolescence and adolescence are important stages in learning masculine and feminine behavior (Maccoby and Jacklin, 1974).

Psychoanalysts who came after Freud[3] varied in the extent to which they supported his views about gender development. Regardless of how far they deviate from the Freudian model, they remain convinced of the sequence: genital awareness leads to fantasy leads to identification leads to gender role (e.g., Person, 1974). The modifications they made lie in the following areas:

1. The nature of genital awareness and the role it plays in gender identity
2. The particulars of the Oedipal fantasy

3. The role of the social environment
4. The age at which gender identity and gender role development takes place

Horney's (1926) explication of the development of gender role focuses on girls and emphasizes quite different aspects of the nature of genital awareness and the content of the child's unconscious fantasy. According to Horney, those children born without penises do not so much experience the lack of a penis as their defining feature, but rather they experience the *presence* of their vaginas. They recognize that they have vaginas and at no point do these children reject their clitorises as inadequate. They are part of their genitals. Anxiety centers around their vaginas, because they cannot be inspected and because the children fear the vaginas will not be large enough to receive their fathers' (fantasized) penises. Children with penises may be envied because it is assumed that they are allowed to masturbate, since they hold their penises when urinating. In normal development, however, this envy disappears when the children with vaginas realize their role in the birth process. There are children with vaginas who continue to envy penises and deny their genitals (and hence their gender), but according to Horney, this is not part of the normal course of development. In sum, she did not see penis envy as playing the important role in development that Freud claimed.

Horney also discusses how the fantasy of some children with vaginas of wanting a penis is reinforced by a society that values people with penises more than people with vaginas. The penis, then, becomes symbolic of greater power and choice. The incorporation of sociocultural influences has become an integral part of contemporary psychoanalytic theory. Unlike Freud, most psychoanalysts no longer see the child's fantasy as occurring within a vacuum.

Some contemporary formulations of psychoanalytic theory (e.g., Stoller, 1975) demonstrate a recognition of the complexities of gender development. Gender identity is not dependent on awareness of one's genitals, but depends on pregenital identification with the mother (for girls) and pregenital separation from the mother (for boys). Identification with the mother is seen as primary for all children, and the development of gender role is also seen as beginning before genital awareness, as a result of the parents' labeling of and interaction with the child. What is hypothesized as arising out of genital awareness and fantasy are the specifics of gender role, particularly such traits as aggressiveness, and dependence/independence (Person, 1974). Even these specifics, however, are seen as grounded in a society where males have certain prerogatives which females do not and vice versa.

SOCIAL LEARNING
THEORY

Psychoanalytic theory postulates a mechanism (identification with the parent having the same genitals) to explain why children learn "appropriate" gender role behaviors, but the theory does not explain *how* the mechanism works. Identification is defined as the imitation and incorporation of complex values and behaviors without specific external pressures to do this. Evidence for identification comes from studies of parent–child similarities in values and behaviors, but such similarity can be due to factors besides identification (Bronfenbrenner, 1958). These factors include direct teaching by the parent in appropriate behaviors, pressure by other people and institutions to behave in certain ways, and genetic factors shared by the parent and child.

With the development of theories of learning in the 1940s and 1950s, psychologists dissatisfied with the lack of emphasis on "how" in psychoanalytic theory began to apply principles of learning theory to explain how identification and other psychoanalytic processes can occur. Eventually, a separate perspective developed, called social learning theory.

Social learning theory, while retaining the idea that processes similar to identification are important in the development of gender components, does not retain the basic theoretical postulates of psychoanalysis. Its major assumption, as stated by Mischel (1966), is that the acquisition and performance of gender-typed behaviors "can be described by the same learning principles used to analyze any other aspect of an individual's behavior" (p. 56). Gender-typed behaviors are defined as behaviors that have different consequences depending on the gender of the person exhibiting the behavior. The learning principles include "discrimination, generalization . . . observational learning . . . the pattern of reward, nonreward, and punishment under specific contingencies, (and) the principles of direct and vicarious conditioning" (p. 57). The emphasis in social learning theory is on observable, antecedent events, rather than on inferred intrapsychic processes, like Oedipal fantasy. The most complete formulation of social learning theory as it relates to the development of gender identity and role is by Mischel (1966; 1970).

In brief, the theory states that through observation children learn behaviors associated with both parents. They learn these behaviors without any direct reinforcement because they see their parents as powerful, effective, and as having control over rewards. (This, according to social learning theory, is the process of identification.) For example, by watching their mother put on lipstick and perfume and observing their father tell her that she looks nice, both sons and daughters learn how to "dress up." However, when the children actually perform the behaviors they have learned, they are differentially reinforced. The daughter may be rewarded for "acting cute," while the son may be disapprovingly told "Boys don't wear lipstick."

Eventually, through differential reinforcement from parents, teachers, peers, and others, children begin to know what they can and cannot do. They begin to anticipate the consequences of various behaviors, and they begin to value gender "appropriate" behaviors because they are rewarded and to devalue gender "inappropriate" behaviors because they are punished or ignored. The child learns the label ("boy" or "girl") appropriate to the rewarded behaviors, and learns to apply that label to her/himself. Through generalization, the child learns to value that label, since it stands for valued behaviors, and to see the label as an important part of her/his self-concept. Gender identity, according to social learning theory, is just another name for this self-label. The male child thinks: "I want rewards. I am rewarded for doing boy things. Therefore, I want to be a boy" (Kohlberg, 1966, p. 89). Social learning theory makes no assumptions about the age at which any of these processes take place; it only states that this is the sequence in which the development of gender role and gender identity occur.

Social learning theory does not concern itself with the question of gender attribution. There are two genders, and presumably children come to learn about physical gender differences in the same way that they learn anything else. It is taken for granted by social learning theorists that gender labels are applied to people on the basis of objective criteria. There is not a great deal of emphasis on "ideas" about gender (and how these might develop) since one of the theory's basic assumptions is that although the *acquisition* of gender-typed behavior may be regulated by cognitive processes, the actual *performance* of these behaviors depends on reinforcement histories. Table 4.1 summarizes the development of gender identity and role, accordingly to social learning theory.

Social learning theory emphasizes the importance of differential reinforcement, but Maccoby and Jacklin (1974) claim that, for the most part, young children are not treated differently by their parents on the basis of gender. If there is differential treatment, it is limited to the parents providing gender-typed clothes and toys, particularly for boys. Others (e.g., Block, 1978) have disagreed with Maccoby and Jacklin, asserting that there is considerable differential treatment in early childhood.

Even if it is true that differential treatment is not strong enough to account for gender differences in behavior, Mischel's statement of social learning theory could still be useful as a way of describing the development of gender identity. A daughter may or may not wear lipstick when she gets older, but she does learn (because the label is differentially applied) that she is a girl and that girls are expected to behave, in at least certain ways, differently from boys. The specifics of gender role behavior may not be well accounted for by social learning theory but, according to Mischel, there is not much to account for—there are very few stable and consistent "sex differences" in behavior. Whether or not a person eventually exhibits a particular gender-typed behavior can be predicted only from a study of past and present reinforcement contingencies and environmental stimuli. These factors are different for each individual. Thus, it is not surprising that there are few consistent "sex differences" in behavior, or conflicting evidence about differential reinforcement for specific behaviors.[4]

Evidence from Green's (1974) study of transsexual adults and children with atypical gender identities provides some support for social learning theory. While Green feels that genetic and prenatal hormonal factors probably contribute to the etiology of transsexualism, he has concluded that a specific social situation is common to the early childhoods of young boys[5] referred to him because of effeminate behavior and to the recollected childhoods of many adult male-to-female transsexuals.

According to Green, these boys, either because they are encouraged by their parents or because of constitutional factors, are attracted from an early age to bright colors, interesting textures, and shiny objects. Feminine clothing and jewelry have these qualities, and, often beginning at age two or three, the boys begin to dress up "like ladies" and start to exhibit "effeminate" mannerisms, like lisps and mincing walks. The power of this "masquerade" is heightened because many of these boys are uncommonly "beautiful." Their cross-dressing is usually encouraged, or at least not discouraged, by their parents. In addition, these boys do not play with other boys, either because no male peers are available or because they prefer the company and less aggressive activities of girls. The father feels that by not liking "boy" things his son is rejecting him, and he becomes psychologically absent from the child's world. By the time these boys go to school, they do not relate well to other boys and are often teased for being "sissies." Eventually the child begins to verbalize, at least to himself, that he wants to be a girl, that he really feels like a girl. He may, when he gets old enough, label himself a transsexual and request gender reassignment procedures.

The most critical factor in the development of a female gender identity in these boys, according to Green, is that there is no discouragement of feminine behavior by the adults who are raising the child. The parents do not realize that by failing to discourage this (particularly the cross-dressing), and by not actively encouraging "boy" behavior, they are aiding him in his developing preference for a female gender role and a female gender identity. Green suggests that the reasoning of these children is as follows: Because I do not like "boy" things, and because I do like "girl" things, then I must really not be a boy. If I am not a boy, I have to be something, so I must be a girl. This reasoning is reinforced by the child's peers who tease him and call him "sissy" and "girl," and tell him such facts as "Boys don't play with dolls." The child's reasoning is, in effect, a restatement of the principles of social learning: "I like girl things, so I must be (or want to be) a girl."[6]

Part of Green's treatment of these children is to encourage them to do "boy" things (e.g., camping with their fathers), and to teach them that (1) not all "boy" things are aggressive, unpleasant (for them) activities, and (2) some "girl" things, like coloring, can be done by boys. In other words, he encourages them to redefine their preferences from "I like girl things" to "I like boy things."

Green may be criticized for being sexist in his treatment program by encouraging differentiated gender roles. We do not think that the criticism is totally warranted, since Green is very clear in his assertion that he is not trying to turn these boys into "supermen," nor is he trying to maintain rigid stereotypes.[7] In fact, Green implies that if gender stereotypes could become less rigid, there would probably be fewer "pretranssexual" children, since there would be fewer nonoverlapping "boys" things and "girl" things. In a world where gender is constructed so that the dichotomy is inflexible and deviance from roles has negative consequences, especially for males, providing treatment for these boys can prevent much of the pain that they would suffer until they became old enough to request reassignment surgery. On the other hand, accepting that these children need treatment confirms the status quo and perpetuates, no matter how humanistically, the gender dichotomy.

As we explain in the next section, there is some question about whether changing cultural ideas about gender roles can really have an impact on the way children think about gender. One of the criticisms of social learning theory is that it does not take into account evidence that children's perceptions of the world are different from adults', and that these perceptions influence the children's gender identity and gender role behaviors. *All* children share "bizarre" ideas about gender, ideas that would not be predicted from knowing their reinforcement histories. The next theory we discuss, cognitive developmental theory, specifically deals with children's ideas about gender.

According to that theory, from a young child's perspective a boy can *become* a girl by changing his clothing and mannerisms. Boys like the ones Green treats may, when they are young, actually believe that they are changing genders when they cross-dress. They may also believe that if they do "girl" things they *are* girls—not just because their parents have encouraged them to act *like* girls, but because, given the way children construct gender, "acting like" is the same as "being" a girl.

These boys do not just exhibit stereotyped "feminine" behavior like wanting to play with dolls, but they also try to move, talk, and dress "like" adult females. They show signs of trying to learn what it takes to "pass" as a female, the same types of things adult transsexuals want to learn. They may be trying to construct a new gender attribution for those around them, rather than just showing a preference for cross-gender role behaviors. Our analysis of children's ideas of gender (which we discuss in the last section of this chapter) suggests that successful treatment of these children must include an awareness of the *children's* rules for constructing gender.

COGNITIVE
DEVELOPMENTAL
THEORY

In contrast to psychoanalytic and social learning theory, cognitive developmental theory (Kohlberg, 1966) emphasizes the child's active role in structuring the world, according to the child's level of cognitive development. The theory, based on the work of Piaget, begins with the assumption that the child's reality is qualitatively different from adults' reality. The way the child sees the world changes in discrete stages until, as a young adult, the individual has an "accurate" view of reality. (From our perspective, children develop until they share the same rules for constructing the world as all other adults. "Accuracy" is a socially constructed concept.)

Before the age of five to seven, children do not have the concept of conservation of physical properties (Piaget, 1952). Adults know that a given amount of water poured from a short, wide glass into a narrow, tall glass remains the same amount of water. Children who have not developed the concept of conservation believe that the amount of water changes when the shape of the container changes. They can give reasons to support this belief (e.g., "It's taller, so there's more water"). Given Western, scientific constructions of reality, both their belief and their reason are "wrong." They have not yet learned the adult rules for reality construction. In Piaget's conceptualization, children are not ignorant, nor have they been taught incorrectly; rather, there is a qualitative difference between the structure of children's and adults' thinking.

We have divided Kohlberg's work on gender into two parts. One is the study of how children's ideas about gender undergo orderly transformations. We discuss this work in the last section of this chapter. The other part of Kohlberg's work is a theory of gender development which can be compared with the two theories we have already presented.

Kohlberg asserts that gender is a physical category based on anatomy, and until children have the concept of conservation despite transformations, they do not have permanent gender identities. Until they understand that, just as the amount of water does not change when poured from one container to another, gender does not change when, for example, someone who plays with trucks starts playing with dolls, they cannot develop a gender identity.

By the time they are three years old children can label themselves accurately (e.g., "I am a girl"). They learn this from hearing others label them, and often can label others accurately, but they do not yet know that (1) a person's gender never changes, (2) everyone has a gender, and (3) gender differences are physical/anatomical ones. By the time children are age five or six, they develop the concept of conservation, including the idea that a person's gender is invariant. Not only does the six year old know she is a girl, but she knows that she will always be a girl. Only at that point, according to Kohlberg, does it make sense to talk about the child having a gender identity.

Once children develop stable gender identities, they begin to prefer gender-typed activities and objects. This is because children value and wish to be like things that they perceive as similar to themselves. As Kohlberg states it, their thinking is: I am a boy. Therefore I like boy things. Therefore doing boy things is rewarding (p. 89).

As they develop permanent gender identities, boys begin to identify with their fathers because they come to understand that not only are they similar to other boys, but they are also similar to men, of which their father is an example. Thus, they want to be like their fathers.

Girls, by the age of five or six, know they are girls; they like girl things, and want to be like their mothers. However, girls are not as "typed" in their preferences or identifications as boys, because they identify with their fathers as well as their mothers. In the reality of the young child, "male" is equated with "big" and synonymous with "more powerful." Consequently, both boys and girls are likely to identify, to some extent, with their fathers and male things in general. Table 4.1 summarizes the development of gender identity and role according to cognitive developmental theory.

Kohlberg presents arguments for why cognitive developmental theory explains the development of gender identity and role better than psychoanalytic or social learning theory. As we have discussed, psychoanalytic theory maintains that gender identity develops from genital awareness. However, Kohlberg has found that children do not have clear ideas about genital differences until *after* they have developed a gender identity. In addition, psychoanalytic theory asserts that appropriate role behaviors are a result of identification with the same gender parent. Research (Kohlberg, 1966) indicates that children are already "sex-typed" in their behavior at an age (four years) when, according to psychoanalytic theory, both boys and girls are identified with their mothers. Finally, Kohlberg claims that social learning theory cannot account for why children have such "unusual" ideas about gender, nor can it account for atypical forms of sexual or gender role behaviors, like homosexuality, despite pressures towards typicality. More importantly, it cannot account for universal similarities in children's concepts and behaviors despite different familial and sociocultural backgrounds.

There are several criticisms that have been made of cognitive developmental theory. One criticism is that being able to label a person "male" or "female," and/or being able to articulate reasons for a label, is not synonymous with being able to make certain distinctions. A psychoanalyst might argue that even if five years olds do not say that men and women are different because they have different genitals, they may still know, on some level, about genital differences. A second criticism, as Maccoby and Jacklin (1974) have pointed out, is that it is not necessary for the child to have the concept of gender invariance in order for self-socialization into gender roles to begin. Three year olds have clear gender-typed preferences, for example, in toys, and it is impossible to discount the effects of this self-socialization on future behavior. Thirdly, cognitive developmental theory cannot account for individual differences in the adoption of gender role behaviors without recourse to concepts like "reinforcement." In general, the theory tends to ignore individual differences. Nevertheless, there is little argument with Kohlberg's general contention that a child's understanding of "boy" and "girl" and the roles associated with these labels are different from adults' understanding, and that that understanding influences the child's behavior and treatment of others.

Of the three theories, cognitive developmental is the only one concerned with the problem of the development of gender attribution processes. At least in terms of labeling, Kohlberg has been interested in the age at which children can correctly label others "male" and "female" and the reasons they give for assigning labels. Implicit in cognitive developmental theory, however, is the assumption that the reasons people give for assigning labels are the reasons they use, an assertion that we question.

As we describe in more detail in the last section of this chapter, children often give physical gender role characteristics like hair length and dress, as reasons for making gender attributions, while adults give primary and secondary physical gender characteristics like genitals and breasts as reasons. According to Kohlberg, these different reasons indicate a shift from seeing gender as a variable category (anyone could be a woman if the way you know someone is a woman is by hair length) to seeing gender as invariant (one's

genitals and secondary gender characteristics do not change). Kohlberg at least indicates an interest in the idea of gender attribution,
although he does not see it as primary, nor as a social construction.
According to cognitive developmental theory, there are two genders,
invariantly dichotomized, which can be labeled on the basis of real,
obvious, factual, objective physical characteristics, and that is what
everyone does—adults and children alike—but only adults know
how they do it.

COMPARING THE
THEORIES

An inspection of Table 4.1 clarifies some of the differences
among the three major psychological theories of gender development. The theories vary in their assumptions about (1) whether
gender identity precedes or develops from gender role, (2) the age
at which these gender components develop, and (3) the ways in
which parents, through identification and/or reinforcement, affect
the development of gender identity and gender role.

Besides these differences, there are similarities among the theories.
Although they all imply that genitals are the criteria for gender attribution, telling females from males is not a concern. This is because
for each theory, and for the psychologists and psychoanalysts who
work within their frameworks, there is no question about the objective facticity of gender. Gender is as real as height and weight and
it can be objectively measured and studied without insurmountable
problems. In addition, gender identity and gender role and the
processes that lead to their development, like identification and
reinforcement, are objective facts. It is assumed that men and women
are behaviorally and psychologically different, and the causes of
these differences can be found in developmental processes. The incorrigible proposition that there are two genders, leads to the assumption that there must be some expression of this dichotomy, even if
the differences are not as extensive as formerly believed, and that
there is a set of psychological factors leading to an orderly, understandable development of gender differences, including gender
identity.

Besides their acceptance of the facticity of gender, the theories,
and the research stemming from them, are similar in their emphasis
on male development. The theories' treatment of both normal and
abnormal development concentrates on boys and tends to offer more

satisfactory and complete explanations of male than of female development—even in the eyes of the theorists (see Kohlberg, 1966; Freud, 1925; Stoller, 1975; Heilbrun, 1973).

Although Freud (1925) claimed that male development is smoother and less precarious than female development, the evidence (e.g., the higher incidence of "gender disorders" like transvestism, transsexualism, paraphelias, among men) indicates that male development is more precarious and more sensitive to environmental influences. Thus, in this case, it might be easier to find more orderly relationships between environmental factors (e.g., parental treatment) and gender role development in boys. Girls' development may occur more independently of external influences. This explanation takes it for granted that scientific research and theory is objective and unbiased—a mere uncovering of what is already there.

On the other hand, some explanations for the concentration on male development take into account the fact that psychological theories and data are not independent of the interests of the people doing the science. Such "accusations" of bias in theory and research have come from a number of sources. Horney (1926), for example, shows how Freud's theory of gender development directly parallels little boys' ideas about gender.[8] The fact that mainly men have created the theories and collected the data may help account for why there has been an emphasis on male development and a relative inability to understand how girls develop. There are several possible reasons: (1) Men are more interested in things like themselves; (2) Men view male development as the norm and try to relate female development to that norm when the developmental processes may be totally different; (3) Men, having been boys, might be able to understand aspects of the development of boys that they cannot in girls.

These criticisms regarding masculine bias share, with the theories being criticized, a belief in the facticity of gender. The implication of the criticisms is that, were the androcentric bias removed from psychology, the "true" facts about gender could then be discovered. These facts, however, would be no more or less "true" than the facts we now have. They would simply be grounded in different incorrigible propositions.

There are at least three theories offered to account for the development of gender. Which one is correct? This question is not one that can be answered. All the theories can point to empirical data supporting their assumptions and/or contradicting the assumptions of other theories. Ultimately, there is no way to determine the truth of theoretical formulations (Kuhn, 1970). Theories are ways of see-ing the world and once one accepts the paradigm of a theoretical orientation, events become interpreted in light of that orientation. Theories may be more or less useful, more or less aesthetically pleas-ing, more or less "in vogue," but their claim to truth is, in some sense, a matter of faith in their basic assumptions. Psychological theories of gender development are special examples, because they are scientific and, thus, more explicit in stating their basic assump-tions, of the general phenomenon of the social construction of gen-der. All assumptions about gender, whether scientific or not, are grounded in the incorrigible propositions which we hold about real-ity. This last statement, is, of course, a statement of our theoretical formulation.

CHILDREN'S IDEAS
OF GENDER

There is no disagreement in the psychological literature that children's ideas about gender differ from adults'. It is the explana-tion for the difference which varies. Psychoanalysts ground the dif-ference in unconscious fantasies and infantile (primary) thought processes. Social learning theorists are not concerned with explain-ing the difference. Cognitive developmental theorists explain it as an example of children's cognitive immaturity. We are interested in children's ideas of gender in terms of what they can tell us about the social construction of gender. We differ with cognitive develop-mental theorists in that we see adult concepts of gender as another stage in reality construction, rather than as the final accurate per-ception of reality.

In the remainder of this chapter we attempt to show how the social construction of reality can be seen as a developmental process, in terms of changes in the incorrigible propositions about gender which individuals hold. We do this through presenting data that we have collected as well as by reinterpreting data from Kohlberg and others.

Concepts of Gender Identity. By the age of three, a child can answer the question: "Are you a girl or a boy?" accurately and consistently. What does being a boy or a girl mean to the child? At that age, ac-cording to Kohlberg (1966), it means no more than being named Sally instead of Susan. It is a characteristic of the child, but not necessarily invariant, and not necessarily a category into which every human being can be placed.

According to Kohlberg, gender invariance develops around age five or six at the same time the child understands conservation in general. According to the positivist perspective this is the point at which the child understands the objective fact that certain transformations do not change the physical characteristics of an object. We take this to be the point when the child begins to share adult rules for gender construction and reality construction. At this point gender identity is "fixed" and reassignments are no longer possible, not because the child has suddenly grasped the facticity of her/his gender, but because the child has incorporated into her/his reality a method for seeing the "fact" that one's gender is unchangeable. It makes no sense to talk about a person having a "gender identity" until that person constructs gender as an invariant characteristic of her/his self. We do not talk about, for example, people having "hair length" identities. In fact, gender is one of the few human characteristics that are constructed as totally invariant from birth. It is for this reason that virtually no attention has been paid to factors in the maintenance of gender identity. Unlike other self concepts (e.g., self-esteem), gender identity is seen as never varying once it is established.

Concepts of Gender Role. By the time they are three, children show preferences for gender-typed toys and activities and have begun to differentiate "boy" things from "girl" things. Their preferences, however, are not yet strongly dichotomized, and the reasons given for a particular preference are egocentric. ("Do boys like trucks or dolls?" "Trucks." "Why?" "Because I like trucks.") Characteristics of the child are attributed to all similar persons. A three year old named "Kate" who liked trucks might believe that all "Kates" like trucks.

By age six, there is a relatively high degree of gender typing in expressed preferences. This does not mean that the child's own behavior is necessarily very stereotyped. The child does believe, however, that gender-typed activities are as inflexible, diochotomized, and unarbitrary as adults believe physical gender characteristics are (Kohlberg and Ullian, 1974). Men are doctors and women are nurses; this is just a statement of the facts. Children will say this despite the fact that their own mothers might be doctors or their own doctors female. Their doing this is not very different from adults, who say that men have narrower hips than women, even though the person making such a statement may believe that "fact" (e.g., by being a man with wide hips); it is still seen as a statement of objective truth.

By early adolescence, children begin to understand that roles are not imperatives the way physical and anatomical attributes are, and also understand that role differences include psychological (e.g., emotional) as well as behavioral components (Kohlberg and Ullian, 1974). In other words, they can construct reality as well as any adult.

Development of Gender Attribution

"Correct and stable gender identification depends on the child's ability to classify a physical object—the body." (Kohlberg, 1966, p. 94). "Gender identification," as Kohlberg uses the term, is the final step in a *process* of deciding whether, through the course of an interaction, the sense of "male" or "female" has been created.

In a recent study of gender identification, Thompson (1975) investigated the development of gender concepts, including the age at which children learn to apply gender labels to pictures and paper doll figures. Three year olds are considerably better than two year olds in attributing the "correct" gender to themselves and others, but one-fourth of the three year olds still made errors. It is not until children are about five or six that they assign gender labels with 100 percent accuracy (i.e., in total agreement with adults) (Kohlberg, 1966). Even then, when they are asked, "How do you know that it is a woman (man)?", their reasons are often "wrong."

We began this chapter with two children's reasons for why their drawings depicted a female or male. Those examples were selected from a study we conducted on gender attribution in childrn's drawings. We were interested in capturing the *process* of gender attribution, in getting as close to the construction of gender as possible, without limiting ourselves to gender identification as other researchers had done. We wanted to see children producing gender cues and wanted to understand the relationship between these cues and children's *post-hoc* constructions through an analysis of the reasons they, and others, gave for attributing gender to their pictures.

In order to do this we asked preschool (age 3½–4½), kindergarten (age 5–6), and third-grade (age 8–9) children[9] to draw two pictures, one of a girl or woman and the other of a boy or man, and to tell us what made their picture a picture of a girl (boy). One month later, each child was shown pictures drawn by children at all three age levels. Included in the group of drawings were the two drawings the child had done a month earlier. Each child was asked to identify the gender of the figure in each drawing, and to tell why that gender was assigned. The drawings were also shown to adults who were asked the same questions.[10]

The principal questions we had were about the relationship between age group and the accuracy of gender attribution. (1) Were the participants more accurate in attributing gender to drawings produced by older children than those produced by younger children? (2) Were older children more accurate in attributing gender to their own drawings, one month later, than younger children? (3) Did participants' ability to attribute gender correctly increase with the age of the participant?

For questions 1 and 2 we found that there was a simple increase in accuracy with age. Participants in all groups were more accurate in attributing gender to drawings, the older the child who had produced the drawing, and were more likely to respond "don't know" to drawings, the younger the child who had produced the drawing. Only third-graders were able to identify the gender of their *own* drawings with 100 percent accuracy. About one-third of the preschoolers and kindergarteners either erred in attributing gender to the pictures they had drawn, or could not assign a gender label, the second time they saw the drawings.

The findings for question 3, however, were more complicated. Older children and adults were not better at making gender attributions to all drawings. Rather, expertise at attributing gender depended on which group of participants was judging which group of pictures. Preschoolers got 13 percent more of the preschool drawings correct than any other group; kindergarten and preschool children attributed the correct gender to 16 percent more of the kindergarten drawings than the third-grade or adult participants; and third-grade and kindergarten children got 12 percent more of the third-grade drawings correct than did the preschoolers or adults.

This finding is quite intriguing. It suggests that whatever cues preschoolers are using, those cues are shared, at least to some extent, by children of the same age, but are not shared by others. The same can be said about kindergarten and third-grade children. If we knew only that older children's drawings elicited more correct attributions, we might conclude that it was a matter of representational ability improving with age. The older a child is, the better she/he can make a dress look like a dress and a moustache look like a moustache. While this is obviously one factor, it does not explain why preschoolers are better, *relative to others*, in attributing gender to preschool drawings or why preschool and kindergarten children are better, relative to others, in attributing gender to kindergarten drawings. If younger children's ideas about gender are as egocentric as they have been asserted to be, then presumably there would be little conceptual information which they shared and little in their drawings which could be sharable. This was not the case. There may be something about gender which young children share with each other, but which is not shared with older children or aduts. We examine this further in Chapter 6.

Some information about the development of gender attribution processes can be gained by looking at the reasons participants in the study gave for the gender attributions they made. The particular categories of reasons (hair length, clothing, size, body features) do not inform us about the deep structure of gender attribution, about whether young children attribute gender differently from older children and adults, any more than asking an adult "What makes someone a man?" does. What we can illuminate, though, is the development of the socially constructed meaning of gender, if we take the kinds of answers participants give to constitute what they understand to be "good reasons" for gender.

Our purpose in soliciting reasons was not to catalog them, detailing stages in cognitive development. Ample evidence has already been collected (e.g., Kohlberg, 1966; Katcher, 1955; Thompson and Bentler, 1971) which shows that young children cite hair length and clothing as gender cues and that adults use biological signs.[11] The reasons that the youngest children gave suggest that they have not yet learned that any reason is not enough; it must be a "good reason." That is, it must be placed within a gender "appropriate" context. For example, both preschool and adult participants frequently gave body parts as reasons. While preschoolers, for the most part, merely named the body part ("Why is this a picture of a boy?" "His hands" or "His face"), the adults characterized the features in a particular way ("Because of the aggressive expression on his face" or "Because his arms are in an athletic pose").

Preschool and kindergarten participants give more "wrong" reasons than anyone else. Their reasons tend to make no sense to adults, to be seen as idiosyncratic and uninformative. Such a list would include: round eyes, long tongue, ears, chin, nostrils, webbed feet. Instead of treating the youngest children's reasons as idiosyncratic and uninformative, an analysis of their "errors" reveals some methodical aspects of their construction of gender and of the development of that construction.

Does the fact that children give these reasons mean that they are using these cues, or does it mean that they are not describing the cues they use and are "merely" trying to give "good reasons?" Although preschoolers were the *least* likely to say "I don't know" when asked to make a gender attribution, they were the *most* likely to say "I don't know" when asked to give a reason for the attribution. Preschool and kindergarten participants were also the most likely to give tautological reasons for their attributions ("It's a man because it is" or "Because I say so").

Giving reasons is not the same as making a gender attribution. It may be that the adults and older children could have made more accurate gender attributions than they did to the preschool and kindergarten drawings, but, not finding anything in the picture that could serve as a "good reason," they assumed that they did not know the gender.[12] The youngest children may not have been concerned with "good reasons," not yet sharing in the adult construction of reality, and thus were not "afraid" to say "I don't know why it's a man" or "It's a man 'cause it is."

The reasons verbalized are not necessarily the cues used. We can postulate that for children, as for adults, gender is attributed on the basis of some, as yet unknown, criteria, and then what is given is a good reason, that is, evidence that supports the way children construct gender and the incorrigible propositions of that construction. For example, Loren, whom we quoted at the beginning of this chapter, said his picture was a boy because it was bigger. Although Loren's boy is bigger than Loren's girl (in terms of face size), in most of the childrens' drawings boy and girl figures did not differ noticeably in size. Several children besides Loren said that their picture was a boy because it was bigger, even though it was actually no bigger than their drawing of a girl. The drawings were the same size, but they were asked to make a differentiation and they did so—either because when they drew the picture they intended there to be a size difference which they were not skilled enough to draw, or because they knew they were supposed to see a difference (otherwise, why would the adult have asked them?). Having classified the drawing, children must give a reason for the classification which displays the factual status of gender, *as they construct the facts.* Since the facts, for many children, are in terms of physical cues like size, this is the reason they give, thus displaying the "objective facticity" of gender.

Adults do exactly the same thing as these children. The reasons adults give for gender attributions display and produce a sense of the factual, objective status of primary and secondary gender characteristics as an invariant dichotomy, regardless of whether, in any particular case, that dichotomy appears "in the picture." When we say, "I knew he was a man because of his broad shoulders and the way he walked," we do not base those reasons on any measure we make of those characteristics. We know he is a man (or at least we know that he is similar or different from us), and the reasons we give display that we know what "man" means; they do not necessarily describe what he did, or how we made the decision.

What differentiates adult gender concepts from those of young children is that adults "know" the socially constructed "signs" of gender and they "know" that these signs are invariant. Some of the differences between the way adults and children understand "reasons" are reflected in the errors some kindergarten children made in attributing gender to their own drawings one month later. (See Table 4.2)

Sometimes "idiosyncratic" reasons are given (" 'cause it has a face"). The same cues may be used, at different times, to signify maleness and femaleness (Example 1). A cue from a particular member of a gender (e.g., "my mother") may be used, but it is not one that is generalized by the child to be an invariant feature of that gender over time (Example 2). These children do not yet know two important things. One is that a "good reason" for gender is dichotomous and generalizable. The second is that gender is a (socially constructed and shared) set of qualities that are "known" to be invariant over time.

It would be a mistake to call the reasons given by the children "gender cues," but they are trying to be methodical; that is, they know they must give a reason, which is a step beyond "I don't know" or " 'Cause I say so." Once they begin to understand "good reason," they start to respond as Loren did. Size and hair length are treated by children at a certain stage as dichotomous, generalizable variables, in the same way as adults treat genitals and secondary gender characteristics.

However, even with an understanding of what a "good reason" is, young children still do not share in the adult method of constructing gender. Children do not "understand" invariance. Five year old children believe that if you put a dress on a man he could change

Table 4.2 Examples of Children's Reasons

	Gender Attribution	Reasons
EXAMPLE 1		
1st Session:	Boy	Because boys have short hair and they don't have beautiful eyelashes. They have boys' shoes like his. Boys don't wear ponytails either.
2nd Session:	Girl	It's a second grader with short hair. Sometimes girls have short hair.
EXAMPLE 2		
1st Session:	Girl	Green eyes just like my mother.
2nd Session:	Boy	Looks big.
EXAMPLE 3		
1st Session:	Girl	This is a girl monster 'cause it has a face on it.
2nd Session:	Boy	It is a cook with no hair.
EXAMPLE 4		
1st Session:	Girl	This is a skeleton mother 'cause it has long legs and she has no colors only red.
2nd Session:	Boy	It's a little kid skeleton. Boys are skeletons.

into a woman. Adults know that this is not "true," but they believe that if you put a penis on a woman and remove her breasts, ovaries, and uterus and give her androgens she could change into a man.

The increasing incidence of persons who get their genitals surgically transformed (transsexuals) poses a dilemma for the adult construction of gender. Since adults hold the concept of gender invariance as an incorrigible proposition, there must be a way to interpret genital transformations so as to maintain the impossibility of gender transformations. The way invariance has been maintained is either by applying a biological characteristic that cannot yet be changed (e.g., gender chromosomes in sports) or, more commonly, especially in psychology and biology, through the development of a new concept, gender identity, which assures that gender will continue to be invariant and not able to undergo any transformations. Genital transformations are seen as not really changing the true gender of a person. It is more like changing water into steam—it is essentially still water, although in another form. Once children have incorporated the concept of an invariant gender dichotomy based on biology into their rules for seeing gender, they become able to collaborate in the social construction of gender, in making gender a "real" fact.

A review of psychological theories of gender development has shown three ways in which it is possible to construct how children come to share with adults the reality of gender. Our own theory is a fourth way of constructing reality and we have shown how it is possible to see the social construction of gender as a developmental process. The next chapter deals with gender construction not developmentally, but as an ongoing process in every interaction.

NOTES

1. Readers are referred to Freud (1925), Mischel (1966; 1970), and Kohlberg (1966) for the most complete statements of these theoretical positions on gender.

2. We are deliberately referring to this group as "children without penises" rather than "children with clitorises" or "children with vaginas," because in Freud's theoretical framework it is their lack of penises rather than their possession of something else which distinguishes them and influences their psychosexual development in a particular direction.

3. This discussion contains only a few examples of modern psychoanalytic treatments of gender development. See Strouse (1974) and Miller (1973) for more complete presentations.

4. Whether there are specific "sex differences" in behavior is not the same as whether there are gender roles (i.e., expectations that males and females are supposed to be different). The area of "sex differences" is too extensive for us to treat it in any detail. (See Maccoby and Jacklin, 1974.) As we have stated before, the question of "real" differences between the genders is separate from the question of the expectation of differences, the formation of a gender identity, and the ability to label others with the "appropriate" gender label and to have oneself labeled "correctly" by others. The assertion by Mischel and others that there are very few "real" gender differences does not call into question the fact of gender identity or gender attribution. If the "fact" that there are few "real" gender differences becomes part of general cultural expectations, there may eventually be changes in gender role expectations. Conversely, as ideas of gender role change, psychologists will find fewer "sex

differences," not just because socialization practices will change, but also because psychologists, who are first of all everyday members, will change their expectations about what they will find, and will consequently look for and "discover" very different things.

5. Green has studied only a few girls who want to be boys, and a few female-to-male transsexuals. Part of the reason why there may be so few is that "boyish" behavior in girls is much more tolerated, and "tomboys" are not seen as needing treatment the way "sissies" are. Based on the cases he has studied, Green hypothesized that the dynamics are similar for girls.

6. Whether the statement is "I must be a girl" or "I want to be a girl" probably depends on whether or not the child has incorporated adult rules for constructing gender. The child who "understands" that gender transformations involve body transformations also understands that although liking "girl" things might make him want to be a girl, that liking does not make him into a girl.

7. There are others (e.g., Rekers and Lovass, 1974) who use behavior therapy, including aversion therapy, to treat effeminate boys. Even though they claim success, their methods and their encouragement of strongly dichotomized gender roles and behaviors as a sign of "mental health" are highly questionable.

8. For example, because little boys have penises, they think everyone has a penis. This does not mean, however, that little girls think that they had a penis and lost it as Freud maintained (Horney, 1926).

9. We thank the following schools for their cooperation: Purchase Children's Center, Sarah Lawrence Early Childhood Center, Quaker Ridge Elementary School, and Seely Elementary School.

10. Ten preschool children saw eight drawings each: their own set, another set of preschool drawings, a set of kindergarten drawings, and a set of third-grade drawings. Ten kindergarten, ten third-grade, and ten adult participants saw twelve drawings each: two sets of preschool, two sets of kindergarten, and two sets of third-grade drawings. The drawings were not presented in pairs, but were shown in random order, with the child's own drawings undifferentiated from the others'. Each of the sixty drawings was seen by at least five participants. Half of the participants were male and half were female. None of the analyses revealed "sex differences."

The children's drawings study has been replicated in Japan by Sheila Sweet. A preliminary analysis of the data indicates patterns similar to the ones reported here.

11. The specifics of our findings on this point are complicated, but, like good positivists, we can mold them into a sensible pattern. Size was not as common a reason as previous research (Kohlberg, 1966) suggested it would be. Only preschoolers used size to any degree, and then mainly in

referring to the pictures they had just drawn, rather than to the pictures
they saw in the second session. Hair length was given as a reason by
all groups. Clothing was not a frequent reason until kindergarten,
whereupon it was used most frequently by each group, including adults.
Although adults did use body parts as reasons (see text), they could not
use many secondary gender characteristics since they were constrained by
the concrete pictures they were looking at. Children do not
draw breasts, hips, beards, etc. very frequently.

12. Gender attribution may not be synonymous with being able to make
a differentiation of some sort, e.g., being able to tell whether another
is similar to or different from the self. This is further developed
in Chapter 6.

5

GENDER CONSTRUCTION
IN EVERYDAY LIFE:
TRANSEXUALISM

There're only two alternatives in
society. You're either a man or a
woman. If I don't feel like a woman
then it's got to be the other way. . . .
Because I didn't feel comfortable
in the first postiion, I'm going into
the second. I'll give it a try.

Robert[1]—a female to male
transsexual, age 26

There are thousands of transsexuals in the United States today.
With few exceptions (e.g., Garfinkel, 1967), the interests of the scientific community have focused either on transsexuals as interesting cases of social deviance (e.g., Feinbloom, 1976) or on the pathology (e.g., Person, 1974), etiology (e.g., Stoller, 1968, 1975), and treatment (e.g., Benjamin, 1966) of transsexualism. In contrast, our interest in transsexuals is not in terms of transsexualism, per se, but only
in terms of what transsexualism can illuminate about the day-to-day
social construction of gender by all persons. To gather information
on this process we conducted in-depth interviews with fifteen transsexuals. The relative uniqueness of our focus was reflected in their
reactions to it. As is common among this group of people, they were
familiar with the scientific literature on transsexualism (Sulcov,
1973; Person, 1974). Some seemed annoyed, some seemed relieved,
and some seemed interested that our only concern was with how their
experience could expose universal features of gender construction.
All, however, were somewhat surprised that we had little interest in
learning the causes of their transsexualism or in questioning their
definitions of themselves. In addition to these interviews, we have
included, in an appendix to the book, excerpts from letters we re-

ceived from a friend who is a transsexual. The appendix illustrates one person's construction of gender and should be read in light of the points made in this chapter.

It is not just specific behaviors of transsexuals that illustrate the social construction of gender. The existence of transsexualism, itself, as a valid diagnostic category underscores the rules we have for constructing gender, and shows how these rules are reinforced by scientific conceptions of transsexualism.

In Chapter 1 we described the natural attitude and the phenomenological method of "bracketing" this attitude. Temporarily suspending "belief" in the independent, objective reality of social and scientific facts like gender allows us to see how the sense of objective facts is produced in everyday interaction. Harold Garfinkel, in whose work this chapter and this book is grounded, has studied several concrete phenomena in order to illustrate general principles of the social construction of reality. One of the phenomena he has studied is gender, through presenting the case of Agnes, a 19 year old genetic male. Although Agnes had a penis, she claimed to have always felt herself to be female and to have naturally developed female secondary gender characteristics at puberty. She requested the construction of the "appropriate" genitals from the UCLA Medical Center, and was interviewed by Garfinkel under their auspices. Garfinkel was interested in the abstract idea of continuous gender accomplishment in every interaction. However, he did draw some concrete conclusions about what it was Agnes had to do to create a sense of being a "real" woman. In the beginning of his discussion, Garfinkel presents the "facts" which form our natural attitude toward gender. He then shows how Agnes' accomplishment was to produce a sense of those facts even though she was an example of how those facts are not always true.

Our natural attitude toward gender (i.e., the real, objective facts) consists of the following (Garfinkel, 1967, pp. 122–128)[2]:

1. There are two, and only two, genders (female and male).

2. One's gender is invariant. (If you *are* female/male, you always *were* female/male and you always *will be* female/male.)

3. Genitals are the essential sign of gender. (A female is a person with a vagina; a male is a person with a penis.)

4. Any exceptions to two genders are not to be taken seriously. (They must be jokes, pathology, etc.)

5. There are no transfers from one gender to another except ceremonial ones (masquerades).

6. Everyone must be classified as a member of one gender or another. (There are no cases where gender is not attributed.)

7. The male/female dichotomy is a "natural" one. (Males and females exist independently of scientists' [or anyone else's] criteria for being male or female.)

8. Membership in one gender or another is "natural." (Being female or male is not dependent on anyone's deciding what you are.)

Our discussion in Chapter 2 suggests that these "facts" about gender are not universal; berdache contradict most of them. Nevertheless, these are the "facts" of gender in terms of Western reality.

It might seem that in light of these facts transsexualism cannot be taken seriously. The existence of transsexuals appears to deny at least points 2 and 5. But if we bracket the "facts," what we find is that the transsexual, through his/her concerns with "passing," and the medical and legal professions, through their treatment of transsexualism, reveal the production of the natural attitude toward gender. The transsexual produces a sense of the facticity of gender in social interactions in the same way everyone produces it. The natural attitude allows no exceptions, so the transsexual, an apparent exception, is seen as not an exception after all, but rather an example of the "objective" truth of the facts. This is the paradox that is demonstrated throughout this chapter.

Garfinkel's assumption (which we share) is that something can be learned about what is taken for granted in the "normal" case by studying what happens when there are "violations." Transsexuals take their own gender for granted, but they cannot assume that others will. Consequently, transsexuals must manage themselves as male or female so that others will attribute the "correct" gender. It is easier for us to see that transsexuals "do" (accomplish) gender than it is to see this process in nontranssexuals. The transsexuals' construction of gender is self-conscious. They make obvious what nontranssexuals do "naturally." Even though gender accomplishment is self-conscious for transsexuals, they share with all the other members of the culture the natural attitude toward gender. The ways transsexuals talk about the phenomenon of transsexualism, the language they use, their attitudes about genitals, and the questions they are unable to answer, point to their belief that though others might see them as violating the facts, they, themselves, believe that they are not violating them at all.

In this chapter we show how (1) the concept of transsexualism as understood by the medical and legal professions, and (2) the practices of transsexuals in everyday interactions produce the sense of the reality of two and only two genders. The process of gender attribution both in terms of what needs to be done to be taken as the "correct" gender and in terms of what rules others apply to make an attribution is also made clearer by studying these "exceptions" who are, after all, only examples of what is more difficult to see in nonexceptional cases.

CRITERIA FOR DETERMINING TRANSSEXUALISM

We defined transsexualism in Chapter 1 and we have used the term throughout the book without explaining how it is determined whether someone is really a transsexual. Sulcov (1973) wrote an exhaustive treatise on the social reality of transsexualism. In it he differentiates two kinds of definitions of transsexualism. One type of definition explains what transsexualism "really is." This would include what Stoller (1968) refers to as a characterological definition—one based on various psychological criteria. ". . . A transsexual (is) a person who feels himself (consciously and unconsciously) to belong to the opposite sex while not denying his sexual anatomy" (Stoller, 1968, p. 132). The second kind of definition, the one that Sulcov found to be in accordance with his perspective, is a definition in terms of a system of treatment: A transsexual is someone who is receiving hormone therapy and genital surgery in order to be seen as the gender other than the one he/she was assigned at birth. Sulcov concluded that the social reality of transsexualism is as a particular kind of treatment that facilitates the routine movement between genders and thus legitimizes that movement. This definition allows us, given our research interest, not to be concerned with whether we have interviewed "real" transsexuals. Defining transsexualism according to a system of treatment does present some problems, however. Not all people who present themselves for corrective surgery and hormone therapy define themselves as transsexuals. For example, there are hermaphrodites who request genital surgery to reduce the ambiguity of their genitals and male prostitutes who may want mammary development to aid them in their trade. A second problem is that not all transsexuals request corrective surgery or hormone therapy. Pauly (1974) claims that female-to-male transsexuals are most likely to request surgery only when they want to legally marry. Otherwise many can live successfully as men without medical intervention. It may not occur to older transsexuals to request surgery until they discover a precedent. Feinbloom (1976) reports a considerable rise in inquiries at the Gender Identity Service in Boston from men over 45 after the publication of Jan Morris's *Conundrum*.

For our purposes we have divided the definition question into two parts: (1) What proof does the medical profession require in order to prescribe hormone therapy and genital surgery? and (2) What proof does the legal profession require in order to allow change of gender status? The answers to these questions reflect society's assumptions about gender. The fact that medical and legal criteria are changing suggests that the social definition of gender is changing.

By what criteria, then, do doctors decide that a person can receive treatment for transsexualism? Before 1966 and the opening of the Johns Hopkins Gender Identity Clinic, transsexualism was not a legitimate diagnostic category and there was no treatment in the United States for such persons. When Agnes first saw doctors in Midwest City prior to her acceptance at the UCLA Medical Center, she was declared to be male. "In the final analysis the capacity to perform the male reproductive function settled Agnes' sex" (Garfinkel, 1967, p. 123). Because her testes could function (although suppressed by large amounts of estrogen), she was capable of producing sperm, and was therefore male. At UCLA, where she finally received treatment, the medical team had different criteria. They performed genital surgery on individuals with biophysical problems. Since they noted high concentrations of estrogen in Agnes' system (and assumed that the estrogen was being produced naturally), they decided that she had a biophysical problem (androgen insensitivity syndrome), and on the basis of that diagnosis and her female gender identity, they declared her to be female. The fact that she was "reproductively male" was irrelevant.

Agnes participated in the decision made about her gender by constructing for the doctors (and for Garfinkel) the "objective fact" of a biological root of her problem. As it was later revealed, she precipitated the pubertal signs of femaleness by taking estrogen which had been prescribed for her mother. Agnes' intention was to display herself, through her talk, as always having been a real woman, *as "real" was defined by the doctors*, so that the doctors would agree to surgery. Not only did she have to present herself to the world as a real woman, she had to present herself to the doctors as a biological woman with an abnormality—a set of male genitals.

Even now, over 10 years later, the medical profession is more willing to recommend corrective surgery for persons who can prove that their "disorder" has a biological root (Pauly, 1974). The Erikson Foundation, one of whose functions was to help transsexuals and educate the public about transsexualism, advised that since health insurance policies allow coverage only for the "necessary treatment of an injury or disease . . . best results (are) obtained when the condition (transsexualism) is presented as a 'neuroendocrinological or psychohormonal disorder,' absolutely requiring and responsive to surgical and hormonal treatment." (Erikson, 1974, pp. 22–23). Criteria for providing hormonal treatment is less stringent than for surgical treatment. There are three reasons for this: (1) Many of the effects of hormone therapy are reversible. (2) Hormone treatment precedes surgical treatment by at least six months while transsexuals "practice" living as their "new" gender. (3) Hormone therapy does not tamper with the essential sign of gender—genitals. (The enlarged clitoris of female-to-male transsexuals that results from androgen therapy is reversible if therapy is halted.)

Most clinicians and medical researchers (except perhaps the most conservative[3] psychonanalysts) suspect that transsexualism has a biological (prenatal hormonal) component. Transsexuals, themselves, talk about having a birth defect and make it clear that their transsexualism is not a matter of choice. Given the state of medicine, however, there is as yet no way of measuring this hypothesized prenatal influence. Consequently, transsexuals must provide evidence that would at least concur with a prenatal hormonal explanation. This evidence consists of proving, through talk, that they have always felt, as far back as they can remember, like the gender other than the one they were assigned. (One drawback of this criterion is that it is difficult to determine the validity of such a claim. Anyone familiar with the literature on transsexualism knows that in order to be considered a transsexual by a medical examining team, one must talk about always having felt like a member of the "opposite" gender.) Transsexuals no longer have to provide biophysical evidence, but they still must provide evidence of always having been one gender, of having had, since birth, an invariant gender identity. The social–psychological criterion of gender identity is grounded in biology, that is, prenatal hormones.

When social–psychological criteria are applied to determine "true" gender identity, certain of society's ideas about gender are revealed. In order for an assigned female to be declared male, he may need to perform all aspects of the male gender role to a stereotypical extent. If female-to-male transsexuals can assume a more feminine role, then they were not really transsexuals after all (Pauly, 1974). A psychiatrist reports (Erickson, n.d.) that he helped a patient realize that he was not really a male-to-female transsexual because he continued relating sexually to women. "So finally . . . I asked him: 'What do you want to be, a Lesbian?' And that crystallized the *contradiction* for him . . ." (p. 7, our emphasis). Thus in order to be a transsexual one must also meet the criteria of being a "normal" member of one's "chosen" gender.

There is some suggestion that not only must one be normal, but it helps to be attractive. A clinician during a panel session on transsexualism at the 1974 meeting of the American Psychological Association said that he was more convinced of the femaleness of a male-to-female transsexual if she was particularly beautiful and was capable of evoking in him those feelings that beautiful women generally do. Another clinician told us that he uses his own sexual interest as a criterion for deciding whether a transsexual is really the gender she/he claims.

Attractiveness is obviously not a formal criterion; however, transsexuals must demonstrate that their public physical presentation is credible enough to allow them to "pass" as their "new" gender. Most gender clinics require that transsexuals live for at least six months as their "new" gender prior to receiving genital surgery. The medical profession considers the transsexuals' comfortableness with their "new" gender and their success in being "taken for" a man or a woman important factors in the gender membership decision. We think that these factors (comfortableness and success) *constitute* gender membership and we demonstrate this point throughout this chapter.

Presumably because clinicians have not agreed upon formal criteria for performing corrective surgery, the legal profession has similarly reached no concensus. In the legal record there are both positive and negative decisions regarding requests for change of gender status.[4] One of the major criteria seems to be the capability of the individual to perform sexual and/or reproductive functions of either gender. (In this sense the legal profession is applying medical standards of 10 years ago.) The courts that have denied applications for change of name have done so on the grounds that the petitioners do not function *procreatively* or *sexually* as the gender for which they are applying. These criteria are somewhat arbitrary since there are clearly nontranssexual females who are unable to conceive and nontranssexual males who are unable to impregnate. Similarly, there are nontranssexual males and females who because of a physical or psychological dysfunction are unable to perform sexually. What the courts seem to be saying is that if a person does not have the appropriate chromosomes, they at least should have appropriately functioning genitals and internal equipment. Given the sexual and procreative criteria, the courts are obviously prejudiced against the female-to-male transsexual who, unlike his counterpart, cannot as yet receive genitals that look and function perfectly. The court has disregarded the opinions of doctors who claim that their female-to-male transsexual patients are true males because they have received mastectomies and are undergoing hormone treatment. The criterion of gender identity does not appear to have had an impact on the courts. Joseph, a female-to-male transsexual without a sexually functioning penis, complains that only when it becomes technically easier to create penises will doctors take female-to-male transsexuals more seriously. The same could be said of judges.

One court decision cites the Committee on Public Health of the New York Academy of Medicine which proclaimed: "It is questionable whether laws and records should be changed and thereby used as a means to help psychologically ill persons in their social adaptation" (Matter of Fernandez, 1976, p. 12). There is other evidence which implies that the legal profession does not see the transsexual as a "real" man or women. Failure to inform one's spouse that one is a transsexual and has undergone corrective surgery is grounds for annulment or divorce since the marriage may be considered to have been entered into fraudulently (Erickson, 1974, p. 32). Fraudulent, in this context, appears to mean more than that the person cannot function reproductively; it implies that he/she is not what he/she appears to be in terms of gender.

It is interesting to note that transsexuals have used legal criteria to their advantage by evoking the negative. They submit that a new or amended birth certificate should be granted because surgical procedures were performed leaving the person no longer a functional female (unable to bear children) or no longer a functional male (unable to impregnate a woman) (Erickson, 1974).

To summarize the legal position of transsexualism, with regard to our interest in decisions about gender, genitals are not merely a clarifying sign of gender; they are its essential sign. To be sympathetic with the legal profession, it is difficult to legislate criteria for deciding what is really a male or a female when this is supposed to be an objective fact, not amenable to legislation.

After seeing Jan Morris on television, one of our students perplexedly inquired: If a person thought he/she were a horse, and surgical techniques were available for transforming that person into a horse, why shouldn't that person have a right to become a horse? His point should be taken seriously. Transsexualism, as a legitimate diagnostic category, exists largely because of advancements in medicine and cosmetology. It is a category constructed to alleviate ambiguity—to avoid the kinds of combinations (e.g., male genitals–female gender identity) that make people uncomfortable because they violate the basic rules about gender. If genitals could not be changed, gender identity would have to be. Since genitals can now be changed, gender identity can now be seen as the less flexible criterion. What we have witnessed in the last 10 years is the triumph of the surgeons over the psychotherapists in the race to restore gender to an unambiguous reality.

Prince (1973) maintains that what transsexuals have is not "gender dysphoria" (the medical category under which transsexualism is subsumed) but "sexual dysphoria." They are not dissatisfied with their gender but with their genitals, because those genitals do not correspond to the gender with which they feel comfortable. There must be congruence between the two, given the rules. In a society that could tolerate lack of correspondence, there would be no transsexuals. There would be men with vaginas and women with penises or perhaps different signs of gender. Similarly, if men could wear dresses there would be no transvestism, as we now understand the category.

Robert, a female-to-male transsexual, speculated about whether he would have had to change in today's world of more flexible gender roles. Although he concluded that he would still have needed to change because he did not feel like a woman, we believe that it was not because he did not feel like a woman that he had to get surgical and hormonal treatment, but rather because he did not feel comfortable having a vagina and breasts when other people who had vaginas and breasts seemed so different socially and psychologically from him.

Science will soon be able to construct perfectly functioning penises. Because of this we will never know what would have been the long-range repercussions, in concepts about gender, of having a group of men in society who do not have penises. We suspect that in a society that allowed men to have vaginas and women to have penises, the biological imperative of gender would weaken. Gender membership would be based on gender identity rather than genitals. Although gender identity is grounded in biology (insofar as current research is seeking its root in prenatal hormones), a biological substrate, inaccessible to public viewing, is clearly less powerful in everyday gender attributions than a biological cue (genitals) which is potentially public.

Now that we have shown how the concept of transsexualism in medicine and law underscores and supports the rules our society has for constructing gender, we will shift to a discussion of how the reality of gender is supported by transsexuals in their everyday interactions.

TRANSSEXUAL BEHAVIOR AND THE NATURAL ATTITUDE

How is transsexualism reconcilable with the "fact" that gender is invariant and there are no transfers? As we mentioned at the end of the last chapter, it is easily reconcilable if we think of the transsexual not as changing gender but changing genitals. Gender remains invariant. For example, one is and always has been a female. It is merely the sign of the gender (the genitals) which must be fixed The fact that genitals *must* be fixed to be the "right" ones to go with the gender helps create a sense of the "fact" that genitals are the essential sign of gender.

This is demonstrated in the ways transsexuals refer to themselves, their bodies, and to the surgical operations they request. A male-to-female transsexual, being interviewed on NBC's "Tomorrow" television program was asked, "How was your beard taken care of?" The transsexual answered, "I was fortunate. I never had much of a *facial hair growth pattern*" (emphasis ours). The fact that she used this particular language is evidence of her belief that real women do not have (and never did have) beards. If they have anything, they have facial hair. Since she was always a woman, she never had a beard.

Very seldom did the transsexuals we interviewed refer to themselves as "transsexual" (although they would all admit to being defined as such); rather they talked about "those of us who have changed." In other words, although they may have at one time been seen as one gender and were now seen as the other, they were never outside one of the two gender categories. In support of their claim to have always been one gender, they request "corrective surgery" not "sex-change" operations[5] (Kando, 1973). They are not changing gender, only correcting a mistake. One female-to-male transsexual wrote to several insurance companies asking them to write policies for transsexuals that would include coverage for "penis reconstruction." This terminology suggests that a penis had been there before, much like a person injured in an accident might request "facial reconstruction." At the very least it implies that the penis always belonged there. Agnes, after surgery, described being treated as a "real female after all" (Garfinkel, 1967, p. 128). The altered sign confirmed the unalterable essence. Garfinkel presents in great detail evidence that Agnes did not see her situation as a matter of choice. She stated that a vagina should only be constructed if it should have been there all along. These are examples of how, through talk, the transsexuals show their belief in the basic invariability of gender, and their belief that the (visible) genitals must be altered to conform to the person's true (invisible) gender.

A psychoanalytic psychotherapist who regards transsexualism as a pathological condition maintains that the emphasis transsexuals place on surgically receiving the appropriate genitals is obsessive. "(It is) as though the sexual organ provides the totality of gender" (Erikson Educational Foundation, n.d., p. 25). What this therapist sees as an obsessive preoccupation, we view as evidence of the transsexuals' acceptance of the natural attitude toward gender. A male has a penis and a female has a vagina. This is a relatively easy task for male-to-female transsexuals, since surgical techniques are available for constructing a vagina. There are no cases cited where a male-to-female transsexual is satisfied with merely the removal of the penis. The female-to-male transsexual has a more difficult problem. How does he reconcile the fact that males have penises, he is a male, and yet he may not have a penis (or at least not a fully functioning one)? Even in this case, though, getting a penis is extremely important. If he does not have a penis, he at least believes that he *should* have one, and, hopefully, will sometime in the future.

One female-to-male transsexual when asked, "What is the most important thing to have to be a man?" answered, "A penis." He then admitted that although he was a man without a penis, it was his biggest preoccupation. The "obsession" with having the sign may constitute, for him, proof that the sign should be there. Occasionally when he has sexual relations with his wife, he thinks about not having a penis, and this reminds him of the period when he tried to be a lesbian. Being a lesbian was catastrophic, since he was treated by his partners as female; his genitals were seen by them as a vagina and clitoris, rather than being treated as "abnormal" male genitals.

Another female-to-male transsexual who did not have a penis stated that the difference between women and men was that they had different sex organs. One way that he handled this apparent inconsistency was to refer to his sexual organs as "genitals" rather than as his "vagina" or "clitoris."

A psychiatrist interviewed by the Erikson foundation said

. . . While it is true that relatively few female-to-male transsexuals insist upon the creation of an artificial phallus, this would not to my mind indicate that a created organ has any less importance in this case. It simply reflects an acceptance of the fact that as her[6] doctor will inform her, the techniques for this surgical procedure are at present far from being perfected, and that the results would leave a great deal to be desired. . . . Mastectomy and hysterectomy are always desired. . . . When the results of phalloplasty are more satisfactory. . . . I would anticipate that the request for this procedure would be accordingly universal. (Erikson, n.d., p. 33)

The importance of getting the appropriate genitals as a sign of belonging to the real gender is not restricted to the transsexual, but is also reflected in the attitude of the transsexual's family. Garfinkel (1967, p. 128) reports that Agnes' family reacted to her preoperative "cross-dressing" with "consternation and disapproval," but once she received the genital surgery they responded with relieved acceptance of her femaleness.

What could be seen as an "obsessive" emphasis is surely less "pathological" than if the individual insisted that she was a woman with a penis. The latter would be seen as "crazy," since it contradicts one of the facts of gender, namely there is no such thing as a woman with a penis. The fact that "preoperative transsexual" and "postoperative transsexual" are major classifications implies that genital surgery is intended and that "proper" genitals are a necessary aspect of the conceptualization.

Aside from the ways transsexuals deal with the fact that they have the "wrong" genitals, the ways they responded to some of the questions we asked shows the work involved in confirming the natural attitude. Almost all the transsexuals we interviewed had difficulty with the following questions: "What did you have to learn in order to be successfully taken as a man/woman?" "Is is different to be a man in this society than it is to be a woman?" "Did you ever make mistakes which caused people to doubt you?" "How do you know if you're doing a good job?" At first we assumed that our questions were poorly phrased; then we thought that our interviewees were just being evasive. Finally, we concluded that their nonresponses were informative. We decided this by asking these same questions of nontranssexual males and female. They could not answer them either. To ask a "real" female if she ever made mistakes is rather senseless, since her gender cannot be doubted. The transsexuals' inability to answer these questions was a way of producing a sense of the naturalness of their gender—proof they are like everyone else, not freaks.

Occasionally a transsexual said something that suggested that he/she was not concerned with displaying some aspect of the natural attitude toward gender. We then found ourselves questioning the "reality" of that person's gender. In other words we found ourselves wondering whether the person was (1) "really" a transsexual, and (2) "really" a member of the gender to which he/she claimed to belong. One middle-aged female-to-male transsexual told us that he was not particularly interested in obtaining a penis, and that he only got a mastectomy because his wife encouraged him to do so. (He did claim to be happy about having needed a hysterectomy for medical reasons.) All of this, we felt, could be seen as evidence of his *not wanting to be a woman* rather than his *conviction that he was a man*. His basically low-keyed attitude toward the penis as a sign of male gender contradicted the behavior of other transsexuals. It may be that he had a male gender *role* identity rather than a male gender identity. This example neither proves nor disproves that the interviewee was a transsexual. It shows that doubt about gender attribution can be generated by a failure to exhibit all aspects of the natural attitude in interaction, even with those who under certain circumstances can bracket the natural attitude. This person unquestionably looked like a man; however, without his presenting himself "properly" it was difficult to see him as a "natural" male. In order to maintain a stable gender attribution of another person, it is necessary to see the natural attitude displayed.

Other transsexuals managed to display the natural attitude in their talk, while at the same time demonstrating to us that they saw the natural attitude *as an attitude*. One young man spoke of "deciding" which gender to be. He said he wanted to be a woman (and he lived as one) because it was easier than being a male homosexual. He eventually "decided" to be a man again. This man and others we have talked with have been affected by their transsexualism in such a way that the natural attitude has become bracketed for them (at least temporarily). It is not that they do not hold the natural attitude in most of their interactions, but rather that by virtue of their transsexualism they have glimpses of gender as a social construction. They do not, however, speak of gender as "socially constructed." One transsexual described it as "seeing masks and hypocrisy" and suggested that everyone should go through a change in order to see how arbitrary gender is. Transsexuals' view of gender as socially constructed in no way caused us to doubt their gender, since while talking about social constructions, they continued to display for us, through their talk, that they were "real" men or women.

One articulate female-to-male transsexual asserted that at least part of the difference between men and women is social. "It's a state of mind on your part and the people who see you." He claimed that he could dress up as a woman and pass. For all intents and purposes he would then *be* a woman. A penis is important to him for his state of mind even though others do not see it. For others he felt that his beard and hairy chest were what was important. Unlike any other female-to-male transsexual we interviewed, he freely labeled himself as a female in his childhood, for example, "When I was a little girl."

Some male-to-female transsexuals when asked whether they felt more like transsexuals or like women answered "transsexuals." Their friends were other transsexuals and they could not conceive of totally passing. One in particular talked about how the "in-between state of being a transsexual" was worse than being male or female because "people don't know how to relate to you." Although attitudes such as this may be due to these women being preoperative, the fact that they were able to conceive of themselves as not really members of either gender at that moment is suggestive. They believe that everyone must be classified as one gender or another, but by seeing that they are temporary exceptions to this rule, they may come to understand that the rule is constructed.

Finally, what Sulcov (1973) calls "proselytizing transsexuals"— those who are celebrities and present themselves publicly as transsexuals—open the way for others to see gender as a social construction. These transsexuals are differentiated from those who pass and in passing seek to preserve the social order of two genders. The transsexual who remains identified as a transsexual is a reminder that one or more of the facts of gender can be violated, and yet we can still make some kind of gender attribution.

CREATING GENDER ATTRIBUTIONS

Everyone must display her or his gender in every interaction. This is the same as saying everyone must pass or everyone must insure that the "correct" gender attribution is made of them. The risks of being "disproved," of not being taken as the gender intended, are minimal for nontranssexuals. Although they must avoid giving grounds for doubt, they are generally not concerned with being doubted and consequently are not concerned with their presentations. If nontranssexuals *are* seen as the "wrong" gender, it is often upsetting, because no preparation has been made for such an event. This is because few people besides transsexuals think of their gender as anything other than "naturally" obvious. A "wrong" attribution in this case turns into an unintentional (and disconcerting) bracketing of the real world. Transsexuals, on the other hand, have planned in advance how to handle these situations and consequently tend to be continually self-conscious about their presentations. They believe that the consequence of not passing is potential devastation.

Goffman (1963) differentiates two kinds of stigmas, those that are externally visible (e.g., a disfiguring birthmark), and those that are hidden (e.g., a secret past as a criminal). Both kinds of stigmas are potentially discrediting. Feinbloom (1976) discusses this notion of stigma in regard to transsexualism and shows how transsexuals must "pass" in order to keep secret their visible stigmas (e.g., an adam's apple in a woman) and their hidden stigmas (e.g., a man having attended an all girls' high school).

The problem with conceptualizing "passing" as discrete management devices is that this emphasizes its deceptive features and overlooks the ongoing process of "doing" gender in everyday interactions that we all engage in. (See Garfinkel, 1967, pp. 164–175 for a critique of Goffmanesque analyses.) We explained in Chapter 1 that in this usage, everyone is engaged in passing, in creating a sense of themselves as being one gender or another. In order for gender to be perceived as "natural," however, it must not be seen as passing. (See Rule 8 of the natural attitude.) According to the natural attitude, real men and women do not pass. When we bracket the natural attitude and see gender as constructed, then passing is not conceptualized as deceptive. It is displaying for others what one intends to be taken as. Passing, in this sense, makes no assumptions about what one "really" is.

To illustrate, Jane Fry, a male-to-female transsexual, served duty on an all-male ship during the years when she was preoperative (Bogdan, 1974). From her point of view, she was "passing" as a male, since even though she knew she was female, she needed to be seen as male in order to remain on the ship. Because she had a penis, she would not have been considered to be engaging in deceptive behavior by most people. On the other hand, Mike would have been. Mike, a female-to-male transsexual, also served duty on an all-male ship. His behavior might have been considered passing, in the deceptive sense, since he had what others would have judged to be female genitals. Nevertheless, both Jane and Mike managed to create a sense of the reality of their maleness for those with whom they interacted.

Robert, a female-to-male transsexual, looked masculine as a teenager. He was not certain he was a transsexual at that time and tried to live as a female. Because it was upsetting when he was mistaken for a male, he tried to do what had to be done to be taken as female. He learned to walk in a feminine way, avoided wearing pants, and in general tried to look like a female (for which he had the corresponding genitals). Although he was usually accepted as a female and would not have been considered by most people as passing, in his words he "faked being a woman." He had to concentrate his energies on being seen as female. When he later began living as a man he no longer saw himself as passing. That, to him, was just being natural. In the social construction sense, however, he was not doing anything more or less to be taken as a man than he had done to be taken as a woman.

It is not that transsexuals know, in any systematic way, what needs to be done to be taken as the "correct" gender. It is not a matter of a recipelike, systematic presentation. We will discuss four broad areas of self-presentation which contribute to gender attributions: (1) general talk (both what is said and *how* it is said), (2) public physical appearance, (3) the private body, (4) talk about the personal past. Since gender attributions are made in the initial stages of an interaction, usually long before a person undresses or talks about her/his personal past, we assume that public physical appearance and general talk are the major contributors to initial gender attributions. We postpone a discussion of how much (or whether) gender attributions need to be maintained over time except to suggest that the private body and talk about the personal past probably play a role in maintenance. The methods by which transsexuals provide others with "information" about these four categories is the substance of much of this chapter. It must be kept in mind, however, that we are studying transsexuals not because they create gender attributions in a particularly unusual way, but because, on the contrary, they create gender in the most ordinary of ways, as we all do.

General Talk

Some techniques for "proper" talk can be learned through observation and rehearsal: learning to say "robe" instead of "housecoat" when shopping for men's clothing; learning to talk "dirt" with other men (a difficult task for someone raised as a girl in a strict Catholic family). Joseph, a female-to-male transsexual, claimed to have learned about behaving like a man from reading the *Playboy Advisor*. While the conventional method is to watch the men and women around you, sometimes professional help is required. There are speech therapists who coach male-to-female transsexuals in raising the pitch and resonance of their voices, introducing softening qualities, developing a more "feminine" vocabulary, articulating more carefully, producing a greater range of inflection, and making freer facial movements. (There is a sizable body of recent research on gender differences in vocalizations and language usage, Key, 1975; Thorne and Henley, 1975). It is sometimes suggested that male-to-female transsexuals speak in a whisper or falsetto; if the voice is still deep, it is advised that escorts order for them in restaurants (Feinbloom, 1976). Booklets published by the Erikson Educational Foundation to advise transsexuals in passing techniques offer hints such as: ". . . When introducing herself on the telephone, (the male-to-female transsexual) should begin the conversation by saying, 'This is Miss X.' In that way, should she still need some practice in feminizing her voice, and if the person on the other end of the line is in some doubt as to her sex, this assertion usually will resolve the question in her favor" (Erikson Foundation, 1974, p. 26). This advice illustrates a fact about gender which we will discuss further; once a gender attribution is made, the particulars (in this case the voice) will be filtered through that attribution and used to confirm it; for example, "It is a husky-voiced female."

Public Physical Appearance

Transsexuals not only learn gender-specific speech skills, but also ways of presenting their bodies that go beyond learning to dress as a male or female. The power of physical appearance in forming gender attributions cannot be denied. Female impersonators, men in the entertainment field whose act (dancing, singing, telling jokes) involves pretending to be female, are aware of how compelling physical appearance is. Newton (1972) notes that in order for female impersonators to prove that they are really men they will sometimes at the end of the act remove their wigs or falsies. Much of the entertainer's skill lies not in merely singing and dancing but in impersonating a female who is singing and dancing. An audience that failed to be convinced of the entertainer's male gender, would be missing a crucial part of the total act.

Transsexuals, in contrast to female impersonators, do not want to give others any reason to doubt what seems to be under their clothes, lest their behavior be seen as a masquerade. "A little extra padding, a scarf, gloves, etc., can all be used to maintain the illusion[7] of femininity . . ." (Feinbloom, 1976, p. 233). In this way, broad shoulders, an adam's apple, and large hands can be camouflaged. Male-to-female transsexuals learn elaborate techniques for concealing the penis, which would be especially important in certain circumstances (wearing a bikini). Female-to-male transsexuals have an opposite problem. They are advised to stuff a pair of socks into an athletic supporter before exercising in a public gymnasium. It is suggested that those who have not had surgery bind their breasts; there are several methods for doing so (Erikson Foundation, 1974).

These techniques are mentioned by transsexuals and in the literature as being things that *should* be mastered in order to be taken as real men or women. We know, however, that people often have very distorted ideas about real men and women. The entire field of "sex-role" stereotyping attests to this. "We define what a man or woman is according to what will enable us most unequivocally to classify ourselves in the desired gender group" (Kando, 1973, p. 28). Women with small breasts who are confident about their femaleness do not use breast size as a criteria for gender decisions. On the other hand, what transsexuals believe constitutes a credible male or female may be related to what troubles them personally about passing. Mike, a middle-aged female-to-male transsexual with a slight physique, talked to us about how important it is for a man to be physically strong. He exercises his hands especially, because he is self-conscious about their smallness. Transsexuals who see gender characteristics as totally dichotomous are reminded by professionals that there are many hairy, muscular women, women with husky and attractive voices, and short, hairless men.

Herschberger (1970) discusses the psychological effects of the word "normal." According to her, the word is so powerful that a man in our society may only feel totally male when in the presence of a woman shorter than himself. When confronted with a taller woman he must either accept his own "abnormality" or conclude that the woman is abnormally tall and even masculine. Marian, a male-to-female transsexual, feels more like a woman in the presence of men than in the presence of other women. She thinks this is because other women are a reminder to her that she is not a "real" woman.

If nontranssexuals, who have minimal concern with being doubted, need to exaggerate maleness and femaleness, transsexuals ought to have even more distorted views. In fact, given their life experiences, it is to be expected. A younger female-to-male transsexual spoke about how "turned off" he was by older transsexuals who seem preoccupied with "How have you been the 'male' this week?" He, on the other hand, claimed to be less concerned with making "that perfect masculine image." He knows that it is not necessary to exaggerate mannerisms, and although he mentioned a number of stereotypical male mannerisms (e.g., loping walk) when we asked him what makes someone a man, he admitted that none of them were really important. What is important is the initial presentation. "Once you tag somebody you're right, and that's it. A lot of transsexuals don't believe that."

The Private Body

Postoperative male-to-female transsexuals have little or no reason to protect their bodies from being viewed. Breast developmnt occurs with estrogen therapy and can be supplemented with silicone implants. Genital surgery is often so successful that even experienced gynecologists do not question the authenticity of the transsexuals' genitals. Janet, a male-to-female transsexual, described a visit to a gynecologist who, not knowing that Janet was a transsexual, told her that there was a cyst on one of her ovaries. Janet protested that this was impossible. The doctor explained that he ought to know since he was a gynecologist, whereupon she countered with, "Well, I ought to know; I'm a transsexual." This example not only attests to the excellence of male-to-female genital surgery, but it also provides a good illustration of the construction of gender. The doctor, having decided by visual inspection (undoubtedly prior to Janet's undressing) that she was female, would interpret anything else he saw or felt in light of that attribution. The swelling beneath her abdominal walls *must* be a cyst; there was no reason to expect it to be a prostate gland. As a nurse who heard this story so aptly phrased it: "If you hear hoofbeats, you don't look for elephants."

Preoperative male-to-female transsexuals and virtually all female-to-male transsexuals manage their bodies in such a way that others do not see them undressed. Major problems center around using public restrooms and avoiding required physicals. The Erickson manual (1974) is quite conservative on these points and advises transsexuals not to use public restrooms if possible and not to apply for jobs with large companies, since most require complete physicals of new employees. The following examples from interviews with female-to-male transsexuals illustrate some of the ways transsexuals manage their private bodies.

Mike, a female-to-male transsexual, joined the merchant marines in his early twenties (even though at that time he had had no surgery and was not taking male hormones). He volunteered for the job of cook not only because it required less physical strength, but because he would have to get up earlier than the others and could use the toilets and showers privately. Even so, he always selected the last shower stall in the row. Once when asked by his buddies, "Did you ever lay a girl?", he failed to think fast enough and told them no. They took him to a whorehouse where, unbeknownst to his friends, he spent his time talking to the prostitute. He explained to her that he did not want to have sex because he had a girl back home to whom he wanted to be faithful. This was apparently a legitimate reason to keep his pants on. Afterwards he told his friends that he had "a great lay."

The Erikson guide for transsexuals (1974, p. 7) suggests that male-to-female transsexuals should always urinate in a seated position with their feet pointed outward. Aside from the concern of being seen, the manual cautions about auditory signs. ". . . Female-to-male transsexuals are advised (to) keep the toilet flushing while making use of the cubicle for urination." The sound of the urinal stream may be one of the more subtle gender cues.

Robert takes a book with him into public toilet stalls. He tries to use stalls with doors, but if none are available he just sits down with his pants pulled high above his knees. At first he was concerned about this but he reassured himself: "Men sit down. So I can sit down without being suspected." He no longer worries that the other men at work have not seen him at the urinal since he does not remember seeing each of the other men standing there. A non-transsexual male probably would not wonder whether he has seen other men at the urinal. A lack of concern with gender is part of its naturalness and highlights how gender is unproblematic in the fabric of everyday life. Until transsexuals understand this, they are continually concerned with "passing" techniques.

The Personal Past

The reason that protection of the genitals from public viewing is so important should be obvious. If genitals are the major insignia of gender (and if, as we will discuss in Chapter 6, gender attribution is essentially synonomous with genital attribution) then it is necessary that everything be done to protect the body. But it is also clear that very few of our interactions involve a public viewing (or potential viewing) of our genitals. We must give the impression of having the appropriate genitals to people who will undoubtedly never see them. This is the same as saying we must give the impression of being and always having been the gender we lay claim to. Gender is historical. In concrete terms this involves talking in such a way that we reveal ourselves to have a history as a male or a female. Transsexuals must not only conceal their real past (in most cases), but they must also create a new past. Marian stated that she worries about referring to her past because she thinks of her past as involving the activities of a social male. Clearly what must be accomplished if the current presentation is to succeed, is for the social past to be reevaluated for the self before it can be constructed for others (e.g., "I wasn't a feminine boy, I was a stereotypical girl").

Some things may be relatively easy to change (e.g., name); other things may be more difficult and in some cases impossible (e.g., school and medical records). At all times the transsexual must remember what details from her/his real past have been included in the new history and which of these have concrete documentation. Feinbloom (1976) states that it is essential for the transsexual to remember what was said in one place in order to escape detection and "to explain the gaps of time produced by those events in the earlier life that he or she cannot acknowledge" (p. 237). For a male-to-female transsexual who spent two years in the army, there are several alternatives: She could tell people that she spent two years in the army as a WAC; or she spent those two years engaged in some other activity like going to college. Or she could be evasive regarding her background and never mention those two years.

Obviously the least problematic course of action (the one that requires the fewest number of additional constructions) is to use actual details from the past. It is because initial gender attributions are so powerful that most biographic details can be credited to either gender category. Once it is decided that you are female (or male), most items you reveal about your past will be seen as female (or male) history.

One female-to-male transsexual in describing his childhood can state with no dissimulation that he played ball, climbed trees, and was generally rough and aggressive. This was, in fact, his childhood as a "tomboy." He supports this description of his past by using such phrases as "when I was a kid."

When Robert is asked about his first dating experiences he describes the girl from his high school he would have liked to date. Thus he draws upon his actual teenage fantasy life to create his biography.

The transsexual's family can be a source of difficulty or they can be a useful tool in passing. Sulcov (1973) claims that most "slips" are made by family members—saying "him" for "her" and vice versa. Wanda, a male-to-female transsexual, told us of her horror when her mother introduced her "new" daughter, Wanda, as "my son." Wanda and her husband were so embarrassed that they left the scene. Wanda assumed that the slip was inevitably discrediting, and yet if we imagine the same event occurring to a nontranssexual female, it is likely that the mother's behavior would be treated as a joke. Everyone would laugh and say something like, "Poor mother must be getting senile." In more intellectual circles the mother might be teased as having committed a Freudian slip. Thus, it is not the slip, per se, which is discrediting; it is the handling of it.

One Hispanic transsexual said her family's solution was to stop referring to her with gender-linked pronouns and names. Another transsexual was aided by his mother who created for the neighbors a mythical twin sister for her son. In this story the twins do not get along and consequently they never visit the mother at the same time. As the transsexual begins to live more continuously as a man, presumably the "sister" will move away.

Part of what it means to give a credible biography involves *giving good reasons*. A good reason is one that does not jar with one's gender presentation—that does not arouse doubt. It may not be clear to a transsexual (or anyone creating a new biography) what constitutes a good reason until a mistake is made. And again, it is unlikely that giving one bad reason would be enough to alter a gender attribution.

Those few times when transsexuals' reasons impressed us as not very good were when they were sweeping generalizations about gender-role behavior. Janet, a thoroughly credible woman, when asked by us what she says when she and her female friends talk about their first menstruation, responded, "Women don't talk about those things." Had she told us that, "My friends don't talk about such things," we would have found her answer less striking. We feel sure that her answer would have gone unnoticed by anyone who knew nothing of her real past, yet it could have been used as evidence of her transsexualism by someone looking for evidence.

A similar example involves a female-to-male transsexual, who when discussing his hesitancy to use public bathrooms, said, "Men don't like to go to the bathroom when other guys are there."[8]

The best kinds of reasons are those that are multifunctional. They not only provide the transsexual with many excuses for the cost of one "fabrication," but they allow other people to use the information for interpreting many of the transsexual's behaviors.

1. Mike tells people that he did not serve in the army because of a bad back. This same reason excuses him from lifting heavy objects.

2. Kando (1973) cites the example of a male-to-female transsexual who told her husband that she was unable to bear children because of a hysterectomy. Her prior hospitalization for genital-change surgery was then seen by the husband as hospitalization for the hysterectomy.

3. Although Robert was self-conscious about his pierced ears, he explained them as having been a requirement for the street gang he belonged to. This story also supports his biography of a "real boy's" childhood.

While we have been careful not to characterize these techniques as deceptive, a number of the transsexuals (especially the younger ones) we interviewed were concerned by what they perceived as the necessary "lying" they must do. Such attitudes ranged from feeling bad about having to give a lot of excuses to actually denying that they had to do so. One woman who denied that she had to "lie" at all may have been trying to prove to us that she was such a natural woman that she did not need to fabricate anything about her past— her past was the past of a "real" woman. Under more careful questioning she admitted that there were some aspects of her life that she could not talk about to most people.

A female-to-male transsexual, prior to a mastectomy, needed to explain to acquaintances why he did not remove his shirt at the beach. Even though he saw his excuse as a good (i.e., necessary) one, he still felt bad. "Feeling bad" would in no way keep him from making the required excuses since he believes his gender status to be at stake. He claims, though, that many transsexuals are not good at giving excuses because they are scared.

Transsexuals who need help constructing biographies and learning good reasons can consult other transsexuals. One physician conducts role-playing sessions where female-to-male transsexuals can give male-to-female transsexuals advice on how to pass as women and vice versa. A male-to-female transsexual was role-playing the following situation. "She's having lunch with the other girls from the office and someone says, as women will, 'I feel out of sorts today. I just got my period. I was going to go to the beach this weekend, but I don't like to swim when I'm menstruating.' And then someone turns to the transsexual and asks, 'Do you prefer to use Tampax or Kotex?' " The role-playing transsexual was stunned by this question which she had never anticipated. It took a female-to-male transsexual with a girl's history to invent such a situation based on his past experience (Erikson, n.d., p. 15).

We have discussed those aspects of gender that may be specifically taught to transsexuals. However, much of what it means to be a woman or a man can not be exhaustively articulated and can not be learned by rote. Many of the transsexuals we interviewed talked about just "picking things up as they went along." The way they talk about learning to pass is like someone explaining how he/she learned language as a child.

The "trick," if there is such a thing, seems to be confidence. Both the literature and the transsexuals, themselves, mention the need to feel and act confident. ". . . The newly emerged transsexual is constantly on guard and overly sensitive to all nuances in relationships. With experience he or she learns that others are not as quick to sense, or as alert to notice as expected" (Feinbloom, 1976, p. 238). ". . . Most people will take you at face value . . . if you are not apologetic in your manner . . . . The key to being accepted by others is your own self-acceptance. . . . An attitude of quiet self-confidence will get the best results" (Erikson, 1974, p. 6, 12). ". . . The transsexual gradually acquires a comfort and spontaneity . . . that smooths the rough edges off his (sic) manner and makes it unremarkable and convincing" (Erikson, n.d., p. 9). The key word is "unremarkable." Several transsexuals mentioned "not overdoing it." One talked about the need to be "cool," not to react without first thinking. Another suggested that if you are really confident, then you do not worry about the "small stuff."

Garfinkel (1967) has explained that passing is an ongoing practice. This is because gender is omnirelevant to the affairs of everyday life. Although transsexuals must be and act confident that no one is going to discover their stigma, they must consciously, continually, make a presentation that will not allow anyone to discover it. Gender is a necessary background to every act. That successful passing requires the continual need to work at routinizing daily activities indicates this background feature of gender.

For Agnes such work involved always anticipating what might be asked of her and answering questions in such a way that they would appear to require no further explanation. She avoided employers' "checking up" on her past by providing them with answers that portrayed her as not unusual in any sense. With the doctors who interviewed her she managed her gender presentation by withholding information—speaking in generalities and pretending not to understand questions whose answers might be used to see her as a male.

For Mike, on board ship, his routinizing involved presenting a total persona of shyness and naivete. Consequently everything he did (any potential errors he might have committed) were seen as arising out of his particular style. His failure to undress in front of others was interpreted in this overall personality context as modesty rather than femaleness. In later years he kept his private life (among people who know of his past) and his professional life (among people who do not) completely separate.

Marian developed a similar technique. In work situations she presents herself as quiet and reserved, thus insuring that other employees will not probe into her personal life. With friends who know about her transsexualism, she is very different.

"Working" at gender can even go so far as creating a physical presence that does not provoke notice. Male-to-female transsexuals who are especially concerned not to be mistaken for drag queens say that it helps to be ordinary looking.

While we agree with Garfinkel that gender is omnirelevant in everyday interactions, and that gender "work" is required, we do not believe that the bulk of the work is required of the one displaying gender. Rather, we assert that most of the work is done for the displayer by the perceiver. The displayer creates the initial gender attribution, probably by his/her public appearance and present talk.

However, after that point, the gender attribution is maintained by virtue of two things: (1) Every act of the displayer's is filtered through the initial gender attribution which the perceiver has made; (2) The perceiver holds the natural attitude (e.g., gender is invariant). In short, there is little that the displayer needs to do once he/she has provided the initial information, except to maintain the sense of the "naturalness" of her/his gender. Passing is an ongoing practice, but it is practiced by both parties. Transsexuals become more "natural" females or males and less self-consciously transsexuals when they realize that passing is not totally their responsibility. This realization gets translated into confidence that the other will contribute to making and sustaining the gender attribution[9] and confidence that unless a monumental error is made, the initial gender attribution will not be altered. "Proselytizing transsexuals" who object to their gender not being taken seriously have made it difficult, or impossible, for others to share in the maintainance of their gender by continually confronting others with a blatant violation of the natural attitude.

The extent to which "errors" can be overlooked is illustrated in the following example. We had met Rachel, a male-to-female transsexual, when she was still living as a male named Paul. When she had just begun to "be" Rachel we were with her in a social situation where only the three of us knew about her background. On this occasion we called her "Paul" several times and even referred to her as "he." Yet she continued to be treated and accepted as a female with no questions asked.[10] An interpretation consistent with the argument we have just proposed is that the other people had made an unambiguous initial gender attribution of Rachel as female and either assumed they had misheard us or did not hear us in the first place. They maintained the gender attribution *for* Rachel. There was nothing that she or we needed to do to "save" the situation. Once a gender attribution is made, virtually anything can be used to support it. (Analogously, once it is discredited, then anything can be used to support the discreditation, e.g., "I always knew he wasn't a woman because his hands were so large.")

The kind of confidence exhibited by transsexuals who recognize other people's role in contributing to gender attributions is illustrated in the following incidents:

1. Jane Fry, a male-to-female transsexual tried to get an I.D. card from a clerk who noted that Jane Fry was listed as John Fry in the records. The clerk asked, "Are you female?" Jane answered

in an inflamed tone, "What do you want me to do? Strip and prove it?" The clerk got flustered and gave Jane the I.D. card (Bogdan, 1974, p. 182). The fact that Jane was preoperative at the time, and if she had stripped would have revealed a penis, is important insofar as it testifies to her confidence that the clerk held the natural attitude toward gender; in seeing Jane as female, the clerk knew the "correct" genitals would be there.

2. Robert, a female-to-male transsexual, needed to get the gender on his birth certificate changed. He self-assuredly explained to the clerk in charge that someone had obviously made a mistake. He said that his mother only spoke Spanish and the error was probably due to that. The clerk, looking at the handsome, bearded young man standing before her sympathetically responded, "They're always making mistakes like that." According to Robert, "If you apprehend trouble, you make it." From our point of view the clerk interpreted Robert's reasonable complaint in the context of the visual and auditory information available to her. The immediate gender attribution was so strong and his presentation so credible that she could not have seen Robert as other than male. The only explanation possible was that there had been a clerical error in issuing the original birth certificate.[11]

3. Robert had a similar encounter with a dermatologist who wanted to give him a full examination. Robert's reaction was, "That's out of the question." While that may seem like a suspicious response to someone reading this account of a transsexual's behavior, it was obviously acceptable to the doctor who responded, "I understand how you feel." The doctor probably interpreted Robert's answer as that of a particularly bashful man. While it may not have been common behavior in a doctor's office, it was legitimate behavior, and thus not discrediting of gender. Once a gender attribution has been made, anything a person does will be seen as congruent with that gender attribution. There is no reason to think that someone is taking androgens unless you have already begun to doubt that they are male. Robert's encounter with the doctor highlights the point that transsexuals can engage in behavior that may bring into question their normalcy, but which need not bring into question the status of their gender. Gender, then, has

primacy over other attributes. When confronted with atypical behavior, one decides that the performer is a "strange" man long before deciding that the performer is not a man after all, but a woman. The latitude that a person has in performing atypical behavior, before that person's gender is called into question, is a crucial issue.

4. Robert made a visit to his old neighborhood as his "new" gender. A friend from high school stopped him on the street, told him he looked familiar, and asked if he had any sisters. Rather than getting upset or defensive, Robert answered "yes" and calmly named all his sisters.

Although Robert is a totally credible man and has "passed" in countless situations, he is still uncomfortable when the topic of transsexualism is discussed in his presence by people who do not know about his past. He is not sure what a "normal" male reaction is and whether he will give himself away if he should defend the legitimacy of transsexualism. He admits that, as in all new situations, he will feel threatened until the first time he tries it; and in trying it he will simultaneously be *doing* "natural" behavior and *learning* "natural" behavior.

What we have been calling "confidence" when exhibited by transsexuals is what, for nontranssexuals, would be seen as a display of the natural attitude. Transsexuals are confident once they accept their gender as unquestionable because gender (in the natural attitude) *is* unquestionable once an attribution has been made.

Gender for the nontranssexual is not problematic. It is a background feature of everyday life, but it need be of no concern. Transsexuals, in routinizing their daily activities, are managing themselves deliberately—sometimes more deliberately than nontranssexuals—but the aim of this management is to keep their gender from being problematic for other people as well as for themselves. The difference between the confident attitude of the transsexual and the everyday attitude of the nontranssexual lies only in the history of the individual. However, in the process of gender attribution history is irrelevant. There are only people who succeed, during ongoing social interaction, in being, for each other, either males or females. All persons create both the reality of their own specific gender and a sense of its history, thus at the same time creating the reality of two, and only two, natural genders.

NOTES

1. All names of transsexuals and any identifying information have been altered.

2. The natural attitude toward gender as detailed by Garfinkel and the "facts" about gender which, according to Kohlberg (1966), young children do not know, are strikingly similar. In light of our analysis of the development of children's ideas abut gender, this is not surprising. It is also interesting to compare the natural attitude with Money and Ehrhardt's (1972) "formula" for insuring that a child develops an unambiguous gender identity (p. 152). The "formula" can be seen as a scientific statement of the natural attitude.

3. We are not the first to note that "liberals" in the field of transsexualism often hold a biological view which is the reverse of what one usually finds. (On issues such as race and intelligence liberals generally look for social–psychological causes.) Some (e.g., Raymond, 1977) claim that this "liberal" perspective disguises a basically conservative and sexist attitude toward gender roles.

4. Judicial rulings regarding change of gender status include: *Anonymous* v. *Weiner* 270 N.Y.S. 2d, 319–324, 1966 (unfavorable ruling); *In re Anonymous* 293 N.Y.S. 834–838, 1968 (favorable ruling); *In re Anonymous* 314 N.Y.S. 2d, 668–670, 1970 (favorable ruling); *Corbett* v. *Corbett* (*otherwise Ashley*) 2 W.L.R. 1036, 2 all E.R. 33, 1970, (unfavorable ruling); Matter of *Fernandez, New York Law Journal*, 3/15/76, p. 12, col. 2 (unfavorable ruling).

5. The term "sex reassignment" is now being used as a substitute for "sex change" in the professional literature on treatment of transsexualism. The former term implies a rehabilitative process, while the latter implies that a person was once one gender and is now the other. Because of our perspective we think "reconstruction" is yet a better term.

6. This doctor's use of the feminine pronoun to refer to the female-to-male transsexual suggests an underlying attitude of skepticism toward the legitimacy of the transsexual's gender claim. And yet this doctor was presented as being sympathetic toward transsexualism and an advocate of corrective surgery. Stoller, an eminent clinician in the field of transsexualism measures the strength of patients' gender identities by the pronouns he finds himself automatically using (Stoller, 1968, p. 235). However, we think the pronoun he uses is a measure of the gender attribution Stoller has made, since as he indicates earlier in his book (p. 192) gender identity can only be measured by asking the person.

7. It is not clear whether by "illusion of feminity" Feinbloom means that femininity in general is an illusion or that the transsexual's femininity (or femaleness) is.

8. We did not find this statement suspicious (having no firmly developed

ideas about males' bathroom idiosyncracies); however a male colleague who listened to the interview tape (and who knew the interviewee was a transsexual) characterized the comment as not a good reason.

9. Under certain circumstances, it is expected that the perceiver will contribute minimally to the gender attribution, and consequently the transsexual must be more self-conscious about her/his presentation. For example, when a transsexual is interviewed by a clinician who must determine whether the transsexual is "really" the gender she/he claims, the clinician may attempt to withhold a gender attribution and try to judge each of the transsexual's acts independently without seeing the act as emanating from a male or female. We believe that this is such a formidable task that this stance can be maintained only for the briefest period.

10. This example illustrates in two ways the resistence of initial gender attributions to change: the power of the other people's gender attribution to Rachel as female, and the power of our initial gender attribution to Paul as male.

11. As transsexualism becomes a more socially shared reality, birth certificate clerks and others in similar positions may come to see that there are other explanations besides clerical errors. In doing so, however, their ideas about gender will necessarily change.

6

TOWARD A THEORY OF GENDER

When we first began to think about gender as a social construction, we devised a "game" called the Ten Question Gender Game. The player is told, "I am thinking of a person and I want you to tell me, not *who* the person is, but whether that person is female or male. Do this by asking me ten questions, all of which must be answerable by 'yes' or 'no.' You may ask any question except, 'Is the person male?' or 'Is the person female?'. After each question, based on the answer I have given you, tell me, at that point in the game, whether you think the person is female or male and why you have decided that. Then ask your next question. You need not stick with your first answer throughout the game, but regardless of whether you stay with your original choice or change your decision you must, at each point, explain your choice. At the end of the game I will ask you to give your final decision on the person's gender."

The game is reasonably simple, fun to play, and is not unlike "Twenty Questions." Our game, however, is not just for fun. Instead of answering the player's questions on the basis of the characteristics of some real person, we responded with a prearranged, random series of "yes's" and "no's." The game is a form of the "documentary method,"[1] and we created it both in order to find out what kinds of questions the players would ask about gender, and, more importantly, to uncover how the players would make sense out of what is, in many cases, seemingly contradictory information. The following is a transcript of a typical game:

Player: Is this person living?
Interviewer: No. What is it?
P: It was an irrelevant question. I shouldn't have asked you that question. No basis for judging it. Is the person over 5'8" tall?
I: Yes

142

P: Male. The probability in my mind of a taller person being male is higher for male and lower for female.
Is the person over 160 pounds in weight?

I: No.

P: Well, now I'm mixed. I'd still say leaning toward male.
Is the person under 140 pounds in weight?

I: No.

P: So, we're between 140 and 160 pounds. I'd say male on the basis of physical characteristics. A person over 5'8" between 140 and 160 pounds . . . I'd tend toward male.
Well, what else can I ask about this person? (long pause) Well, I mean, there're obviously some questions I can't ask .

I: Like what?

P: Like does this person wear skirts?

I: Yes.

P: The person *does* wear skirts. Then it's female I assume because I assume in general when people wear skirts they're female. The exception being Scottish males perhaps under some conditions, but I assume on the basis of probability that that's it. I've established in my mind that the person is probably—without asking directly questions about the sex of a person. I have to ask five more questions?

I: Yes.

P: Is the person a mother?

I: No.

P: Well I can't—that's a sex-directed question . . . Well, I'm still leaning toward female. (long pause)
Does the person have a 9 to 5 job?

I: No.

P: Well, I'm leaning toward female.

I: Why?

P: Skirts, the physical attribution make possible—physical characteristics makes possible female and not having a renumerative job makes less likely in my mind that the person's male. (long pause) When the person was a child, I don't know if this is a legitimate question, did the person play with dolls a lot?

I: No.

P: No? Well I'm still leaning toward female, because females don't have to play with dolls. I'm avoiding—I mean there're substitute questions for "is the person female or male," but I assume I can't ask those question.

I: Yes you can ask anything.

P: But if I ask some questions it's essentially . . .

I: You can ask me anything.

P: (long pause) Well, there's a system to this. If one thinks of good questions one can narrow it down very well, I imagine—any other physical characteristics . . . Well, you can't ask questions about physical characteristics if they determine whether the person is male or female.

I: Yes, you can.

P: Does the person have protruding breasts?

I: Yes.

P: Then more likely to be female. (long pause) I'm trying to think of good questions. We covered physical characteristics, job relations . . . I'll ask another physical question.

Does the person have developed biceps?

I: Yes. I'd like your final answer.

P: Well, I think the answers I've been given—the answer to the last question about developed biceps, leads me to doubt whether we're talking about a woman but the—and the physical characteristics describe, that is height and weight could be both man or woman in my mind although I tended a little bit toward man, but the several questions tip it in my mind. The wearing of skirts, the protruding breasts, the nonrenumerative job make it more likely in my mind that I'm talking about a woman than a man. Although the developed biceps, as I understand it, throws a monkey wrench in it because I don't know if it could be accurate to characterize any woman as having developed biceps, but perhaps you can.

We have played this game with over 40 people. A summary of what occurs includes the following observations: (1) Players exhibited the rule-guided behaviors described by Garfinkel (1967, pp. 89–94), including perceiving the answers as answers to their questions, seeing patterns in the answers, waiting for later information to inform earlier information, and so on. (2) Specifically in terms of gender, all players were able to make sense out of the apparent inconsistencies in the answers, such that players were led to postulate bearded women and men who were transvestites. In one case the player concluded it was a hermaphrodite, and in another that it was a transsexual. In all other cases the final decision was either "male" or "female." (3) Only 25 percent of the players asked about genitals in the first three questions. Most players asked questions about either gender role behaviors or secondary gender characteristics. When asked after the game why they did not ask about genitals, players explained that it would have been tantamount to asking "Is this person a male (or female)?", which was an unacceptable question since finding the answer was the object of the game. Players knew that their task was to discover the gender of the person without asking about gender specifically, synonymous, to them, with asking about genitals. Some of the players who did ask about genitals and received answers refused to ask any more questions, claiming that there was no reason to do so. They were absolutely certain of the person's gender, even if that decision conflicted with the other pieces of information they received. (4) Only two people who asked about genitals asked about a vagina before asking about whether the person had a penis. One was told "yes" the person had a vagina, and the other was told "no." Both of them then asked if the person had a penis. Of the fifteen people who asked about a penis first, eight were told "yes," and none of them then asked about a vagina. Of the seven who were told "no," only four then asked if the person had a vagina.

The way in which persons played this "game" suggested to us that (1) Gender attributions are based on information whose meaning is socially shared. Not just any information will inform a gender attribution, and certain information (biological and physical) is seen as more important than other information (role behavior). (2) Once a gender attribution is made, almost anything can be filtered through it and made sense of. (3) Gender attribution is essentially genital attribution. If you "know" the genital then you know the gender. (4) In some way, knowledge about penises may give people more information than knowledge about vaginas.   *Lacan?*

⌐   **THE OVERLAY STUDY**

In order to investigate further the relationship between gender attribution and genital attribution, and to collect additional information about the relative importance of physical characteristics in deciding gender, we designed a more formal study. A set of plastic overlays was prepared. Drawn on each overlay was one physical characteristic or one piece of clothing. The eleven overlays were: long hair, short hair, wide hips, narrow hips, breasts, flat chest, body hair, penis, vagina, "unisex" shirt, "unisex" pants. When the overlays were placed one on top of the other, the result was a drawing of a figure with various combinations of typically male and female physical gender characteristics. The overlays, in combination, produced ninety-six different figures. Each figure had either long or short hair, wide or narrow hips, breasts or a flat chest, body hair or no body hair, and a penis or a vagina. Figures were either unclothed, wore a non-gender-specific shirt and pants, or wore one of the two articles of clothing. All figures had the same, non-gender-specific face. (See Figures 6.1 and 6.2 for two of the figures used.)

We assumed that the figure that had many typical female characteristics would be seen as female, and the figure that had many typical male characteristics would be seen as male. What, though, would people decide about the "mixed" figures? Would the figures be ambiguous stimuli, stumping the participants, or would sense be made of them as in our Ten Question Gender Game? How would the presence or absence of particular cues, especially genitals, affect the participants' perceptions of other physical characteristics?

Each of the ninety-six figures was shown to ten adults, five males and five females. The 960 participants were asked three questions: (1) Is this a picture of a female or a male? (2) Using a scale of 1 to 7, where 1 means not at all confident and 7 means very confident, how confident are you of your answer? (This was, in part, to give us information about whether the forced choice in Question 1 was a clear gender attribution or merely a guess.) (3) How would you change the figure to make it into the *other* gender?

From the participants' answers, not only would we have an "objective" measure of the relative weight of various characteristics in making gender attributions, but, in seeing how people construct gender from "contradictory" cues, we would gain some understanding of the phenomenological reality of femaleness and maleness. As we have pointed out previously in this book, people who are designated "males" and "females" vary within gender and overlap between genders on every social and biological variable. How, then, is gender dichotomized such that, phenomenologically, there are only males and females? By controlling the variables and by slowing down the gender attribution process by means of this overlay study, we hoped to see the construction of gender. Although making judgments about drawings is not the same as making judgments about real people, insights gained from the former are valuable in understanding the latter.

What constitutes gender? George Devereux, a psychoanalytic anthropologist, claims that ". . . much of mankind's high degree of sexual dimorphism is due to the *woman's* conspicuous femaleness;

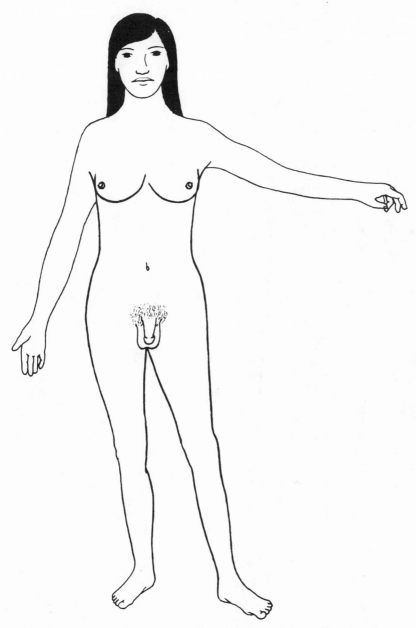

Figure 6.1 Figure with penis, breasts, hips, no body hair, and long hair.

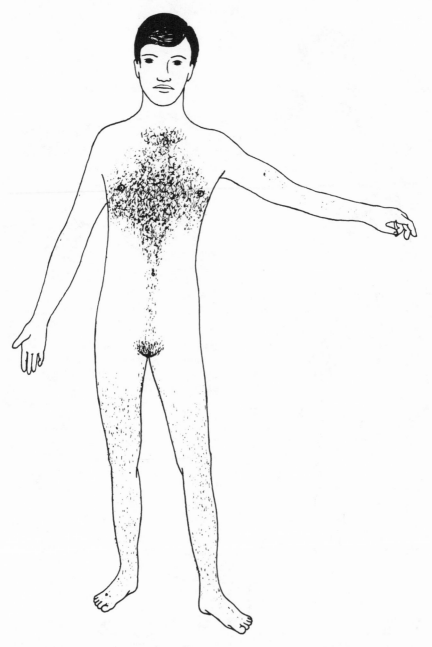

Figure 6.2 Figure with vagina, no breasts, no hips, body hair, and short hair.

she is sexually always responsive and has permanent breasts. Man is not more obviously male than the stallion; woman is more conspicuously female than the mare . . ." (1967, p. 179, italics ours). The findings of the overlay study are in direct refutation of Devereux's assertion. It is the penis which is conspicuous and apparently impossible to ignore, and it is the male figure which dominates the reality of gender. These findings hold for both male and female viewers of the figures.

One way to analyze the relative importance of the genitals is to ask how many participants made a "male" gender attribution and how many a "female" gender attribution when the figure, irrespective of all other gender characteristics, had either a penis, a vagina, or had its genitals covered by pants. Considering first the thirty-two figures whose genitals were covered, ten of these figures had predominantly "male" characteristics (at least three out of four), ten had predominantly "female" characteristics, and twelve had an equal number of "female" and "male" characteristics. If "female" and "male" gender cues were equally "powerful," we would expect that 50 percent of the participants would provide a "male" gender attribution to the covered-genitals figure, and 50 percent would provide a "female" gender attribution. This did not occur.

There were a disproportionate number of "male" gender attributions—sixty-nine percent —to the covered-genitals figure. This finding can be understood in light of other data collected. Seavey, Katz, and Zalk (1975) report that adults who interacted with a baby without knowing its gender more often thought the infant to be a boy. (The baby used in the study was female.) In another study (Haviland, 1976), men and women incorrectly labeled girls "male" twice as often as they labeled boys "female." In Chapter 4 we discussed the children's drawings study but did not, at that time, present data regarding the direction of errors in gender attributions. Kindergarten, third-grade, and adult participants attributed "male" to a female figure more often than they attributed "female" to a male figure. Preschoolers, who do not yet participate in the adult social construction of gender, did not show this bias. On the other hand, kindergarteners, who hold the most rigid and stereotyped ideas about gender, erred in saying "male" five times more often than they erred in saying "female."

This predisposition to think and guess "male" irrespective of external stimuli is reflected in other cultural phenomena such as the use of the generic "he." Had our participants been asked to attribute gender to an inkblot, they might have responded "male" more often than "female." However, the participants were not just "thinking male" (making judgments irrespective of stimuli) but actually "seeing male," filtering the external stimuli through "androcentric" gender attributions. In other words, not only is there a tendency to respond with a "male" answer, but on practical occasions people's perceptions are such that the stimuli *look* "male."

Our evidence for asserting this comes from an analysis of the distribution of gender attributions for the figures with various secondary gender characteristics. Virtually all the "female" cues (long hair, wide hips, breasts, no body hair), and even the cues we intended to be neutral (clothing), were seen by at least 55 percent of the participants as male cues. Never were male cues (short hair, body hair, narrow hips, flat chest) seen by more than 36 percent of the viewers as female cues. We cannot blame this on poorly drawn female characteristics, since these same "female" cues *were* perceived as female in a predominantly female context. For example, overall, 57 percent of the figures with breasts were seen as male. Three and a half percent of the participants who made a "male" gender attribution to the figure with breasts said that adding breasts was the first thing that should be done to make the figure female. However, of those participants who saw the figure as female, over half of them mentioned "remove the breasts" as the first thing to do to make it male. Thus, in a female context the female cue was salient, but in a male context it could either be "ignored" or seen as a male cue. In phenomenological reality although the presence of a "male" cue, may be a sign of maleness, the presence of a "female" cue, by itself, is not necessarily a sign of femaleness. As we shall see, the only sign of femaleness is an *absence of male cues.*

Our discussion thus far has been limited to "secondary" physical cues. Presumably figures without pants, showing either a penis or a vagina, provide viewers with additional gender information and move them further from the fifty-fifty split we hypothesized. If genitals were the definitive gender cue then we would expect that figures with penises (irrespective of any other combination of gender characteristics they had) would be seen by 100 percent of participants as male, and figures with vaginas would be seen by 100 percent of participants as female. While genital cues increase the number of gender attributions toward the "appropriate" gender, the difference between the presence of a penis and the presence of a vagina is profound. Those participants who saw a figure with a penis responded like our hypothetical sample for whom the genital was the definitive gender cue, but those participants who saw a figure with a vagina did not. The presence of a penis is, in and of itself, a powerful enough cue to elicit a gender attribution with almost complete (96 percent) agreement. The presence of a vagina, however, does not have this same power. One third of the participants were able to ignore the reality of the vagina as a female cue.[2]

If we conceived of the processing of gender cues as additive, then we would conceptualize our findings in the following way: There existed in participants a tendency to think and see maleness which produced "baseline" gender attributions of 69 percent male and 31 percent female. Participants who saw the "undressed" figure had one more piece of information to produce an attribution. Genitals provided approximately 30 percent more information. "Female" gender attributions increased from 31 percent to 64 percent when a vagina was added. "Male" gender attributions increased from 69 percent to 96 percent when a penis was added. According to this conceptualization the genital is just one more piece of information. It is not that the penis is a more powerful cue than the vagina, but that each genital has a 30 percent power which is added onto a differential baseline (not based on genitals).

We do not, however, interpret the findings in that way. We conceive of the processing of gender cues multiplicitively. Cues work in a gestalt fashion. The genitals function as central traits (Asch, 1946), affecting the interpretation of each of the other cues. Once participants decided that the figure had a penis, they were even more likely to see the long hair as "reasonable" male hair length, ignore/misperceive the width of the hips, and see the facial features as "masculine." Similarly, once they accepted the reality of the vagina, they were more likely to see short hair as "reasonably" female, and see the facial features as "feminine." If the vagina were as definitive a gender cue as the penis and functioned as a central trait, then it would produce female gender attributions with 96 percent agreement—overcoming the bias against such an attribution in the covered-genital condition. In fact, as some of our other findings indicate, the vagina does not function in this way. It is either ignored/misinterpreted in the first place or when recognized does not have the power to influence the other cues.[3]

Penis equals male but vagina does not equal female. How many additional female cues does the figure with a vagina need to have in order to produce female gender attributions 96 percent of the time? In other words, how female did a figure have to look before virtually all participants said that it was a female? There is no single female cue that *in conjunction with a vagina* produced female gender attributions more than 81 percent of the time. Figures with a vagina and *two* other female cues produced female gender attributions more often. If the two other female cues were long hair and breasts, female gender attributions were given 95 percent of the time—as often as male gender attributions were given when the penis was present. Even adding another female cue (vagina plus *three* female cues) brings the percentages of female gender attributions above 95 percent in only two conditions: the figure with wide hips, breasts covered, long hair; and the figure with no body hair, breasts, and long hair. Even when the figure has a vagina, the remaining male cues are obviously operative and powerful.

The differential reality of the genitals is noted again when we look at the participants' certainty answers. Young children are "better" at attributing gender to clothed figures than to naked ones (Katcher, 1955), presumably because genitals are not part of the way they construct gender. However, adults are not always more certain of their attributions to naked figures than to clothed figures. They are only more certain of their attribution to naked figures when the genital exposed is a penis. When the genital is a vagina, they are no more certain than when the genitals are covered. Participants were most certain of their gender attributions when the figure they judged had a penis, and least certain when the penis was strongly contradicted. If we consider the sixty-four conditions where the genitals were exposed, in twenty-five of them at least one-half of the participants gave certainty scores of "7", indicating they had no doubt about the figure's gender. The penis was a cue in twenty-two of those conditions. There was only one condition where at least one-half of the participants were very uncertain (scores of 1,2, or 3). In this condition the figure had a penis and four female cues.[4] The participants' uncertainty in that condition was also reflected in the fact that one-half identified the figure as male and the other half as female.

More evidence regarding the phenomenological reality of the penis comes from participants' responses to how they would change the figures with genitals. We coded the "change" answers relating to genitals into three categories: (1) remove genitals, (2) add genitals, (3) change genitals. If the penis and vagina are equally real features then we would expect just as many participants to have said "add a vagina" to create a female as said "add a penis" to create a male. And similarly we would expect as many to have said "remove the penis" to make a female as "remove the vagina" to make a male. We did not find this.

In changing a male to a female 38 percent of the participants mentioned removing the penis, but only one percent said that it was necessary to add a vagina. When changing a female to a male, the findings are reversed. Thirty-two percent of the participants said that a penis needed to be added to make a male but only one percent said that the vagina need be removed.

Thompson and Bentler (1971) examined the relative importance of physical gender cues, testing responses to nude dolls with various combinations of male and female gender characteristics. If we compare the data they collected with the findings of the overlay study there is a significant similarity. The adults in Thompson and Bentler's study gave the doll with a muscular body structure, short hair, and male genitals the maximum "male" score; they gave the doll with a rounded body structure, long hair, and female genitals the maximum "female" score. When the cues were gender-consistent they were equally weighted. When the cues were in contradiction, however, the genitals clearly had differential meaning and power. Participants rated the doll with muscular body structure, short hair, and *female* genitals only somewhat less masculine than the maximum male score, while they rated the doll with rounded body structure, long hair, and *male* genitals considerably less feminine than the maximum female score. The power of the penis lies not in its absence, since the masculine doll minus the penis was still seen as very male, but in its presence. The feminine doll with a penis could *not* be seen as female.[5]

There seem to be no cues that are definitely female, while there are many that are definitely male. To be male is to "have" something and to be female is to "not have" it. This proposition is related to our earlier discussion of a "male response bias" and both are integral to the social construction of gender. The implications of this are explored in more detail in a later section of this chapter.

To summarize the overlay study: Gender attribution is, for the most part, genital attribution; and genital attribution is essentially penis attribution. In the next section we argue that penis attribution takes place irrespective of the biological genitals and on the basis of the cultural genitals.

CULTURAL GENITALS

Garfinkel (1967) makes a distinction between the possession of a penis or a vagina as a biological event and the possession of either

[handwritten margin note: what about pregnancy? (albeit temporary)]

genital as a cultural event. The cultural genital is the one which is assumed to exist and which, it is believed, should be there. As evidence of "natural sexuality," the cultural genital is a legitimate possession. Even if the genital is not present in a physical sense, it exists in a cultural sense if the person feels entitled to it and/or is assumed to have it.

According to our perspective and the language we have been using, cultural genitals are the attributed genitals, and since it is the penis which is either attributed or not attributed, we maintain that the only cultural genital is the penis. It belongs to males and is attributed by members as a part of the gender attribution process in particular instances. Physical genitals belong only to physical (genderless) bodies and consequently are not part of the social world. Attributed genitals are constructed out of our ways of envisioning gender and *always* exist in everyday interactions. Males have cultural penises and females have no cultural penises, even cardboard drawings wearing plastic pants. How else are we to understand the participants in the overlay study who claimed that the way to change a clothed male figure into a female was to "remove the penis," or the child who sees a picture of a person in a suit and tie and says: "It's a man because he has a pee-pee."

Physical genitals are a construction of biological and scientific forms of life and are relevant only to that perspective. Penises do not exist in isolation. They belong to, and are presumed to be attached to, males. When what looks like a penis is found to be attached to a female, it is treated as a penis only in the physical (nonsocial) sense. Janet, a male-to-female transexual we interviewed, told us of one or two occasions prior to surgery when she had sexual encounters with men. These men did not treat the (physical) penis between her legs as a (social) penis. They seemed to have decided that it was "all right" that Janet *appeared* to have an inappropriate physical genital because they had already decided that the genital had no reality in a cultural sense. This example illustrates that if the physical genital is not present when it is expected (or vice versa), the original gender attribution is not necessarily altered. When expectations are violated a change in gender attribution does not necessarily follow. It is the cultural genital which plays the essential role in gender attribution. (See also Garfinkel, 1967, p. 157.)

The overlay study has confirmed Garfinkel's (1967) analysis that in the natural attitude genitals are the essential insignia of gender. More specifically the findings suggest that it is the penis which is essential. Garfinkel argues that when we "do" gender in particular instances we are creating the reality of gender as a construct. It is apparent, though, that we not only create gender as a construct, but we create the specific categories of "female" and "male." We must be doing more than gender; we must be doing *female* or *male* gender. While Garfinkel's analysis of the natural attitude toward gender provides us with the best (and only) guide to how gender is accomplished, he does not tell us how *female* and *male* are accomplished. When he discusses Agnes' concern with being a "real woman," his emphasis is on what *real* means for Agnes and for those making judgments about Agnes's gender. What does gender have to be in order to be taken as real? We are emphasizing the *woman* part of "real woman." A male and a female may engage in the same practices for the purpose of convincing others that they are *really* the gender they assert. They must, however, engage in different practices if they want to convince others that they are one particular gender and not another. To say that attributing "penis" leads to attributing a male gender does not explain how we attribute penis in the first place, nor under what conditions an attribution of no-penis occurs.

The relationship between cultural genitals and gender attribution is reflexive. The reality of a gender is "proved" by the genital which is attributed, and, at the same time, the attributed genital only has meaning through the socially shared construction of the gender attribution process. Reflexivity is an intrinsic feature of reality (Mehan and Wood, 1975). The question of how members reflexively create a sense of themselves as female or male, as well as make attributions of others, is the topic of the next section.

DOING FEMALE AND MALE

Theory and research on how "normal" people present themselves as either female or male has been almost totally absent from the literature. The most suggestive is a brief, but important paper by Birdwhistell (1970). Taking it for granted that there are two genders and that, in order to reproduce, the two genders must be able to tell each other apart, Birdwhistell raises the question of what the critical "gender markers" are for human beings. He rejects genitals as a marker because they are usually hidden and because children do not treat them as a relevant characteristic. He also rejects "secondary sexual characteristics" as being far from dichotomous, at least when compared to those markers in other species (e.g., plumage in birds). Birdwhistell believes that "tertiary sexual" characteristics" (nonverbal behaviors such as facial expression, movement, and body posture) are the predominant gender markers for humans. Using data and informants from seven cultures, he demonstrates that members can recognize and sketch out, in a rough way, typical and atypical nonverbal behaviors for females and males. In a study of American "gender markers," Birdwhistell indicates some of the body postures and facial expressions that differentiate males and females, concentrating on behaviors that convey sexual interest. He emphasizes that no nonverbal behavior ever carries meaning divorced from the context in which it occurs.

We agree with Birdwhistell on the importance of understanding gender display and recognition, as well as with his assertion that genitals and other physical characteristics are not the critical signs of gender. It is informative that people can describe and recognize typical and atypical gender displays, but if a display can be characterized as typical or atypical, then the gender of the person who is displaying has already been attributed. Therefore typical displays are not necessary to make a gender attribution nor are atypical displays grounds for doubting an attribution. A woman is still a woman, regardless of whether she is being (nonverbally) masculine or feminine.

Birdwhistell's work does not uncover particulars of the gender attribution process. His data on American gender displays was collected in the same way as every other study on "sex differences." People were sorted in the first place into one of two gender categories, and only then, after an initial gender attribution was made, were these displays compared. This technique, as we have stated before, involves assumptions that militate against uncovering the gender attribution process. By accepting the fact of two genders and pre-categorizing people as one or the other, the researchers have already (implicitly) decided that there are differences. Given their ideas of what female and male mean, certain differences take on importance, while others are seen as irrelevant. On the one hand, variables may be chosen for study because they fit the list of differentiating characteristics which researchers already "know" men and women have (e.g., "preening" behavior). On the other hand, some cues may be ignored, either because they seem so obvious that they are not worth studying (e.g., wearing a dress) or because they are not considered relevant; that is, they are not part of the social construction of gender (e.g., the color of the person's hair).

In order to fully understand the role of nonverbal behaviors in the gender attribution process, it is necessary to understand that the social construction of gender determines why and how we study certain phenomena. Rather than asking people to notice or describe the typical and atypical behaviors of their own and the other gender (which, as even Birdwhistell notes, can never result in an exhaustive list), information could be gathered on which, if any, nonverbal behaviors are "conditions of failure." In what nonverbal ways could a person behave such that her/his gender is questioned? Although our own interests are theoretical, such concrete knowledge has practical implications for transsexuals and others. If the conditions of failure could be described, then people could be any gender they wanted to be, at any time.

The gender attribution process is an interaction between displayer and attributor, but concrete displays are not informative unless interpreted in light of the rules which the attributor has for deciding what it means to be a female or male. As members of a sociocultural group, the displayer and the attributor share a knowledge of the socially constructed signs of gender. They learn these signs as part of the process of socialization (becoming members). In our culture these signs include genitals, secondary gender characteristics, dress and accessories, and nonverbal and paralinguistic behaviors. As we established in Chapters 2 and 4, these concrete signs of gender are not necessarily universal, nor are they necessarily the same signs used by children.

In learning what the signs of gender are, the displayer can begin to accentuate them, to aid in creating the gender dichotomy. For example, as Haviland (1976) has demonstrated, height of the eyebrow from the center of the pupil differs considerably between adult American women and men, but is virtually identical in male and female infants and young children. The difference in adults is obviously aided, if not caused, by eyebrow tweezing and expressive style.

Along with the displayer learning to accentuate certain signs, the attributor contributes to the accentuation of gender cues by selective perception. For example, members of our culture may look for facial hair, while in other cultures this might not be considered something to inspect. In learning to look for facial hair, the attributor perceives in greater detail signs of facial hair than would be the case if facial hair were not a cue. Selective perception occurs in many other contexts. Eskimos differentiate various kinds of snow (Whorf, 1956); people see more or less aggressive behavior in a football game, depending on which side they support (Hastorf and Cantril, 1954).

Although within a positivist framework it is important to delineate specific gender cues and unravel the process involved in learning to accentuate and selectively perceive these cues, doing so glosses over the deeper structure of the social construction of gender. Members do not simply learn rules for telling females from males. They learn how to *use* the rules in their relation to the socially shared world of two genders. There is no rule for deciding "male" or "female" that will always work. Members need to know, for example, when to disregard eyebrows and look for hand size. Gender attributions are made within a particular social context and in relation to all the routine features of everyday life (Garfinkel, 1967). Among the most important of these features is the basic trust that events are what they appear to be and not performances or examples of deceit (unless one is viewing a performance; in that case the assumption is that it is a "real" performance which carries with it other routine features).

Given basic trust regarding gender, successfully passing transsexuals, by virtue of being successful, will be impossible to locate (Sulcov, 1973). To be successful in one's gender is to prevent any doubt that one's gender is objectively, externally real. We do not live our lives searching for deceit, and, in fact, classify people who do as paranoid. In contexts where deceit regarding gender is made salient, everyone's gender may begin to be doubted. For example, Feinbloom (1976) reports that when she speaks on panels that include "real" transsexuals, she, presenting herself as a "real" woman, is sometimes asked if she is a transsexual. The context in which persons appear reflexively create the possibility or impossibility of being real or "only" passing.

If there are no concrete cues that will always allow one to make the "correct" gender attribution, how is categorizing a person as either female or male accomplished in each case? Our answer, based on findings of the overlay study, reports from transsexuals, and the treatment of gender in the positivist literature, takes the form of a categorizing *schema*. The schema is not dependent on any particular gender cue, nor is it offered as a statement of a rule which people follow like robots. Rather, it is a way of understanding how it is that members of Western reality can see someone as either female or male. The schema is: *See somone as female only when you cannot see them as male.* Earlier in this chapter we stated that in order for a female gender attribution to be made, there must be an absence of anything which can be construed as a "male only" characteristic. In order for a "male" gender attribution to be made, the presence of at least one "male" sign must be noticed, and one sign may be enough, especially if it is a penis.[6] It is rare to see a person that one thinks is a man and then wonder if one has made a "mistake." However, it is not uncommon to wonder if someone is "really" a woman. The relative ease with which female-to-male transsexuals "pass" as compared to male-to-female transsexuals underscores this point. It is symbolized by the male-to-female transsexual needing to cover or remove her facial hair in order to be seen as a woman and the female-to-male transsexual having the option of growing a beard or being clean shaven. The female may not have any "male" signs.

The schema, see someone as female only when you cannot see them as male, is not a statement of positivist fact. It is not that "male" gender characteristics are simply more obvious than "female" ones or that the presence of a male cue is more obvious than its absence. The salience of male characteristics is a social construction. We construct gender so that male characteristics are seen as more obvious. It could be otherwise, but to see that, one must suspend belief in the external reality of "objective facts."

To fail to see someone as a man is to see them as a woman and vice versa, since "male" and "female" are mutually constitutive. However, the conditions of failure are different. The condition of failure for being seen as a woman is to be seen as having a concrete "male" characteristic. The condition of failure for being seen as a man is to be seen as not having any concrete "male" characteristics. In the social construction of gender "male" is the primary construction.[7]

GENDER ATTRIBUTION AS AN HISTORICAL PROCESS

The gender attribution process is simultaneously an *ahistorical* and an *historical* process. It is ahistorical in the sense that we have been discussing; gender attributions are made in the course of a particular, concrete interaction. It is historical in the sense that it creates and sustains the natural attitude toward gender and hence gender as a permanent feature. The historicity of gender is constituted in the course of interaction. In ongoing interactions, once a gender attribution has been made, it is no longer necessary to keep "doing male" or "doing female." What Garfinkel, Agnes, and many others have failed to recognize is that it is not the particular gender which must be sustained, but rather the sense of its "naturalness," the sense that the actor has always been that gender. In sharing the natural attitude, both actor and attributor can assume (and each knows the other assumes) that gender never changes, that people "really" are what they appear to be. As a consequence of holding the natural attitude, the attributor filters *all* of the actor's behaviors through the gender attribution that was made, and the actor's behaviors are made sense of within that context. As we have illustrated in Chapter 5, almost nothing can discredit a gender attribution once it is made. Even the loss of the original criteria used to make the attribution might well become irrelevant. The man might shave his beard; the woman might have a mastectomy. The gender attribution will not change, though, merely because these signs no longer exist.

Since discrediting gender attributions is a matter of discrediting naturalness, this can only occur over time through a violation of the gender invariance rule. The person must create a sense of having "changed" genders. She/he must violate the naturalness of the gender (i.e., its historicity) before discrediting occurs and a new gender attribution is made. Even then, a discrediting of the original gender attribution will not necessarily occur. Gender attributions are so impervious to change that the person will be seen as "crazy" long before she/he is seen as being the other gender. For this reason, transsexuals find it most difficult to be seen as their "new" gender by those people who made their acquaintance in their "original" gender. The first impression will not dissipate for a long time (Feinbloom, 1976). If, however, the first impression is made when the transsexual is in his/her "new" gender, it will be most difficult to discredit *that* attribution, regardless of the information given to the attributor. We have had transsexuals lecture in classrooms and have had students question the authenticity of the lecturers' *transsexualism*. These students were unable, after a conscious search, to specify any cues that would unqualifiedly classify the transsexuals' gender as other than that which they appeared to be. The knowledge that these people had admittedly been assigned the other gender at birth and had lived 30 years as that gender became problematic for the students (and fascinating to us) because that information by itself could not be used to discredit the gender attribution.

If transsexuals understood these features of discrediting they would (1) focus on creating decisive first impressions as male or female and (2) then stop worrying about being the perfect man or woman and concentrate on cultivating the naturalness (i.e., the historicity) of their maleness or femaleness.

Just as any concrete cue can be cited as a reason for making a gender attribution, once an attribution has been discredited, anything concrete can be used as a "good reason" for the discrediting. "I knew she was 'really' a woman because of her slight build." In the case of discrediting, just as in the case of original attributions, the "good reasons" given are not necessarily the cues used during the process.

The reason that "normals" do not walk around questioning the gender attributions they make or wondering whether people will see them as they "really" are, is not because gender is a given, but because gender invariance is an incorrigible proposition. Rather than violating invariance, people use what might be seen as discrediting information to reflexively support this proposition. "I know that Greta has a penis, but that's irrelevant, since she's really a woman." All of us, transsexuals and "normals" alike, are in as little or as much danger of not being able to be seen as what we "really" are. It is our method of applying information which maintains our gender, not some intrinsic quality of our gender, itself.

GENDER DIMORPHISM:
THE PROCESS AND
ITS IMPLICATIONS

Once a gender attribution is made, the dichotomization process is set into motion. The cues involved in the schema which led to the attribution are seen as connected with a myriad of other cues which are consequently also attributed to the person. All of these cues taken together, or any of them separately, can then be used as reasons for having made the attribution in the first place. For example, people might decide that someone is male partly because they notice the presence of a beard which is a socially constructed "male" cue. If asked, "How do you know the person is male?" the attributor might answer, "Because he had narrow hips, a beard, and he walked like a man." The attributor may not have originally noticed the other's hips or walk, and in terms of a measurable distribution, the other might not have narrow hips or a "masculine" kind of walk. Since the other has been dichotomously placed into the gender category "male," and since the attributor "knows" that men have narrower hips than women and walk in a distinctive way, these features come to be seen as having been important in the attribution (see, e.g., Seavey et al., 1975). They are important, however, only because of the way we construct female and male as dichotomous, nonoverlapping categories with male characteristics generally constructed to be more obvious.

It has become increasingly acceptable to assert that the dichotomous behaviors which we attribute to the two genders (i.e., gender roles) are not necessarily the way women and men actually behave. There is growing evidence that the genders behave in very similar ways; and yet many people continue to make differential attributions of motives and behaviors, and to interpret behavior and its consequences in a dichotomous way, depending on whether the actor is female or male (e.g., Deaux, 1976; Rubin et al., 1974). Dichotomous gender role behaviors are overlayed on dichotomous *gender* which has traditionally meant two dimorphically distinct biological *sexes*. In the same way that behavior is dichotomized and overlayed on form, *form is dichotomized and overlayed on social construction.* Given a constitutive belief in two genders, form is dichotomized in the process of gender attribution at least as much as behavior is. As a result we end up with two genders, at least as different physically as they have been traditionally thought to be behaviorally.

The social construction of gender and the gender attribution process are a part of reality construction. No member is exempt, and this construction is the grounding for all scientific work on gender. The natural attitude toward gender and the everyday process of gender attribution are constructions which scientists bring with them when they enter laboratories to "discover" gender characteristics. Gender, as we have described it, consists of members' methods for attributing and constructing gender. Part of members' construction involves seeing gender as consisting of, and being grounded in, objective biological characteristics. Our reality is constructed in such a way that biology is seen as the ultimate truth. This is, of course, not necessary. In other realities, for example, deities replace biology as the ultimate source of final truth. What is difficult to see, however, is that biology is no closer to the truth, in any absolute sense, than a deity; nor is the reality which we have been presenting. What *is* different among different ways of seeing the world are the possibilities stemming from basic assumptions about the way the world works. What must be taken for granted (and what need not be) changes depending on the incorrigible propositions one holds. The questions that should be asked and how they can be answered also differ depending on the reality. We have tried to show, throughout this book, how we can give grounds for what biologists and social scientists do, and how the everyday process of gender attribution is primary. Scientists construct dimophism where there is continuity. Hormones, behavior, physical characteristics, developmental processes, chromosomes, psychological qualities have all been fitted into gender dichotomous categories. Scientific knowledge does not inform the answer to "What makes a person either a man or a woman?" Rather it justifies (and appears to give grounds for) the already existing knowledge that a person is either a woman or a man and that there is no problem in differentiating between the two. Biological, psychological, and social differences do not lead to our seeing two genders. Our seeing of two genders leads to the "discovery" of biological, psychological, and social differences.

In essence we are proposing a paradigm change in the way gender is viewed, a shift to seeing gender attribution as primary and gender as a practical accomplishment. In the remainder of this chapter we outline some of the theoretical and practical implications of such a shift.

One consequence of the shift is a new focus for research. Instead of concentrating on the *results* of seeing someone as female or male ("sex difference" research), scientists can begin to uncover factors in the gender attribution process. We have offered some suggestions on how this can be done, and will end the book with a few more. However, unless this research is undertaken with a concurrent acceptance of the proposition that gender is a social construction, there will not be, and cannot be, any radical changes in either how science is done or in how gender is viewed in everyday life.

Many of those concerned with sexism and the position of women in society have suggested that what is needed is a change in the concept of, or even the elimination of, gender roles. The assertion is that, even though the genders are physically dimorphic, except for a few biological differences related to reproduction, there is no necessary reason for any sort of differentiation. Rubin (1975) has written an excellent article, taking a strong position on this. She sees gender as a product of social organization, as the process by which "males" and "females" (the two sexes) become transformed into "men" and "women" (the two genders). Her analysis demonstrates the possibility of "the elimination of obligatory sexualities and sex roles, . . . of an androgynous and genderless (though not sexless) society" (p. 204). Rubin's analysis of gender, while compatible with ours, still is grounded in, and takes for granted, the objective reality of two biological "sexes." Such a position does not question the facticity of two genders, as we mean "gender." An "androgynous society," by definition, retains the male/female dichotomy by agreeing to ignore it. Because accepting the facticity of two genders (or sexes; the former includes the latter) means accepting the assumptions which ground the gender attribution process, a "simple" elimination of gender role will not change what it means to be female or male. The social construction of gender revealed through the gender attribution process creates and sustains androcentric reality. "Male" characteristics are constructed as more obvious; a person is female only in the absence of "male" signs; there is a bias toward making a male gender attribution. In the process of attributing "male" or "female," dichotomous physical differences are constructed, and once a physical dichotomy has been constructed it is almost impossible to eliminate sociological and psychological dichotomies. Given that the physical dichotomy is androcentric, it is inevitable that the social one is also.

Whenever science has offered evidence of a biological continuum, but everyday members insist (because of the way reality is constructed) that there are discrete categories, there have been attempts to legislate against the continuum. Laws in the United States on what constituted a "Negro" and laws in Nazi Germany on what constituted a Jew are two of the most obvious examples. These laws did not reject biology, since biology is a crucial part of the construction of Western reality, but used biology. Race was seen as grounded in the amount of biological matter ("blood," or genetic material) of a certain type within a human body. Rulings in sports (see Chapter 3) which legislate a person's gender are not very different from such laws. As scientists find fewer biological, psychological, and social dichotomies and more biological, psychological, and social continua, it is not impossible that legislators will attempt to legally define "female" and "male," rather than relying on specific judicial rulings. As long as the categories "female" and "male" present themselves to people in everyday life as external, objective, dichotomous, physical facts, there will be scientific and naive searches for differences, and differences will be found. Where there are dichotomies it is difficult to avoid evaluating one in relation to the other, a firm foundation for discrimination and oppression. Unless and until gender, in all of its manifestations *including the physical*, is seen as a social construction, action that will radically change our incorrigible propositions cannot occur. People must be confronted with the reality of other possibilities, as well as the possibility of other realities.

Scientific studies of gender are ultimately grounded in the biological imperative of reproduction. Dimorphism is seen as necessary for sperm and egg cell carriers to identify one another. Many of those who argue against the blurring of gender roles, against androgyny, against the claim of transsexuals to be a different gender, base their arguments on this "biological imperative." One extreme form of the argument is that if there are not clear roles, functions, and appearances, people will not develop "healthy" gender identities, no one will know how to, or want to, reproduce, and the species will become extinct.

The major premise of such arguments is that "male" and "female" are the same as "sperm carrier" and "egg carrier." However, what we have been demonstrating throughout this book is that they are not. "Male" and "female" are grounded in the gender attribution process and are social constructions. They are more encompassing categories than sperm and egg carrier. Not all egg carriers are female and not all females are egg carriers; not all sperm carriers are male, nor are all males sperm carriers.

The only requirement for the "biological imperative" of reproduction is that sperm and egg carriers must be identifiable to each other for reproductive purposes. However, not every human being can reproduce, nor does every human being who carries reproductive cells want to reproduce. Reproduction is not even a possibility for human beings throughout much of their life cycles. Sperm cell carriers are rarely younger than thirteen or fourteen, and probably have an increasing number of defective sperm cells as they grow older (Evans, 1976). Egg cell carriers are usually no younger than eleven or twelve, and can reproduce for only a few days each month for 30 to 40 years, which totals perhaps 3½ years over their life span when they could be identifiable as capable of reproduction. Thus, for all people, reproduction is not a continuous fact of life. In addition, technologies like artificial insemination, the development of techniques for ovarian and uterine transplants, and genetic engineering may, in the future, change our ideas of what the "biologicol imperative" for reproduction is.

The argument that certain "suitable sex differences" or stable secondary gender characteristics are necessary in order to make a differentiation between egg and sperm carriers is not an argument for the biological imperative. Rather, it is an arument for the maintenance of gender. Such arguments are based on the social construction of gender, of being female and male, which is much more than reproduction and, in fact, has little to do with reproduction. Gender, in science and in everyday life, is constructed to be dichotomous not only from birth, but even after death. A woman who dies remains a woman forever. If there were cultures whose dead became neuter, then this would suggest very different ideas about gender.

There are alternative ways we can begin to think about gender, new constructions for which "gender" is probably not even the most appropriate word. Some people, at some points in their lives, might wish to be identified as sperm or egg cell carriers. Except for those times, there need be no differentiation among people on *any* of the dichotomies which gender implies. Because the reproductive dichotomy would not be constituted as a lifetime dichotomy, it would not be an essential characteristic of people. Even the reproductive *dichotomy* might someday be eliminated through technology. No technological development related to reproduction, however, is necessary in order for a new social construction to appear.

Our description of this alternative possibility is not meant to be read as a prescription for a new social order, but as a theoretical "blueprint." Perhaps some readers will feel that we are describing myth or science fiction (see LeGuin, 1969, 1976). That is not our purpose here either, although both myth and theory serve important functions. It would be naive to assume that any statement of alternatives could, by fiat, change the way members view reality. We do not expect that there will develop a whole new social construction of gender in everyday life. What we are arguing is that the world we have now is no more or less "real" than any alternative. What we are demonstrating is that through our theoretical framework exciting alternative possibilities for understanding the meaning of gender present themselves.[8]

As we have reexamined the literature on gender, and as we have analyzed the data we collected on the gender attribution process, we have become convinced of an intriguing possibility. The process of *gender attribution* (deciding whether some one is female or male) and the resultant *gender identification* (assigning the label "female" or "male") may not be the same thing as *"gender"*[9] *differentiation*— knowing whether the other is similar or different from oneself, perhaps in terms of some basic reproductive criteria.

Although children are not 100 percent accurate in assigning gender labels until they are four or five, and although they cannot give "good reasons" for their identifications until they are somewhat older (see Chapter 4), Lewis and Weintraub (1974) reported that infants, before they are a year old, can make some kind of differentiation between "females" and "males." Male infants looked at pictures of other male infants longer than at pictures of female infants, and the reverse was true for female infants. What is most interesting about this study is that Lewis reports (Friedman et al., 1974, p. 191) that adults could not make accurate gender attributions to the pictures which the infants differentiated. The adults could not say, beyond a chance level, whether an infant pictured was female or male. Lewis, however, did not report whether the adults could differentiate in the same way the infants did, that is, on the basis of length of eye contact with the picture.

Lewis terms what the infants did "gender differentiation." Both Kohlberg and Green (Friedman et al., 1974, pp. 192–193) assert that the infants' behavior has nothing to do with gender and that it is "merely" a self–other distinction, since the infants were too young to have gender identities and/or gender concepts. We agree. Gender attribution and gender identification are not possible before the individual shares members' methods for seeing and doing gender. It is possible, however, that infants can make "gender" differentiations —the differentiation necessary for the "biological imperative" of reproduction—a process very different from gender attribution.

Were the infants using cues that adults could not perceive? Their behavior seems to be related to our finding in the children's drawings study (see Chapter 4) that preschoolers were better at determining the "gender" of the other preschoolers' drawings than any other age group. It is also interesting that several transsexuals have mentioned to us that they have the most difficulty "passing" with young children. Is it possible that there is some ability which human beings have to differentiate sperm and egg cell carriers which is then overlayed and superceded by learned members' methods for constructing gender? Obviously a great deal more research on infant and children's gender attribution and "gender" differentiation processes is needed, as well as research on how these processes change over time. It is also important to know more about nonverbal (e.g., eye contact) indicators of "gender" differentiation in adults.

It has become clear to us that within the paradigm of contemporary science we cannot know all that can eventually be uncovered about what it means to be a woman or a man. All knowledge is now grounded in the everyday social construction of a world of two genders where gender attribution, rather than "gender" differentiation, is what concerns those who fear change. With the courage to confront, understand, and redefine our incorrigible propositions, we can begin to discover new scientific knowledge and to construct new realities in everyday life.

NOTES

1. This is the method (Garfinkel, 1967) by which members decide meanings and assemble a body of knowledge on the basis of documentary evidence. In Garfinkel's demonstration with a "rigged" question and answer format, he showed how, in searching for patterns, members make sense of incomplete, inappropriate, and contradictory material, and how they hear such answers as answers to their questions.

2. This was the one case where we found a difference between our female and male participants. Twenty-eight percent of the male participants said "male" when the figure had a vagina, but 43 percent of the female participants said "male." Why should the presence of at least one male cue in the context of a vagina be more salient to women than to men when they are constructing gender? If constructing "femaleness" requires an absence of "male" cues, perhaps those who have been so constructed ("women") are more sensitive to violations. Our sample of 960 participants was selected from those who happened to be on the campuses of eight of the colleges and universities in the New York Metropolitan area on the days the data was collected. It is possible that a sample of feminists would have placed more emphasis on the reality of the vagina.

3. Even when participants were asked to judge a nude figure with no genitals, they more often responded "male." In addition to the ninety-six conditions already mentioned, we had sixteen "no-genital" conditions. We expected that "female" gender attributions would predominate, since the drawings would approximate what some have called the "hidden" female genitals. In fact, though, 58 percent of the participants labeled the figure "male." The "male" cues (short hair, narrow hips, body hair, flat chest) were obviously impossible to ignore.

4. In order to partially check the validity of using a drawing, we replicated this condition (penis, breasts, hips, long hair, no body hair) using a photograph of an actual person (taken from a popular "sex" magazine). The findings for the photograph were almost identical to the findings for the drawing. Six participants identified the model as male and four as female. At least one half of the participants had low certainty scores. In addition, we showed ten participants a photograph of the same model with the penis hidden and pubic hair showing so that it looked like there might have been a vagina. Thus, we were able to closely replicate the condition: vagina, breasts, hips, no body hair, long hair. Again, the findings for the photograph were very similar to our overplay results. Eight participants identified the figure in the photograph as female.

5. Newton (1972) notes that the most amateur mistake a female impersonator can make is to fail to conceal the "telltale" bulge of the penis. Apparently that error is considered damaging enough to destroy the illusion of femaleness. This piece of evidence in conjunction with our

data suggests why the female-to-male transsexual is not as overtly concerned with obtaining a penis as the male-to-female transsexual is with getting the penis removed.

6. Freud was right about the "obvious superiority" of the penis. However, he considered the emphasis on the penis as an inevitable psychological consequence of its objective reality. We are treating the belief in the penis' objective reality as problematic. Those who read Freud as being concerned with (socially real) phalluses, rather than (physically real) penises, see psychoanalytic theory as being grounded in meanings that come very close to our schema for differentiating females from males: "The alternative (is) between having, or not having, the phallus. Castration is not a real 'lack' but a meaning conferred upon the genitals of a woman. . . . The presence or absence of the phallus carries the difference between the two sexual statuses, 'man' and 'woman' " (Rubin, 1975, p. 191).

7. Several features of psychological and biological research and theory on gender seem to have an intriguing relationship to this schema. The specifics of the relationship are unknown and open to speculation, but these features include the precariousness of the development of a male gender identity and male gender role behaviors (as opposed to female), the prevalence of theories of male gender development which cannot explain female gender development, and the scientific fact that, beginning with conception, something (genes, hormones) must be added at every step to make the fetus male.

8. The major dilemma of the ethnomethodologist is the problem of infinite regress. If we assert that reality is a social construction, why stop at gender as a social construction? Why not assert that "sperm carriers" and "egg carriers" are as much of a construction as "male" or "female"? We all have to make a decision to take *something* for granted, to stop somewhere; otherwise it would be impossible to get out of bed in the morning. Our decision has been to stop here; others may wish to go on. (See Mehan and Wood (1975) for a discussion of this problem and an explanation of what Garfinkel (1966) meant when he said "Ethnomethodologists know 'tsouris.' ")

9. We have used "gender" as a modifier because no other word exists to convey our meaning. However, we have set it in quotation marks to differentiate it from gender, as the term has been used throughout the book—the socially constructed, dichotomous categories of "male" and "female" with all their layers of implications.

LETTERS FROM RACHEL

The following letters were written over a two-year period by a male-to-female transsexual named Rachel. We first met Rachel in 1975 and began corresponding with her shortly thereafter. At the time we met, Rachel was 27 years old and a graduate student in biology at a university in the southwest. She had begun estrogen therapy and electrolysis, but had not yet undergone any surgery. When we met Rachel she was still living as Paul, a male. Our first impression of her was of a very feminine (but not effeminate) male. Because she knew of our professional interest in transsexualism, she told us she was a transsexual. Paul looked so androgynous that at first we were not certain whether this person was a male-to-female transsexual or a female-to-male. Our thinking of her at those first encounters as a male was based more on what she told us about her present situation (e.g., that her name was Paul and that she had not begun living as a woman) than on her physical presentation which, by itself, did not *compel* either a male or female gender attribution.

The letters we have included here are not a complete account of Rachel's life during the years when she made the transition from Paul to Rachel. Additional information about her life was conveyed in phone calls and during visits. Also, there is obviously material that Rachel chose not to share with us, and consequently there may be areas about which the reader will have unanswered questions. We have edited the letters, changing the details that would disclose too much of Rachel's identity and deleting redundant material and comments that were not directly relevant to the purpose of the Appendix, which is to provide an extended example of the social construction of gender.

When we decided to include this Appendix as part of the book, we asked Rachel if she would reread her letters and comment on her feelings as she looked back at herself over the last two years. She wrote a brief autobiography and also her reactions to some of the things she discussed in her letters. Following the letters, we have included excerpts from her retrospective account. The final part of the Appendix consists of our analysis of the ways Rachel has become a woman.

(1) Winter, 1975

I just got your second letter and was really very disappointed to hear that you didn't even get my first letter for a variety of reasons. . . . The letter was handwritten and was seven pages long—a tome. The other reason that I was disappointed is that it included photos you requested, that meant quite a lot to me. They were the only ones that existed and I did want them back. I'm sure that the letter will be reconstructed when we get together. I'm very much looking forward to it. I have been writing another letter to you and interrupted it to write this in order to be able to make a quick reply.

I agree about the name Monique. I didn't come up with that name. The woman to whom I was engaged to at one time, who is still a special and undefinable friend offered that name because she wanted it to be a name that she had never run into before. I have long been conscious that it probably does have a little too much flash and glitter. But I don't like Monica. That's a little wicked. Other friends like Rachel. It seems to fit. I appreciate your feedback which is honest and straight off the hip. Although it's painful, it's also the most needed. In my next letter I will briefly unfold the details of my recent trip to Dallas where some important firsts, albeit small ones, occurred. But I'm beginning to see that this whole thing or process is a series of small steps. The other day in the lab when I am as straight as I ever get I met a woman and conversed with her for a long time. She assumed that I was a woman until someone called me Paul. It really blew her mind. Other interesting events have been happening like that.

It appears that I may be among the ranks of the unemployed soon. The company I have worked for is cutting back. Part time people are the first to go. I will do everything possible not to let this interfere with my trip to N.Y.

About my dissertation. Tentatively good news! The event that I related to you (on the phone) was a real blessing in disguise. Rather than do that group all over again, I talked it over with my adviser and convinced him that part of the study wasn't necessary anyway. And got him to agree. So my dissertation has been cut in half. It seems much more finite now. I have set Dec. as the time I will get out and hopefully make the big transition. I'm really excited. This week I'm working on my proposal which is only two years overdue. I hope to get it in first thing next quarter and take prelims by the end of the quarter. I also have been looking over the works of my forerunners and am much encouraged. Some real junk has been put down on paper in pursuit of Ph.D.'s. Poor trees!

I hope that my first letter gets back to me. I did return address it. Please take care. . . . Would I be wearing out my welcome if I came and stayed from one weekend to the next? My schedule is completely flexible. My finances will be anywhere from good to bad depending on

my job situation. Oh the ravages of uncertainty. At least I don't have
to worry about being drafted.

If I get a Watts line at work I'll call.

Oh yes, one more question? What's the weather going to be like in
N.Y.? You might tell me what to pack. My wardrobe is not extensive.
But it's nice. In my first letter I commented that one of my big conflicts
was between my liberated self and wearing some really traditional
clothes that I feel like I have been deprived of for so long. Eventually
after I am thoroughly entrenched in the role, I'm sure that a liberated
unisex thing will be my motif, but right now I still have some things to
get over. I grant you full license to give me as much guidance as you see
fit. Somehow I don't think that the license need be granted.
Some of your comments have really helped.

Take care. Hurry and reply so I can make plans around yours. Until
then, and unless I get another name change. By the way is Rachel all
that bad? Or is it more of the same. Let me know with both barrels
if you think not. I have to nix Monica.

In sisterhood,

Rachel

(2) One week later (responding to a set of questions we sent her)

Hi.

I've been trying to find time to sit down and answer your
questionnaire. In doing this I can answer the questions and perhaps
make comments on the questions themselves.

Before I do, though, I wanted to tell you about some of the nicer
things that are happening to me at least historically. Last weekend I
visited some friends in Dallas. It seems that everywhere I go there are
things to learn and especially nice people to meet. A notable feature
of this trip was that I got to be Rachel (which they preferred to Monique)
for the duration of the trip. One of many small milestones. Another
tiny one was that I fought back the compulsion to wear a dress at least
one day and wore a pants suit. This is more in keeping with the liberated
image I have of myself. A third and most important thing I think was
that I met people as Rachel, who had never heard of Paul or TS and
who never knew that there was anything out of the ordinary about my
womanhood. It was all very nice. Woman to woman communications are
different than male-male and male-female communications. It was
refreshing in a very vital dimension reminiscent of the old science
fiction where the protagonists were just running out of oxygen and

suddenly a fresh new supply is found or generated in the nick of time. I met some neat every day people. Where I stayed, there was a sort of a little community where everyone was very close and were really with one another. I really liked it. There are so many attractive things in life and so little time. Que es la vida.

Let's see, the questionnaire. Do I think of myself as a woman or a TS? In one respect I think of myself as a woman or many respects, increasingly more all the time in fact. I also see myself as having been latent in the old sense that the analytical schools see homosexuals. I am "becoming" in the Rogerian sense if that says anything. I don't naturally identify myself as a TS, only when a very unliberated interaction spells out "I won't buy your act—I won't let you be a woman." My response is that "OK, then I am a TS in the process of becoming a woman."

What does it mean to be a woman or a man? It initially begins with where your head is, with your own identity, then internalizing, and reflecting those things that are consistent with that identity, and acting upon the world in ways that are consistent with those identifications. That's an ideal definition. Generally all the identifying and role playing is done for us, as we are socialized. A more personal answer, which is what you're after, is that the roles are very different. The masculine role in our culture is typified in isolation through competition, stoicism, aggression, etc. The feminine role is different and makes more sense for me; it has been described (I agree with these) as being more tribal and more together; there is a sisterhood where the male role is antithetical to there being any brotherhood. Women have by far the upper hand in sociofacilitative skills. That seems to be very important to me.

How does anyone know they are a woman? Most people that know they are women are fortunate in that they were born as little girls. I wasn't. I do not *know* that I am a woman. But then again being interested in epistemology I don't *know* anything. I will say that I feel that I experience things more the way women do than men do. I am also more comfortable existing with expectations that our society makes of females than I am with male expectations. I feel more real as a female than I do as a male. Another thought—I'm sure that a lot of naturally born women define themselves as women because they aren't men.

In this world of hard core two genderism, to borrow Margo's terminology, if a person's sex and gender is coincident, all is well. However if there is conflict, the result is a whole lot of dissonance that must be reduced. In evaluating oneself, a TS may come to see figuratively that she is leaving a prescribed gender for one that is better suited to her. Now then there are only two in our society. And I'm sure that if a person rejects one gender one must come to feel that they must be of the other. But it seems to me that this is only part of the process and is certainly not the core or heart of the issue as Green it. People expect a TS to adhere more rigidly to the traditional stereotype and set up pass/fail scales in their heads. I've watched people watch me do things like take my shoes off, etc. and heard them comment on how femininely I did it. Yet one would not watch a gender consonant woman take her shoes off and if she deviated from "being feminine" while doing it—so what?

I am the woman that I am seen as being. I ask only that people grant me that.

I know that I am "passing" (I don't like that word. It isn't appropriate to TS's really, as you know it's borrowed from TV's, but for lack of a better one . . .) when no one pays too much attention to me in public. When I am being scrutinized carefully would be an indication that something is amiss.

I deliberately softened some of my gestures and smoothed my walk a bit. Actually, losing 40 lbs. of bulk meant that I had to deal with the world in a very different way. A store's glass door is something to be negotiated with now rather than brushed aside. But so many things came naturally. And my acquisition seemed to be one trial learning, in doing a lot of things.

No one taught me anything.

Convincing other people hasn't been difficult or in any way a discrete task. Nor has it been a main objective, in that, well, life wouldn't be really livable if my main fears and worries were—gee, am I going to pass? There are lots of everyday women who are much further away from the traditional female stereotype than I and we never question their femininity or womanhood at least.

I have seen women or people trying to pass who after scrutiny turned out to be males. Not having conversed with them I don't know what their thing was. It was in the French quarter in New Orleans and I was out walking around and suddenly I became especially aware of a woman who was walking at a much faster than normal rate. Her rate of travel was what gave her away. It was at night so it took me a while to notice that she had on a rather improbable red wig. But not even it was aberrant in the French Quarter.

If I looked very masculine and could change only one thing . . . I would change my tenure here on earth. It would depend on what was making me look masculine really. That's a hard question to answer.

If I were counseling other TS's I would tell them that the biggest danger is overstatement. To gravitate toward the mean in all possible dimensions and not to call attention to themselves. That there is much more to being a woman than physical appearance and to always remember that.

All TS's do not want unusually big breasts. I don't. To answer your question, I would have to say first possibly because they have gone a long time without any at all. More importantly because breasts are the most overt of discriminators because of their association with femininity

seems to think. He has missed taking into account the streng
striving and approach that a person shows when making the
If things were as the hypothesis suggests then the TS paradig
be basically an avoidance paradigm. There are strong elemer
transsexuals. It is very painful for people to include me in the
males. But it does me a gross injustice to say that my behavic
really positive striving as I see it is due to my *not* wanting to
identified. You'll remember the classic self report of the little
saying that they wanted to be little girls ever since they can re
I don't recall them saying, "I didn't want to be a little boy," bu
"I want to be a girl." I remember this very clearly. I really w
like my sister and her little girl friends. It seemed like a very c
that I wasn't. As I see explaining the motivation of gravitating
femininity because of one rejecting a masculine identity and tl
only one alternative is basically an avoidance response.
I really don't feel like that's what's happening.

There are two sets of acquaintances, not friends, that do not
that I am a TS. The first are those people at work where it wou
much less than prudent to make the disclosure. Hmm, now tha
about it they are about the only ones who don't know and who
as a male. The other set knows me only as Rachel. By the way I
you the letter at this point, I'm really sorry you didn't get my i
haven't had extensive experience with those people who know
as Rachel. (Gee I hope you two don't dislike that name too—but
you do please let me know.) Those people are heterosexuals wh
pretty cool heads and seem to be quite liberated and comfortabl
themselves. It's interesting the dimensions that a person picks tc
describe people when the question is open ended.

How do I decide to tell someone? I'm most comfortable aroun
when I can truly be myself. I can't be me when people are makin
assumptions about me. To do so makes me uncomfortable, and tl
not really relating to the real me. I can expand this and pin it dov
you a little better. Males relate on the basis of charisma and brav
in general. Meaningful interpersonal exchanges are made by
rare males and by women much more often.

The way that I tell them varies, depending on how long I have I
them, the extent of our mutual investment in each other, the natu
the commonalities in our relationship and, earlier, status different
were important, but very much less so now. As of late I guess the
that I told you was typical. Although I don't think I needed to tell
you. I had a strong feeling that you two knew.

I think perhaps there are slight differences in my behavior with
people who know me as a woman and those people who know me
as a TS. Those differences come from my feeling more comfortable
with myself and feeling more authentic when they don't know. Wh
people know I'm a TS they monitor my authenticity and I am aware

and because they are unique to the female 52% of the world. Possible sexual reasons are that breasts are important in the male interpretation of femininity.

Up to now I have made no errors that I have regretted. I haven't made any slips. My friends have, however. I've been out in restaurants and had them say, he'll have another drink. At that point I'd like to drop under the table, but just pretend like I didn't hear it and hope it had no significance to the waiter. These friends are people who work beside me in lab, etc. where I have to be a guy.

I haven't done anything inappropriate but I have done some things that aren't necessary. Lately when I'm not swollen from electrolysis I find that I am not perceived as a male. In fact after befriending a new grad student I was surprised to find that she didn't know that I was a "male" until someone used my name. Prior to that we had been engaged in conversation for about a half hour. What a compliment. To tie things together and to answer the question, as of late apparently I don't need a dress and a "face" and other accessories to be perceived as a woman. However, the opportunity to wear these occurs so infrequently that it's really rewarding. I don't think this is the best way to be but I feel that when I do move into the role full time that it will lose its reward value; at least I hope so. The styles that I tend to buy are the sort of things that Mary Tyler Moore wears and the other night she was accused of impersonating a Barbie Doll on her show. Just nice clothes. The sort of things a well-dressed woman would wear.

To my knowledge I've never been doubted as a true woman with only one exception. I was frequenting a bar in both roles, and the personnel had a better memory than I thought . . . although I make a fairly unremarkable female, as a male I stand out a bit, at least I do here in Houston. It wasn't until several weeks later that I found out that I had been detected. I haven't been back to that establishment since then.

It's improbable that anyone would ask me if I used to be a guy. If it did occur, it would depend on who it was as to what I would do. Knowing that the person themself must feel pretty awkward in asking such a question, I think I would perhaps make a humorous reply tinged with incredulity to try to get us both off the hook. I might reply, why yes . . . in my first and fourth incarnations. One thing for sure I wouldn't be facilitative unless perhaps the encounter were on a one-to-one basis. The proposition is a basically mortifying one.

Do people treat me like a woman? I would have to say yes. Your question is a loaded one. To be treated as a woman is a highly stylized matter depending on the individuals involved in the interactions. It first of all depends on how they interpret gender roles and the expectations that each person sets up as a result of those interpretations. Those things that are most meaningful to me might be the nature and content of interpersonal communications I engage in. Male-male communications, as I think I have stated somewhere before, are based on a lot of bravado and charisma, modes of communicating which are mainly without substance, potentially isolating and highly competitive. Female communications can be meaningless just as male communication can be sensitive, but in general female communications (based on the women that I know) have more depth and is based a lot more on sensitivity and empathy than males muster. There are real differences in support and nurturance, qualities that are very important to me. I also perceive that there are some real differences between the way that females communicate among themselves and in mixed groups. For these reasons I am much more comfortable being a woman among women than a male.

Although [Jan] Morris has been criticized for being very unliberated across a lot of dimensions, some of the things she says are in agreement with my own views. The world *is* nicer to women than men. I find that as a man I am treated with neutrality and indifference; as a woman there is always a smile and people are just nicer. That doesn't mean that I groove on impedestalizing women to the point that we are treated as if we are helpless. That's not where I'm at at all. If any of the TS's I have known treated me differently it was a couple of years ago when I was much more of a neophyte and that was how I was treated.

Being a woman is pretty much as I thought it would be.

I don't think there will be many significant changes in my behavior after surgery. I think there might on the part of other people. I think perhaps surgery to everyday people symbolizes and in their eyes solidifies commitment. In their own heads I think they say, "Well, if you're willing to go through that much trouble and pain then I can at least treat you as a woman." In a lot of people's heads, sex, gender, gender roles, and genitals all have to be consonant. Surgery to me is important to achieve some of this consistency. I'm really looking forward to it but I'm aware that my head is as important in being feminine as my genitalia. There are people with vaginas that are much more masculine than I and people with penises that are more feminine.

I do know post surgical TS's. They do report that the surgery doesn't make much difference in how they are treated. They were pretty completely female prior to surgery.

Buying women's clothes never was much of a problem. The local stores generally employ senile old women for exploitative reasons and they are easy to approach with a "shopping list" of things "for my wife" without their thinking much about it. The more male and more nervous and least interested one appears, the easier it is.

[WE ASKED RACHEL HOW SHE WOULD HANDLE SOME SPECIFIC POTENTIALLY DISCREDITING SITUATIONS.]

It all depends. A lot of things could be explained such as my pills, no children, and the absence of the menses if I said that I had had a hysterectomy because of a cervical malignancy. If I didn't want to go that far, I have been on several BC pills. I know how they make me feel and can talk about it the same as any other woman. The menses— obviously I never have had them but I've been included by women enough that I think I can pretty well make anyone think that I have them or have had them. Children—never had any and am a professional woman who doesn't know if she is really dedicated enough to properly care for a child. It's not big on my list at the present.

Being with a guy who wants to touch below the waist: This hasn't happened yet. I've never dated in the traditional sense. When I have gone out with males it's with friends who are quite aware of my situation. I suppose the thing to do would be to tell them that this isn't the right time of the month for that, or that I'm not that kind of girl (tongue in cheek) or just coming on a little cold.

Past histories don't have to be heavy on gender-specific information. When an occasion calls for it, I can be fairly honest and therefore consistent. I had sisters so I know what a female adolescence is like. And there is plenty of overlap. High school idols, I loved the Beatles and saw them in high school. My date was a photographer and we saw them from the UPI pressbox. . . . How exciting!

You know how I feel about the women's movement. Homosexuality in concept is fine and is up to the individual. At this point in my own life sexuality is very low on my list of concerns. I'm a little confused as just who or what is appropriate to relate to in terms of my own identity. Male homosexuality as it is practiced can be cool, but it is very objectifying and gamey usually. Female homosexuality can be beautiful and on the other hand it can be very destructive. So can heterosexuality for that matter. To sum it up homosexuality is pretty much of a non issue.

I don't spend much time thinking about drag queens. In general I don't think I really like the idea that much. Unsophisticated people tend to confuse TV's TS's and DQ's. And when I make a self disclosure I have to go through a lot of shit because of the existing confusion. DQ's are parodying something that means a lot to me.

Your questionnaire was interesting. I don't know how far you go in interpreting your data. As I understand it your primary interests are gender and not the TS as such. That's cool. I think that you should pay special attention to the TS's concept of her/his self. You had a few questions at the beginning but I'm not sure they're the best. I'll think about it. A lot of your questions are aimed at determining the individual's role definition/expectations. I think that's good. Your questions on gender errors are good. Have you ever recognized a TS and if so how? is good. The situational questions weren't too threatening or challenging. But then again I'm a good anticipator/manipulator. It seems to be a good questionnaire.

I hope I've given you some food for thought, without having made too big of a fool of myself.

It looks like I'll be driving to N.Y. Do you have any suggestions as to what to do with my car? I'd like to park it somewhere safe and free if possible. That may be a pipe dream but if anyone would know it would be you. Please keep in mind that it's a little sports car on which the door locks have failed. It would be *easy* to steal for anyone who knew what they were doing. But it's all I have. I am so much looking forward to coming.

As I said in the lost letter meeting you two has precipitated a lot of good things. Since meeting you in Chicago so many right on things have happened! Another question . . . The garment district is up there. I may have a little money for some clothes. Are there outlets for good clothes at reasonable prices, or should I just go on and buy here?

Pardon my typing, I'm in the process of switching from two fingers to ten, self taught. I'm not the dingbat that my typing would indicate. I'm also a little more coherent.

Take care. Please write soon.

Love,

Rachel

(3) Two weeks later

I can't tell you what a lift it was today to see your bright yellow letter in my box. I'd been anxiously waiting for your letter, too. I've got a lot things to say.

First of all, I'm glad we got the name thing straightened out. I had [so] many names. . . . I was beginning to feel like Sybil.

It was great talking to you two. I'm certainly not rich so we'll have to color me extravagant. Actually my friend John and I sat to make plans for the trip. I said to him, "John, let's make plans for the trip." From then on it went like the ballad of Gerald Ford . . . because we realized that no plans could be made until I talked to you two. And being the woman of action that I am, I called. . . . I got so excited talking about the trip that I didn't get any sleep that night, which isn't really that unusual. I keep Sominex in business.

After sitting down and thinking things over John and I got it together enough to come up with an itinerary which is completely compatible with your suggestions. We will leave Houston in the midge Saturday morning and travel to Ohio. There we will have a mission of quixotic proportions. I haven't seen my mother in a year since she learned her son is really a daughter. So we are meeting on neutral territory at my aunt's, to whom I am closer to than I am my mother. She's a child of the flower and is truly enlightened. My mother is directly descended from the vinegar berry and I must face her. As a matter of fact I'll have to face my Aunt too and their whole family whom I was very close to. They'll have some adjusting to do. The first part of the trip could be rough. . . . Oh well. To make matters tighter, Tuesday morning I'd like to leave Ohio as Rachel. I hope they serve drinks on the train. Anyhow sometime Tuesday morning we'll depart from Ohio to arrive in N.Y. Please pay close attention to this part. It would be groovy if we could arrange our schedule in such a way that it would be convenient for one of you to meet us at the train station. It's not a necessity, but it would be appreciated. The last time I was there I didn't have trouble navigating, but I don't know how far I have regressed in ten years. Besides that, I was cleverly disguised as a teenage male (actually that's not too clever, but for reasons now unclear it seemed to be the thing to do). Please remember that my luggage and I will be thinking . . . somewhere in this city of eight million plus is Suzanne and Wendy. It probably won't be easy carrying that baggage around without getting mugged (and worse). I'm really wide open for suggestions as to what to expect.

I have a couple of requests. It would be nice to resign as resident TS for a little while. I don't know how many you know or see as friends. I'd just like to be one of the girls to those around us. How sensitized will your friends/associates be? Secondly, on your accommodations I'm not particular. I'd like to spend as much time with you two as I can without putting you two out. If possible if your apartment and house come without other people that would be preferred. I would be less than perfectly comfortable around unfamiliar males I think. (The more traditional, the less comfortable.) The week in N.Y. will be my first sustained attempt "in coming home." I think the time, place, and people will be right. You asked about anything special . . . maybe a play? and I love good food. Who doesn't? A party? that would be cool if I'm still together and you're into it. Really nothing concrete. Serendipitously I have found you another TS. John's people gave him a really hard time when they heard he was coming with a WOMAN. So he elaborated. His friend has just lost a lover to the operating table. If you're looking for someone to interview maybe after I am introduced I can arrange for you to do so. By the way I know after you read my tome that you'll have questions so we can go into things in depth then.

I've been going through some neat things here as I have met some people who are very understanding and have faith in me and what I'm going through. I've gotten a chance to meet some nice people who have never heard of Paul. All of these things are sort of new and nice. I doubt that you will miss the fact that I'm highly reflective to the point of dwelling on minutia and I'm sure that in the natural course of events that I will have some shit to go through. Things will precipitate. But I seem to be able to handle these things by anticipating them. I'm a realist. I also know that in being me I can't see me the way other people do. So any feedback you can provide for me will be highly appreciated. If you see any rough edges break out your polish.

Oddly enough the last time I was out I, by virtue of having been seated at a table beside this guy, encroached on some other woman's territory, her guy. It took me a while after the get-together to understand the meaning of those poison darts she was shooting at me. The interesting thing is that friends heard her describe Rachel as one of those tall slim brunettes—highly sophisticated, the kind she just couldn't stand. I think she mistook my bashfulness for sophistication. I can be very shy, a quality which John mislabels as my southern charm.

All other things aside, the last couple of weeks have not been good ones. It's certain that I will lose my job now. Other employers do show interest but I fear that I am highly diversified to a point that it is a disadvantage. Everything from brain research to x-ray physics to computer programming. I'm not really interested in these things any more. But until I get my degree they are my marketable skills. I'll be glad when I don't have to do them any more. I'm also considering just taking unemployment as a government assistantship and concentrating on my dissertation, but that certainly would decrease my options right after I get out of school. I would even have a hard time affording hormones, one of life's necessities.

I also had a car accident. The other driver was a huge black who insisted on trying to relate in a very male-male fashion. Thirdly, Vivian, my long-term companion of four years, having realized that what I am to be cannot fulfill her, has been accepted for overseas teaching. I think I'll be alone for a long time.

So this trip, the planning, and seeing you two will have important maintenance functions for me. Overall, my spirits are pretty high. I've been taking my Geritol and taking care of myself, etc.

Write soon

With love,

Rachel

(4) Late Spring, after her visit to New York, where she was Rachel for the whole time.

We're back and I know that Houston can never be the same. As John and I pulled into town and saw the skyline we both burst out laughing and looked at each other and said at the same time—It's not exactly New York, is it? Do adaptation levels ever shift and in a very short time, too. I think I know now where I will want to settle down at least for a while.

The trip did a lot of good and brought out many changes mostly for the good. I made the trip just before I was due to make major (professional) changes anyhow, so I have a lot of adjusting to do other than dealing with my newfound addiction to lox.

My own accomplishments amaze me. Keep in mind that I had attended only one party publicly in my new identity where people did not know about me. Then I came up there and met the people up there. I had never considered what size bite I could chew. But I don't think that I would have chosen the size that somehow seemed to present itself. I do not mean to sit here and let my head swell; actually my humility is intact.

I usually can make rather accurate predictions about me, upcoming situations, and how I will respond to them, but coming back was harder to bear, a bigger down and far less comfortable than even I would have predicted. There are some things that I have done here since I have come back that have surprised me, too. I guess I'll start at the beginning for a change, making a little more sense than usual. (You can't imagine how I'll hate relinquishing my reputation for the "idiosyncrasy" of my usual style.) So you won't have to work as hard to understand this letter.

We arrived in Ohio and went to my cousin's house. I have only learned to appreciate him recently. His wife, Sharon, is also a child of the flower. They both are very accepting of my transition and Phil finds me much more likeable as a female. A very special cousin Susan who is one year to my senior came over that night. She also was very complimentary and accepting. We went out to a nice Italian (at last) dinner and really capped off the entire week with some very human experiences.

The next day was the day to drive home, but I found that I really couldn't make the switch. I found it impossible to go into a men's room. I just couldn't do it. So even Monday I just carried a purse with me and used my feminine credit cards and everything was a little easier. I decided then to go more public at school and to make an unofficial name change around the lab, etc. This wasn't as easy as I had thought it would be. You'll remember that I said I don't make errors and can be consistent, but other people can be impossible with the best of intentions. I simply requested that around the lab people refer to me as Rachel. This took much effort because not only had habits been built up but people grew nervous because they didn't know who knows and who doesn't, and as it turns out there are a large number of fringe people that you don't notice usually, who become painfully apparent when such a transition is being made. Observation: No matter how ready—or how much surgery or how womanly I am, I'll have to leave here before I can begin to make a realistic change. So much depends on the people around. As you found out yourselves, the set is very difficult to break. By the way I did feel very real and genuine there. I felt real oneness with myself there with no conflicts at all. But it's impossible

to do this around people who have known me in a previous
role (with for-the-most-part-exceptions like John).

Other advances have been made. The not having a past bit has
captured my attention. There are several publications going out of here
in which I was acknowledged for technical assistance. People were very
easily persuaded to change the name on the acknowledgements.
Secondly, a couple of journals have requested that we publish a couple
of articles on my methodology. Guess whose name will be on those
papers. So many good things are happening, and I'm learning some
important things about human nature.

One thing I feel is significant. I can't really feel at all comfortable in
behaving the way I did in New York in the lab, although I feel that
the me that came out in New York was really me. I feel that there are
tremendous gradients that will not let me do "those things." Specifically,
the fantasies that I have about coming across the way I did up there
here are that I would be consumed. The fantasy is oral, but I think I
would in a real way lose all my credibility with the people
I interact with. It's a real bind; I can't be ME.

Vivian and I are adjusting to the fact that we have to part. Tonight
we were listening to Denver and his song Leaving On a Jet Plane
was playing and suddenly we were both crying our hearts
out and holding each other. It was heavy.

So all in all there are no more doubts or cobwebs; there are only
those things I must do in order to get to where I want to be. I was sorry
we didn't get to spend more time together. I hope you didn't feel like
you were babysitting or that you had a neurotic hanging on to your
coat-tails at times. Please remember that a lot hit me at once and there
was much to be digested. Things are happening very fast. I think,
however, that all in all my equilibrium is good. It's hell to have to be
two people. I think that perhaps you got a brief glance at how
complicated life can be. I have never been so aware
of the gap between academe and experience.

There were a couple of things that will seem mundane to you that
were touching to me. Joy was starting her period at the time and asked
me discretely if I had "any equipment with me to start it with." I wish
I had. I will never have to (I don't see this as a plus) but I'll carry a
few tampons on occasion for those who might want to borrow them.
Kathy took me aside and told me what places on the machine would
snag your pantyhose and a couple of other in things that would be only
of interest to women. So much for that; it's late and
I'm getting unusually nostalgic.

Take care, keep in touch. I feel more legitimate than ever in signing,

In sisterhood,

Rachel

(5) One month later

Hi,

I just thought that I would drop a note to inquire if you have received my last letter which I sent a week after my return. I haven't heard anything from you. The other alternative may be that you have written and it got lost—if so you should know.

Things are much better these days. I was very upset at the prospect of having to return to such a schizophrenic life style and I'm happy to report that I haven't. I have informed the majority of my acquaintances of my plans and have been pleasantly surprised at the response. It's been pretty warm and receptive. Even the provincials of provincials, our department chair, knows these days. To be "known" is not nirvana of course but it means I can be more me which is important. As I said in my last letter I'll definitely have to leave here and start over. I have gotten involved with a very intimate group of people who have never heard of PW and I value being a member of their group highly.

Things have been pretty exciting here lately.

Both of you take care.

Rachel

(6) One month later

Dear Sisters,

Your letter arrived at a most opportune time. As usual a tremendous number of important things have occurred since I wrote last.

I've mentioned that things have never been the same since N.Y. and it's really neat that things are increasingly not the same. In a controlled way I have gone public in the department, not something that in itself is gratifying at all, other than it allows me to make the transition while I'm still here in school, and that's gratifyin'. As John puts it, it seems that N.Y. released a lot of action-specific energy. Now even our department head knows. I don't know if I mentioned this or not. I must report that all overt interactions with other parties have been most human and quite accepting.

Things have changed so fast that it seems that Vivian has left, or at least the relationship is cooling rapidly. She has become involved with a very straight grad student (in Physics) who lives about one hundred feet from me. I don't know of any way to communicate in words the extreme pain, excruciation, and agony that this caused me.

For awhile I felt very suicidal. Loneliness doesn't scare me, but it sickens me. I have a high regard for myself to the point that it seems almost a waste for me not to have someone to give to, to share with, and to love. I can, however, understand Vivian's frustration. I am the changing entity in the relationship and am not the same person she fell in love with four years ago. She has been constant and I still love her tremendously, in a non-erotic but very affectionate and physical way. What is happening, though, in reality, is probably the best for both of us. She did something that was extremely cruel and sadistic in what represented the redefinition of the relationship. This occurred on Wednesday of this week and I was all but nonfunctional. Every time I would start a protein fractionation I would burst out into tears. I had to see committee members the next day and really looked horrible and had to really try to fight back the tears while I was talking to them. The one bright thing that happened was that I got your letter which dented the all encompassing numbness. In the last couple of days I have seen her and it seems that we will still be casual friends or more but nothing has settled down yet. In losing her I do have more freedom; you'll remember that's just what Joplin sang, freedom can be very cold and lonely. Today I saw an attorney and she is going to see the court Monday about my name change. I'm pretty excited about this. This means that my six-month trial period is starting? is about to start? I don't know what constitutes it.

I see my doctor in Baton Rouge on May 20th. So I'll know much more. I did find out that Blue Cross and Blue Shield does have a two-year preexisting conditions clause. HMMMMM. BUMMER especially when I just found out that my mother just let my policy go, which would have counted as time, about five years' worth. My only hope for quick cash is developing a prototype commercial system of the protein fractionation equipment that I developed here. I'm not sure what the odds are that we'll be able to find a real world entrepreneur. I never have been too functional outside my ivory tower world, but then I never have wanted to be.

I'm readjusting to poverty which, as it turns out, is not as much fun as it used to be after having been affluent. If nothing else money can buy pleasant diversions.

I'm trying to get up my courage to take prelims this quarter.

Something really funny happened the other day. My car had broken down and since my income is zilch I had to do the work (which I hate) on my car. I do it in surgical gloves to protect my manicure. I hate grease. I was fuzzy because I had been doing electrolysis, dirty, unclean, greasy, and my hair was very dirty. In short I was disgusted with myself. I went to the store to buy parts for the car and talked to the guy in the store for a while and was more than a little surprised when he said, you don't see many ladies working on their own cars these days! I just smiled and said I had taken a course in school on it. He said he'd heard about the course and thought it was a great thing. Things definitely aren't as schizophrenic as they used to be. My record is still consistent, I haven't been called sir since N.Y. even when I called the hardware store and asked for liquid wrench.

I do have a hard time empathizing with your distress over not accomplishing anything in a month or so. I feel bad in admitting it but I sort of feel that if I were where you are I would be resting awhile, at least for a couple of years after my degree. I have a lot of life to live after school. Maybe I'm fooling myself—I don't know. Could be that I have some latent achievement need that will explode into actualization after school; but if it's there, it's pretty latent.

The more I think about it the sorrier I am that I missed seeing more of the city. Really, I don't have any regrets except that I didn't get to stay longer (the important part of the trip was more than accomplished). I see a lot of the things I whizzed by on TV regularly and get a little homesick for that place. I really liked it. I definitely need more than Houston.

Please take care and write soon. Your last letter came at the perfect time. No telling what kind of ups and downs I will have gone through in the interim.

Love,

Rachel

(7) Two weeks later

Hi,

Someday, perhaps in the near future even, I promise not to open a letter by telling you that a lot has happened since I wrote last but not this one because a lot has happened since I wrote last.

I am now legally me. It is amazing how a piece of paper with legal hocus-pocus creates legitimacy. The name change has helped make things more real and concrete for people around me too. I'm learning so very much about human beings but I don't think it's generalizable to other situations.

In reading the literature you will remember that prior to surgery there is no *legal* reason for me to have female status. I pulled a moot trick in writing up the court order itself by using female pronouns instead of their alternative. The judge didn't notice this in signing the order. When creditors and other people that must see the order see it those pronouns greatly facilitate things requiring much less discussion. Last week I was a little surprised that people didn't catch on faster when changing credit cards, etc. Many never questioned that I had not always been a woman. Even when handed the court order.

I went through a bad period due to being all alone and I think that it was only natural that I questioned what I was doing. At no time, however, could I generate any kind of male alternative to the direction I am going, and am all the better for it. I hope that makes sense to you. It's a little like religion to more conventional people.

Last Tuesday saw me in Baton Rouge to see the surgeon for my checkup. We began talking about financing this thing which looks very grim. Hopefully, the local Voc Rehab is considering two other women like myself and possibly I will be a third case. I have some very new literature dealing with Voc Rehab and the TS which I will donate to them.

Today . . . I talked to two of my committee members; the first was in molecular biology, my outside member; he is very straight but we have always gotten along extremely well. Today was no exception even after I told him. His response was that mine was a choice that everyone has to make, which is remarkably enlightened for that type. I'm beginning to stop dealing in terms of stereotypes; they just don't seem to hold anymore not even for biologists. My second member is a neat guy. He taught me my basic biochem course and is a bit like Burt Reynolds so I had things both good and bad going into our meeting. I conduct myself no differently around him or dress no differently and he hadn't noticed or suspected. Oddly enough I felt that I was in control in this conversation. After taking his course I pretty much knew what he looks for as far as body language and nonverbal communication is concerned and was in control enough to come across exactly as I wanted to. That isn't to say that I was at all dishonest in what I communicated but I was aware of precisely what messages he was getting.

Also today a friend, Michelle, was approached by our secretarial staff who is very interested in a humane way rather than a voyeuristic fashion. She explained the relevant things to them to their satisfaction. They were one element that I had not known how to deal with because I had pictured them as rather hard core traditionalists. The one thing that I had failed to take into account is that they are sisters and that transcends so very much if not all.

So as you can see it hasn't been a dull week.

Rachel

(8) One month later

At last things do seem to be settling down to a dull roar and I'm grateful. I'm completing the documentation on my protein fractionation technique and am looking forward to getting that completed.

I've gone ahead and entered and seem to have completed the evaluation (pencil and paper part) in Baton Rouge. They do have a compulsion to ask me to drive up there every month and tell them I'm doing fine. They seemed initially to be a little threatened by me not because I'm a TS but because I'm completing a Ph.D. The shrink and I have clashed once as he needed to establish a "me-doctor . . . you-sicky patient . . . I'm always right in what I say" relationship. But he only got far enough to satisfy himself on that round. They are definitely into the male-dominated medical model there. I really don't think they can even imagine that there are any alternatives. I was complimented one day when I overheard a candid conversation between the shrink and the surgeon. They both agreed that if I hadn't told them that I had once been a male that they wouldn't have known.

Back at school my committe members have all individually accepted my proposal. I have informed them all of my change of status and have received nice patronizing responses. In reality though it seems that the members that I don't see very often (3 out of the 4) are very threatened. I think that my committee meeting will have all the elements of a three-ring circus. I want to take prelims by August 1st.

I keep having dreams of N.Y. I really liked it up there. A large company has sent down some informal feelers down here concerning offering me a job on Long Island. It might be worth it just to live up there for a while. Oh yes, I have found a place right around the corner that serves lox but without bagels which seems most incomplete. So when I can afford it I treat myself to lox and crackers for lunch. I'm not affording much these days. I'm completely a ward of the state being on unemployment and just having qualified for food stamps. By the way, it seems that Voc Rehab has paid all expenses for several TS's. I have contacted them to find that this practice has a temporary (and maybe permanent) hold on it because 1.) they suddenly realized that they had no fixed policy on it and one is needed, and 2.) new Federal guidelines have everyone confused on just what is permissible and what isn't as far as Voc Rehab is concerned. It seems that in the case of the TS that the whole policy will be contingent on the attitudes of the members of the state board. Word has it that the conservatives are maintaining that TS surgery is elective and therefore not fundable. But there are good people (my surgeon for one) who are working very hard to get it through. Voc Rehab hopes to have the issue cleared up by early July. Keep your fingers crossed.

So that seems to be it. Please let me hear from you soon. Take care—

In sisterhood,

Rachel

(9) One week later

Hi!

Such a dynamic greeting deserves a no less enthusiastic letter. And not only that, I'm going to refer to myself in first person. It sounds like you have been busy. I'm glad to hear that you two are forging ahead with your book.

My work is coming along well; for the past three weeks I have been doing the initial work on my dissertation, which will be completed in another couple of days. Not only that, I am having a committee meeting either this week or next, something I have feared for years because of all the horror stories, and the fear has abated and I'm even scheduling prelims for August 1st. If you knew me as well as I do, these things can only mean one thing—BUSINESS, I want out. I'm really tired of the piracy/lunacy and desire a little sanity.

Regarding camping, I don't mind eating in the woods. I'll eat anywhere but I think that I'd probably opt to sleep in a hotel room. I guess that makes me a semi-sissy. You see, I did a huge amount of camping when I was a little girl (I don't choke when I say that these days—I guess it comes with practice) and spent all my spare time in the great out-of-doors. Now it seems that I have lost all rapport with chiggers, ticks, and mosquitos, value a shower in the morning above all, and feel huge frustrations when I can't find a place to plug in a hair dryer. On the other hand it seems that oh so many of my peers are into this outdoors thing. I have a feeling that when time permits (what a cop-out . . . time will never permit) I'll get back into it.

I have one piece of very exciting news. I have designed a small "clinical/research" version of the apparatus that we use at school for the protein separations. Currently there are no units that will do this on the market (our technique is highly refined). We have submitted the plans to my former employer and they're very interested in it. They are supplying us with the facilities to build a prototype. If they like it they will buy the rights and pay a royalty. It would be more than a year before they could go into production on it, but just think maybe I always won't be on foodstamps . . . sauteed mushrooms might be just around the corner. I wish this had come a little earlier so I wouldn't have to be starving. It's really a gig when we are showing people around the lab and they ask "who designed this system" and the colleagues say—she did. People's eyes bulge. It really gets to them when they see what a woman did. It's good for us all. Take care.

Love,

Rachel

(10) Fall—2-1/2 months later

Dear Wendy and Suzanne,

I'm glad I got your letter when I did because I had started writing
one to the both of you several times only to discard it midletter.

There is not a whole lot that is new for me to report. I think I
have passed prelims and will soon be admitted to candidacy soon.
That's a groove.

Our newest capitalistic venture has had some snags but is still
making remarkable progress. We've had incredible legal hassles.

At any rate we have our first customer, which is not at all as paltry
as it sounds. Each unit will sell for nearly $7000! I have to fly to
San Francisco on our first consulting trip. That will at least pay for the
calculator that I had to buy to get through prelims. The interesting thing
is that the design I have developed is sound, there is no competition, and
it could really go somewhere. However I know that given enough rope,
at least a few inches, I can hang myself in the business world. I'm
not particularly an advocate of the profit motive—but owning and
running my own company would certainly let me be my own woman
which is an important plus.

The world has grown to be at least quite accepting. I think with
time poeple can get used to anything, even me. In fact, things are going
very well as far as settling down is concerned. I have noticed a gradual
change in the people who know and I can't see any discriminable
difference in the way XX individuals and I are treated, which when
you think of it is a little mind bending. I'm getting to feel quite
legitimate. In fact, there are males who are sure that I really need
their own "special" kind of attentions. But I have kept my distance.
Remember the unicorn (they only made one).

Your comments about Medical Center struck me as being a little
harsh. I know there were some gross inaccuracies, because yes it was
commercial TV. But I am thankful that it was on TV at all. It was done
in a way that was minimally acceptable to the confused and
homoerotophobic public. I really remember going through those exact
things that Pat did in one form or another. The whole show was
certainly better than no show. I was a little surprised at some of my
own responses. My own transition was gradual as you will remember.
At a biology convention the hotel staff were calling me ma'am and I
was thrown out of the men's room before my transition. My change
compared to Pat's was evolution compared to revolution. He,
phenotypically, would make a less than probable woman, meaning
that such a person would have a questionable probability at being
happy postsurgically. John was less generous than I—"Pat was definitely
a drag," he said. I did feel a little less than comfortable in the last
five or ten minutes of the show. And would have a little harder time

at using "she" than you did in your letter. But she has every right to try and that is what is important.

A couple of weeks ago I had a terrible case of gastroenteritis either from the flu or from food poisoning so I had to go to hospital. It was my first time to seek treatment in this life and needless to say I was a little nervous. The nurse told me to take my blouse and bra off and slip into a hospital gown. I kept my slacks on under the gown as I was supposed to. The doctor came in and started to examine me—kidneys, chest, breasts, etc. and I thought it was all over and there would be need for no frank discussions until he started to unzip my slacks to examine my lower half. At that point the conversation went:

Rachel: Before you do that I think there's something you should know.

MD: Yes?

R: I'm a preoperative TS.

MD: A what?

R: (I explained.)

MD: Gee, if you hadn't told me I'd never have known. Have you lived as a woman all your life?

R: Since May.

MD: Amazing.

Then he really got off on the whole thing. I wanted him to fix my stomach. The sad thing is that the only reason he unzipped my pants was to listen to my stomach. He really never would have gone further south. But I guess it was good for him. As it was it still took me six days to recover (from the gastroenteritis).

I keep having dreams of N.Y. I liked it so much.
Houston is such a burg.

I've met a really neat guy with whom we founded a really intense but platonic relationship, which is great because he's married to a radical feminist who hasn't moved here yet from their home town. He has perhaps the most fantastic head of any male I have ever met. He's in computer sciences and we have ever so much in common. Intellectually, the relationship has been very stimulating, which has been a much needed ingredient.

You know this has been a really upbeat letter. And it's Friday nite which is usually a very blue time for me. But that doesn't even spoil things.

Take care and write soon.

Rachel

(11) Six weeks later

Hi you two!

I must say that I was really glad to get your last letter as I was
in a very good mood and I received it at an opportune time. Because of
the way things have been going for the last couple of months almost
any time would have been a good time because everything has
been going very well for a long time now. How strange.

My dissertation is going very well. But how could things not go
well during the initial fractionations. There are many interesting
phenomena in the offing. Since I am the senior student in my lab and
I have a lot of say in what goes on in it, several of the new first-year
persons have decided that I must be their one and only mentor. At
times I find myself being followed like Lorenz and his little geese.
I think what they really want is a little mothering.

My social life has exploded. The only trouble with being very
much sought after is that it is definitely fattening. I'm counting
calories again. Tch Tch. I'm certainly having more fun.

Business seems to be going well too, which will eventually lead me
around to answering your question about the system you've asked about.
After a brief struggle with my adviser, which I won, corporate harmony
seems to be ours. Actually we incorporate Wednesday. It's all very
exciting. It really has blown a lot of male minds (a very narrow and frail
entity at that) when visiting the lab to see what a woman can
accomplish. I think the phenomenon is good for all concerned. That
reminds me, I'm teaching a course in several different techniques on
bioassays at the graduate level as a result of a multitude
of requests from student peers.

I can't tell you how excited I was about last spring's trip to N.Y.
I'll be very much more real on the next trip. I think you'll find that my
bashfulness has pretty much dissipated and I've even acquired
a little polish where there were rough edges.

I'm not sure what I want to do yet. It will depend on what we do
with the company and how much potential it seems to have. The system
being developed, by the way, is an advanced method for blood protein
separation using an electrophoretic technique that I developed for my
dissertation. It is very fast and reliable and relatively inexpensive. By
the way, how is Harry's research going? I hope he got it off the ground.
I never got a letter from him. And I'm not even the dark lady of
Houston anymore! Tell him that I'd like to hear from him and that if
he needs any consultation when I get up there I'll be glad to help
him within the limits of my meager talents.

I even find that one of the reasons that I have been so content
lately is that I have been accomplishing so much.
Sounds a little perverted doesn't it?

I'll have to tell you that I have been perfectly chaste since N.Y. which has been absolutely no strain, and I have made no commitment to any kind of an orientation so I'd at least like to see what it's like. I must say that many men have become very interested but they seem rather monolithic and predatory. Sometimes being just another pretty face can be quite a burden. But on the other hand I've never been so happy. I've never regretted what I've done for a moment.

I'm going to visit home for the first time in a couple of years over the holidays. I haven't taken a vacation since I saw you two and it will be a logical breaking point in my dissertation. It also may be a breaking point for me. It's quite probable that I will regret it. "You can never go home again" will probably be very true for me.

I had some very straight friends, some who have never learned to spell cosmopolitan much less become one, so I am one of the things in heaven and earth of which they have never dreamed. It's really sad. The tragedy is theirs however, not mine.

It looks like I have given you enough to chew over. I'll be looking forward to your next letter. Write soon.

Love,

Rachel

(12) Four months later, Early spring, 1976

Someone borrowed my typewriter so I thought I'd handwrite you a letter since I've found time to take a breath and write you a letter. I'm sorry that I've been such a poor writer but you wouldn't believe the schedule I've been keeping lately. It's been rough. I've been doing my dissertation, teaching a graduate course, and running our mini-company. It's demanding being President/secretary/designer and the sales/marketing division all at once.

Spring arrived here very early and it's been a pleasant spring. I've been very much in demand and have been having a good time learning the bump with some of the other students. I find that women partners are much better than males. My measure is a bruise count after each dance. The score is Harvey 117 and Jennifer 0. I'm sure Harvey would be a great linebacker, however.

It seems that with every plateau there are always new slopes to climb. I've been very comfortable becoming me but looking back I'd have to say I've been very tentative socially, and have buried myself in work. Part of the reason has been financial, but probably the residual reasons have just been self-confidence and a pause while I get my head together. The woman, Jennifer, whom I have mentioned, is a very close friend. She is very honest and a good friend who provides some very supportive feedback, the net effect of which has been to help me with my self-confidence. We've had a lot of talks about a lot of things. It's strange, we love each other a lot but she really wants a guy and I respect that. I am looking more and more toward surgery. I think I'm going to put a small ad in the *MS.* personals saying: Woman grad student financially depleted needs money for surgery. Please help. And see what happens. Right now that's the only thing I can think of.

The other night Jennifer gave my hair a *light* frosting (light meaning subtle). It looks pretty nice.

I don't know what I'd like to do when I get out next fall. Maybe I'll put another ad in an international magazine. Position wanted: Potential countess or potential princess desires countessship or princessship. All counts and princes invited to apply. I'm an equal opportunity employee. P.S. White horses preferred.

All kidding aside—one really unfair thing. The automatic assumption and hence pressure is that I do a nice straight heterosexual thing and pair off with a male. This I think is a compliment, but a little unfair. Even Jennifer, I think, assumes this.

Gee what a mellow night this is. It's Saturday and I took a night off from the world after having been rock and rolled to death last night. For the first time in my life I'm listening to FM easy music station. Hmm, just my luck the wine cellar's locked.

Actually I feel like there are so many things to tell you that I'll just have to wait to see you. It's only a month off you know. . . .

In sisterhood,

Rachel

(13) Summer, five months later

I'm trying to resist the temptation to spend several paragraphs apologizing and explaining why I haven't written. However, suffice it to say that I haven't. . . .

So much has happened! The reason you didn't hear from me immediately after the trip to N.Y. was that I went through a real *blue funk* for a month or six weeks and was seriously depressed. I just sat around and stared at the walls and seemed very down. I think I was very worried about employment as my unemployment was running out. Along about then Ted came into town and we did the town as well as it can be done. Later he called and offered me a job with his firm. At the time it seemed almost like a good idea so I said yes. Since then, I've reconsidered as he wants to move his company to Kansas City.

The net effect of the job offer was to lift me out of my funk. When I'm depressed I become even less disciplined than usual and procrastinate a lot.

Oh yes: My dissertation research is finished. I haven't started writing yet and don't intend to until fall because I want to play this summer. It's the first time in my life I've ever really done my own thing and I sort of enjoy it.

I've had my first affair. Well as much as I can have had one. It had its good points as well as its bad ones. He was piddling around as an undergraduate, is beautiful, rich and a gourmet. For the last two weeks we lived together. At the onset of the relationship I told him that I had been through some recent traumas and wasn't ready for any sex. He said OK and away we went. He has exquisite taste. All and all we were good for each other. And he never knew. He has offered to fly me to San Francisco to go on a cruise on his yacht. I spent last nite writing him a letter to let him know that yes, I would come, but along with it I supplied what I'm sure will strike him as being some unusual insights into my past life.

Our company has delivered the first instrument. Many people want to buy stock and several companies are calling and will visit the lab this fall. After almost exactly one year of incredibly hard work we brought home less than $900.00 which will go into my medical fund as a first deposit. I don't really want to continue with the company. My education in this field is pretty complete and it's time for me to move on to other things. I don't want to be shackled with a business venture. Who knows if I continue I might even be a success—an outcome which I will avoid. I'm starting to do some consulting in Oregon which may develop into a job which is very exciting. It has to do with electrophoresis and the analyses therein. . . . I'm glad I've found something that turns me on. So as you can see there have been very few dull moments, and I really have been busy with virtually no time to myself, even for maintenance. So forgive me.
Now I have more time and will write.

Love,

Rachel

(14) Late fall, 1976, three months later

Dear you two,

Perhaps you have noticed that I've fallen down in my letter writing
for which I must apologize. But in your last postcard you told me to
expect a letter soon. Oh well. . . . I've been both busy and not busy.
I've finally gotten so fed up with things at school that I am working
concertedly at finishing the dissertation. All I have to do now is
to do the data analysis, for which I have written computer programs,
and do the writing. It seems to be at times formidable and
wholly unrewarding in itself.

I have come to realize that I spent the last several months in at
least a mild depression and have been working at a very low energy
level. A lot of it has to do with my professional aspirations or lack of
them. I've said many times that a professional life seems a bit too
regimented. I'm laid back enough that the so-called rewards of the
profession, i.e., publications, a prominent reputation, etc., are pretty
meaningless. It seems to me that since we really are here only once and
in that our stay is as short as it is, that I can't feel particularly
positive about dedicating that much time in my life to just fill pages in
journals. At the same time I do envy people who don't share
those feelings.

The fact that I have interests and expertise in so many different
fields and could never get them together also bothers me. This week
I was asked to be a guest speaker at three different seminars, one on
electrophoretic separations, another to a psych of women class on sex
differences and biology, and a third to a computer sciences class on
computers in the biological sciences. I can't figure out where home is.
Although many colleagues admire this, such a widespread
distribution of expertise makes me feel rather insecure.

I endured one major trauma very recently. Several companies have
indicated a strong interest in our apparatus. I don't know if I told you
but the one in Utah is installed and is working fine. Anyway we have
been negotiating with several companies for the eventual sale of the
rights. That fell through. Meanwhile I had started making firm plans
with Baton Rouge. At the same time when I was talking to Baton Rouge,
I found out that the procedures were much more expensive than I had
thought they were going to be. Net effect experientially was that I had
gotten very close and then been yanked much further away than I was
to start with. Gee . . . I lost some insulation (emotional) that I'll never
be able to replace. But now looking back on it the crisis had some good
effects because it's gotten me off my derriere and I'm doing something.
But what tantamount agony. The real world can indeed be ruthless.
So we are still negotiating with the two largest companies. They came
to the lab to see the unit and commented that our unit is the most

elegant and sophisticated process they have ever seen. Company A will be here at the end of next week. Company B wants me to come to Boston for a job interview. Every time I come into contact with a company I get a job offer. Ted got down on his hands and knees and almost begged, but his company is gnat sized. I went to Cleveland a few weeks ago and saw him and wasn't taken particularly good care of, and I'm sure that Ted doesn't even know how really grim his treatment was. He lodged me in an apartment with no heat, and all there was to sleep on was a mattress with a bedspread and a sheet. I was just beginning to recover from bronchitis. . . .

Robert came up for a visit. He was the summer fling I wrote about. I had written a letter to him explaining my situation to him and I don't think it made the slightest bit of difference to him, that is to say that there were no cognitive shifts on his part that I could see. The sad thing about Robert is that he is as existentially lost as I am but much more anxious. He was here for four nights and completely drunk for three which was typical of the summer. We're both aware that to each other we're nice people to visit, but haven't enough in common to live together. But it was really nice to see him. He wants me to come visit for Christmas. As of yet I haven't made any definite plans.

I know this letter has had consistently down overtones which for the most part is where I've been, but things seem to be taking an upturn. After the ordeal last month which precipitated so much I'm definitely less passive about most things. I'm still refusing to look for jobs yet so I can keep my options open. It's so much more fun to be a dilettante. The puddle I'm in is seeming ever smaller. My advisor is asking me to stay here after my degree and research with him, which usually ends up being *for* him instead. He's very gifted. He's gotten a good national reputation based on research that I have designed (and others, of course). It's an interesting tack that I have too much conscience for and too little ambition. My forte is really problem solving and I am most happy when I'm challenged. He loves this.

How are things going?

Take care and write.

Love,

Rachel

Rachel's Comments: Winter, Early 1977

I'm very touched at the opportunity to help the authors with their appendix, first because they've found value in something I've had to offer and secondly, because here I have the chance to make detailed commentary on a journey I took that most people rarely think about, and yet is quite human. We rarely are provided with the occasion to go back and make a "here and now" commentary on something that happened there and then.

I can remember in my own experience that people could only relate to small pieces of my existence, which was an ever present source of frustration. Now I find that there are things in the transition, as it becomes more remote in my past, that I can no longer relate to.

I met Suzanne and Wendy in February of 1975, and it was during the summer of 1972 that my struggle to repress that which was undeniable faltered and I acknowledged to myself that I was a transsexual. At the time I was a hard working graduate student in molecular biology in a southwestern university which was filled with some incredibly provincial people. I was very happily engaged to a woman and then things inside me began to surface. It should not have been such a surprise because I had been privately aware of these things all my life. I certainly did experience the classic phrase of the M-F-TS, "the very first thing I can remember as a child was wanting to be a girl."

During elementary school and junior high I never missed an opportunity to either disappear out into the woods and cross-dress or to do it when no one was at home. I kept my secret so well that my parents were completely unaware of this and when I finally told them of my plans and admitted my childhood activities they absolutely refused to believe it. This had to be my ultimate irony where when I needed to discuss these things with them, that my secret had been so well kept there was no way to prove it.

I remember that during the fourth grade years I was particularly feminine, playing with the girls, often wearing my shirts tied around my waist to symbolize a skirt. It was a happy period but frustrating because I didn't have full feminine privileges; I wasn't going to grow up and be a woman.

There was no one in my elementary school with the sophistication to realize the implications of my behavior and I don't know how far I could have gone with it. I do remember, however, that I gradually became aware that if I continued with the feminine behavior that some pretty bad things were going to "come down." No one ever said this to me, nor do I think it was recognized that a problem existed, I just remember a feeling that I began to get—to stop behaving like girls do and behave like boys do. Although Christine Jorgensen had come and gone from the public view at the time, I had never heard of her. I couldn't read at the time, and my parents never discussed her in front of me. So there seemed to be no alternatives but to grow up male. What pain, what a trap to be stuck in a body that was going to shape your existence and sort of carry you along with it whether you wanted to go or not. I felt like a honey bee that has used its sting; the life had been pulled out of me. This realization and the related decision was private. My teachers, of course, had no way of knowing this, and every time there was an odd number of girls forming a team for games or whatever, I was put with them, a happy and sad eventuality. How was I to compete in a male world if all I knew how to do was jump rope?

My secret cross-dressing continued on into high school. High school had its own set of more adult horrors. There was gym class where I was introduced to the concept of the "jock" or athletic supporter, which I'm happy to say I never used once. There were public showers, which I don't think anyone noticed that I never used once in five years. There were some things that were just too "male" for me to tolerate. These differences were differences that I kept well hidden, and I don't think anyone noticed at all. I can say this because if anyone had noticed I would have been a target for much derision and cruelty, and I never was.

I did become consumed by one sport and that was basketball which became a compulsive year-round sublimation. It was a good sport where there was no crushing body contact and, since I was medium height and very light weight and fast, I was rather proficient. It took me a long time to earn respect in sports. Since I had never played any real sport until high school, my motor skills lagged behind my classmates'. It seems that by my junior and senior years that these differences had disappeared in my one sport, and I could play well enough to be on the school team, which I did not do.

During undergrad school I lived at home for the first two years and whatever education I was getting was strictly academic. My social skills were notably lacking. With this in mind I decided to join a fraternity (a large national). It was not until I was twenty or twenty-one that I began dating and oddly enough was rather successful.

Sexual experiences with women followed. Although I had a good reputation I didn't find sex to be at all what people advertised it to be and explained it away by feeling that I had yet to find a really compatible partner, a feeling that continued for several years.

My senior year in college was a depressing one due to tiny finances and I found that the only thing that would lift the depression was to resume my cross-dressing, which continued into graduate school as I was really unable to discontinue it. Had anyone ever asked how I explained the behavior or how I classified it I would have said that I was a transvestite. But there was more than that and during my early years in graduate school I was becoming increasingly aware of it. I began going to the library and reading books on transsexuality. I must say that the contents certainly seemed weird to me then and even now as I look back at them. It seems that they are written in tones that suggest that the transactions therein had to have occurred under an eerie green light as strange and bizarre people went through some rather unusual rituals. It must have been the clinical tones (with the underlying implication that these people are sick) of the books that gave the texts this flavor. I had difficulty identifying with the people and their desperate struggles while at the same time there were strange and undeniable feelings surfacing in me that would soon equal the poor souls in the book. From one summer to the next I asked myself the question—Am I one of these people? It seemed not, for one thing thing my existence had certainly been punctuated by what appeared to be success in a "male role" even if it did feel most vacuous and empty. I remember uttering many male utterances and doing many things now that I would consider offensive and distasteful. I can only look back at the models I was supposed to conform to and wonder why.

I had a split awareness, not in the schizophrenic sense at all, but I know that except during my few most unaware years I did not perceive women as the other, the alien, the incomprehensible as most men do. I felt a genuine sameness under the skin. And I began to ache all over and deep inside when I acknowledged that, yes, although seemingly not "classical" (a figment of the imagination), I was a transsexual.

What to do about it. I looked genuinely male and behaved that way. I had the feeling that I would make a rather improbable woman, less than attractive and light years from any kind of ideal. It seemed then that my alternatives were either to live a male life of ineffable spiritual pain that permeated my entire inner existence, or I could become what I thought would be an externally grotesque, rather sad, caricature of a woman. It seemed to be a difficult decision. These decisions, I think, were paramount in the summer of 1972. It was during this year that I decided to discuss the issue with a close friend and thusly make a twenty-four year old privacy slightly public. The results of the conversation weren't as shattering as I had thought. The conversation turned out to be a marathon catharsis, and at least one person in the world shared the burden of my secret.

Very little happened in the following year that I can remember other than I began to take some BC pills for their estrogen content (something that I wouldn't recommend without a physician's supervision because many contain progestins which have androgenic effects).

Significant things did begin to occur the next summer, or in April, actually. I went to Dallas to see a friend who was a physician and who was very understanding and did a number of favors such as track down a pair of TS's for me to talk to. That was a weird experience in itself. One was in her sixties with a very deep voice, and I wondered at many of her self-delusions. The net effect verified many of the fears I had of my own self-potentials.

It was the year that I went on my perennial crash diet and lost 45 pounds in four months going from 170 to 125. This brought about a happy state of affairs as I felt much better about my body. It was the year that I contacted Gay Liberation to find if there were any known transsexuals in town to talk to. There was one with whom I spent a very happy evening in a funeral parlor (they chose the location—I didn't). She was very encouraging and I saw that, yes, there was such a thing as an attractive transsexual. She was a hair dresser with a high school education and clung to rather traditional definitions of what femininity was, and as it turned out we had little to share intellectually. She couldn't fathom university life, much less graduate school.

I made a conscious decision to stay away from gay society. It's strange but I felt that the average gay had an equally dim awareness, when compared to heterosexuals, of the transsexual phenomenon, and had some rather contaminated expectations of me from their experience with cross-dressers who are frequently encountered in the gay world. I did not want to have to expend energy bucking these gradients of expectation nor did I want to acquire any of these mannerisms as I felt that they were only a parody of womanhood. There is much misogynism in the gay world, and it is generally a very male world and as such held little for me.

I did befriend a gay male however, who because of his active role in the field of gay awareness was also a significant and appreciated person in my life. I'll never forget the night that I, in becoming Rachel, took my first walk around the block with him. Later in the summer he took me to my first party which was at least slightly magic. It was not without cost for him because his friends were surprised to see him with a woman and there were jokes about his being a latent heterosexual.

There were internal or "head changes" that were equally important as the cosmetic changes that were taking place. I began to think in terms of what and who I wanted to be and as such, how was I to get from where I was to be this person mentally. Here words begin to fail because it is so difficult to describe how one takes oneself apart, in terms of her basic assumptions that make the foundation for all that the person is and says and does. I had to remold my most molecular assumptions. I pictured all of these little assumptions as little building blocks that make up our automatic and reflexive behaviors. It was my task to take each one of these building blocks out of the foundation, examine it in the light of who I wanted to be, internally modifying it to work the way I wanted it to work, and put it back into the foundation, only to pull out another block and do

the whole thing over. This is as close as I can get to putting the
process on paper. During the process I really believe I became
acultural almost, because I examined some cultural assumptions we
make and for some reason remember that I became particularly
critical of the work ethic and product-oriented culture we are
immersed in. What an unusual by-product.

So there were personality changes as well as physical changes.
I did my own electrolysis to remove my beard. It seems that I did
a very good job as I have no more facial hair and there
is no scarring, pits, or discoloration leaving only a soft, smooth face.

This was the time that I began to venture out in public in my
identity of Rachel. Things did seem brighter and the air did seem
lighter as Morris proclaimed, but I knew about the power of
suggestion. I continued to grow.

There is no doubt that there were external changes becoming
apparent in the person people knew as Paul. There were rumors
that I was dying of cancer when I lost the weight. There were
awkward moments such as when a technician rushed into the lab
and was disappointed to find that it was I who had walked into the
lab rather than "a new girl."

Most of all I can remember the pain and the agony. Momentary
satisfactions of going out and being Rachel were too episodic
and far apart. Perhaps one of the cruelest things, and here again
my words fail, is that the transsexual is constantly immersed in the
world where that which she wants most is constantly around her
and interacting with her. At times it seemed so extraordinary how
the women around me could be so very unaware of themselves and
of their womanhood. Womanhood seemed such a privilege. No one,
I think, unless they have been through it can understand the
frustration. Now the frustration has completely faded and I'm
only glad that I remember it as I'm writing so I can put it down here
on paper. I don't think I did a particularly good job. At the same
time I find that it is ever easier to take myself for granted in my
day-to-day life and it must be that much easier for the rest of
womankind to do so in that they have never known any other
gender or sex role.

I think I have included the necessary biographical data to bring
the reader up to date to the point where I met Suzanne and Wendy
and began to write to them.

When I met Wendy and Suzanne, it was a time of great uncertainty
of how the world was going to respond to me in my everyday
life. Apparently I was right at the point where I was giving no
gender cues or better yet, I was a strange mixture of both. A way to
look at it would be that I had reached the androgynous ideal a
long time before the world was ready for it. I had a unique
opportunity to see what the world was like when its inhabitants

could not tell what sex I was. There was an equiprobability that when I would approach a stranger in public to buy a toothbrush or book that I would be addressed as sir or ma'am. My clothing was uniformly unisex at the time. They weren't the garb associated with any alternate life style. Frequently, at work, people would come up and ask me where I got those pants or that "shirt." The men would say, "wow, I really like those clothes but haven't been able to find any like it, where did you get them?" I would reply, "in some of the campus stores," while neglecting to tell them, "not in the men's department." It's also interesting to note that once the people, say at work, had known me, they saw nothing really unusual about my behavior even as naive people were perceiving me as a woman. A perfect example was one day at lunch while on a trip to Washington: Many of us were seated at a table, supposedly all males, when a waiter came up and presented me with a customary rose "for the lady." That had to be one of my most embarrassing moments. There was also the time I went in to the store to buy an ice cream cone and the waitress looked up and said, "Can I help you ma'am . . . . ah sir . . . . ah ma'am . . . . ah sir." As she continued to flip-flop her face became more panic stricken as she found herself facing true ambiguity. She finally just stopped using any gender-related words, a technique I saw frequently. These events all came before the transition.

In part I think my answer to the question "How do you know that you are a woman?" [second letter] was partially an evasion. Please note that these answers were written pretransitionally. Possibly, it was premature for me to answer some of these questions and possibly not. They are at least valuable in contrast. My hiding behind epistemology was philosophically consistent, so I can only answer the question experientially and the answer is quite simply stated. When I am out sitting down at a table in a discussion with a group of women I do not feel, or am I aware at all, that there is any difference between us (unless the topic of discussion is on having periods). I do feel that I am different from men. These experiences, derived from settling into the role and being much more comfortable, are more recent than I was able to offer previously.

There is also a newly evolved set of rules for telling someone. The new rule is—if at all possible—don't. Previously when I was less secure in my role there was a conscious striving to establish necessary intimacy to tell someone about my past. This was self-protective so I wouldn't have to go through any trauma in case of discovery. There was also the need to talk about it. Later as I became more comfortable this was no longer necessary. Now my strongest wish is to be just ordinary and not have my past known at all. Here in the department in school there is a most effective grapevine which includes students, faculty, and secretaries who have deprived me of the privilege of making disclosures to those people that I see fit. It seems to me that this process strips me of a valuable personal right, but it is a sad reality of life. Those relationships that are spared this treatment are among my most treasured. I long to be seen as just an ordinary woman. I have a widespread academic reputation on campus, and at times it's hard to tell if my name is known because of my achievements or transition. The phrase "I've heard a lot about you" is scary to me because of the possibility that it has more than one meaning. At the same time I have learned to take these things in stride and assume that these things will evaporate after I have graduated and relocated.

The way that I tell people when it's necessary varies with the person. At times I start out by saying that I wasn't born a lady. Media coverage has made it easier. I've considered saying that Renee Richards and I have more in common than tennis. Actually the grapevine takes care of most of it for me and acquaintances who are interested in gaining insight into the phenomenon ask me about it at times. It does create a class of people at school who "may know" but I'm not sure. If they are closely connected with the biology department experience has shown me that I should assume they do. This doesn't always work out though, as I have found out that people who have worked next to me for years, meeting me just after the transition have not known; so there are exceptions.

I now wear a wide range of styles. It's rare that I ever look like Mary Tyler Moore. There are times that I dress smartly and there are times that I dress in a unisex fashion. Just recently I bought a pair of leather boots that are in the fashionable western style and my clothes need no longer be strictly feminine in the traditional sense. I remember recently that I was in the Colorado mountains on a hiking/skiing trip where there is only one way to dress. I was particularly happy with my appearance which I thought was rather androgynous with boots, several sweaters, and several pairs of pants and was considering the possibility of a bulky appearance and was amazed when a friend (naive) said, "Rachel, you get the *Seventeen* magazine award of the day."

A very important parallel can be made to the person who grew up very obese and sometime after adolescence loses a significant amount of weight. Although the weight is gone and the clothes worn are many sizes smaller, the individual's self-concept takes a much longer time to "catch up" with the external realities. I certainly experienced this phenomenon where I was buying clothes that were too large. Over the years I have come down from a size 13 to a comfortable 9.

I'm 5′9″ and weigh 128, which is rather thin. When people ask me
how much I weigh they are surprised by my answer. Their response is
that, "I can't believe you weigh that much, you certainly don't look like
you do." I will diet much sooner than people think is necessary even
though I have the kind of frame that will not show an extra 10 pounds.

It hasn't been until lately when I've found that some really attractive
women friends wear clothes larger than mine, have shoulders wider
than mine, that my negative feelings about my frame have begun
to fade away. The basis for these things has to be the old memory
of looking over a shoulder that was much larger and much more
muscle bound and hating myself. It's taken awhile for those feelings
to dissipate.

My return to Houston after New York was most significant. I had
had a joyous week in New York. I liked the new me and the thought
of returning to Houston to a male existence was untenable. It
would be asking too much. It was getting very close to time
to make the switch.

In a way I had prepared things well. I had let people know
discretely, knowing that the word would get out like wildfire. I would
not have to tell many people; things would be rather obvious. It
was a crucial depressing time. I was claiming what was mine but the
emotional expenses were tremendous.

I made the request to lab personnel about the name and gender
pronoun change and there was a tremendous amount of variability in
people's response. I must say they all tried very concertedly. There
were inevitable slip-ups. There were awkward very tense moments.
Simple mechanical operations become difficult. Outside people would
make professional calls into the lab for Paul. What were lab
personnel to do? Yell for Rachel or Paul? How was I to answer the
phone? Pain . . . embarrassment. But we all tried and ever so slowly
Rachel became more and more of a reality. One of my most effective
tools was a confrontive behavior modification approach. When
someone would yell for Paul I would not respond until I heard a yell
for Rachel. When in conversation someone referred to Paul I simply
looked at them squarely and asked sharply, "who?" No one but me
will ever understand or appreciate how painful that process was. My
advisor tried and seemed to have difficulty making the transition,
showing a definite lag. From conversations with others I heard that he
was inconsistent in his use of names and gender pronouns when I
was not around. This was a style I saw from time to time which I
referred to as "not doing homework," and as such was something
that I couldn't directly operate on. Time was needed for complete
healing. The process seemed to take a few months before everything
settled out.

A quite different kind of encounter, contrasted to lab personnel, was encountering acquaintances, near and distant. These were people who I knew at a distance. They were perhaps the most surprised and awkward. But some of them became good friends and others just shook their heads and dropped out of my life's picture completely.

Needless to say that this was radically affecting the relationship between Vivian and myself. Our relationship in the past was not sexual but very loving and very affectionate. We have since realized perhaps that we had played special unique parts in each other's life, that we'll never find anyone for whom we'll care about as much as we cared about each other. But at the time things were more than strained. She did have her sexual needs that were going completely unsatisfied. She really tried to stay with me far longer than she should have for both of our own good. But it was very soon after this that she left. Amidst all of the other things I had to deal with, I would soon have to deal with it all alone.

I thought I would have to leave Houston before I could make a realistic change. Time has shown that this is not true with *qualifications*. After two years, life is rather simple and routine in the same place and in the same lab. The qualifications are two. The first is that damned grapevine and the other is myself. I find that to new acquaintances my past makes no difference. The report is rather uniform that they can't imagine me as a male. Those who have asked to see pictures of me in the past simply shake their heads and acknowledge that they would never recognize me as the person in the picture. My face does seem to look almost entirely different, and there is something seemingly very different about my cheekbones seeming higher or more prominent. This may be because of the weight loss. I'm not sure.

My reality is that even though it makes no difference to new friends and acquaintances, their knowledge does make a difference to me. I don't feel quite as good around people who "know" as I do around people who don't. I know that a psychologist would say that the dichotomy is artificial and the distinction is in my own head. There seems to be some truth to this as people seem to forget completely, but it's harder for me. These things are a little painful to talk about but they're necessary for the record. The difference is that it's more pleasant for someone to make a completely "female" set of assumptions about me than a partial set. By this I am specifically referring to questions about my past, etc. Actually when people learn of my past they tend to forget it. It's me who has the hard time forgetting. It's more pleasant for someone to ask me about didn't I love horses when I was a little girl, etc. That's about the most concrete example I can generate immediately. Just let the statement ride intuitively; the relationship with those people who don't know feels better and freer. The air seems fresher to me. I would say that there is no difference in my behavior between the two populations.

There are several humorous stories about events that occurred after my name was legally changed. In May I decided to go to a department store and get my credit card changed. Remember, at this point I am now legally Rachel, supported by a court order specifying that Paul Wright (she) is now and forevermore Rachel. The conversation went like this:

Me: "Good afternoon, I'd like to have my credit card and name of my account changed."

Clerk: "Fine. My name is Mrs. Givens and I'll be happy to help you."

Me: "I've received a sex reassignment and I have the legal documentation."

My voice must have dropped in volume as I said this because she did not hear it, or did not want to hear it.

Clerk: "May I see your card, Dear?"

I hand the card to her and watch a perplexed look cross her face.

Clerk: "Is this your father's card, honey?"

Me: "No."

Clerk: "Are you married? Is it your husband's?"

Me: "No, it's mine and I want the name changed."

Clerk (now obviously confused): "Your name was Paul Wright?"

Me: "It was."

Clerk: "Oh you poor dear. No wonder you want your name changed! Did your mommy really name you Paul?"

Me: "I'm afraid so."

Clerk: "Just a moment, let me get your records."

She disappeared into a door into an inner office and reappears studying my portfolio with a more perplexed look on her face.

Clerk: "I don't understand Miss, this record says male on it."

Me: "That was more or less true at one time."

Clerk (now pale with a sick look on her face): "Just a moment, let me talk to the manager."

She disappears suddenly into the inner office and after a brief interlude suddenly people start leaving the office and making mass exoduses toward the bathroom which conveniently is on the ante room where I am. Others seeing that the bathroom was full just peeked out of the door. There were many sets of eyes upon me and I felt rather mortified. The clerk approaches with a manufactured smile and says, "Won't you have a seat," and begins to pour over my record.

The transaction was completed and I received my card promptly in the mail. But I still had not learned my lesson and besides really had to make a public appearance to get my driver's license changed. This was much more dangerous as my *legal* status at this point was very nebulous and poorly defined, putting me at the mercy of the people at the motor vehicle division. I remembered that they all carried guns and felt a little alarmed. Phil, aware of the possibility that very bad things could happen, offered to go with me.

When we arrived the division was set up with three desks numbered 1, 2, and 3, respectively, in large three-foot numbers. There was a moderate amount of activity at each desk. Anticipating the potential for chaos I tried to wait until no one was at desk 1 before I approached it but a guard blankly yelled, "Next step up—Don't hold up the line." Suddenly it was my turn in a crowd of people. Phil was in the background watching. It was time for a renewal luckily. The interaction went this way:

Policewoman: "What's the nature of your business?"

Me: "Renewal and name change."

I had no idea what they were going to require for proof of change of sex.

PW: "There is a form for a married woman changing her name."

Me: "I didn't get married; I'm just changing my name."

I showed her the court order.

PW: "Fine."

Me: "I'd also like to change the address and the sex."

PW: "Fine."

It seemed she was going to fall asleep as I watched her write on the top of my application for renewal:

"Change Name"
"Change Address"
"Change Sex."

PW: "Just move on to the next desk, please."

Phil told me that at that point our stoical policewoman #1 turned sunset red from head to toe. My job now was to carry the paperwork to the remaining two desks where there was no necessity to show the court order.

Policewoman #2 (cursorily looking over the changes needed for the license): "Let's see, Change name—OK, Change address—OK, and . . . Change sex." *She stopped and thought for a second and looked at me.*

"Gee. The division of motor vehicles really messed up this license. Wrong name, address, and sex."

She stamped the application.

PW #2: "Take this to desk 3."

As I left Phil overheard Policewoman #2 say to the now beet-red #1: "I've never seen so many mistakes on one license."

PW #1: "You dummy . . . . That's one of them transsexuals."

PW #2 (blinks): "Oh."

Nothing eventful happened at desk #3.

Had anyone asked, "whom do you think will make the most bizarre unempathetic response to your transition?" I would have replied the secretarial pool in the departmental office. I was correct as I found out later. They vacillated between face-to-face empathy and a horrored acceptance. Later, as the years passed I think time cured much and I became rather ordinary to a degree. One thing was humorous, though. I couldn't leave town for any amount of time without rumors floating to the effect that "the surgery" was at hand. All this was quite predictable.

Our department head, a rather rigid ex-naval officer, had always disliked me. My advisor once told me that genuine talent threatened him. With my transition he refused to use feminine gender pronouns in relation to me. The secretarial pool and students were supportive enough to discourage this, an act of untold courage for which I will eternally be grateful. However, even a year later when he absolutely had to speak of my accomplishments to strangers, as he advertised the department, he would refer to me as "he" and use my old name.

Looking back on the events I'd have to say that this was certainly the most uncomfortable time of the transition, and later things *concerning the transition* just kept getting easier and easier.

In my eighth letter there are references concerning my first trip to the psychiatrist with whom I would be working until surgery. I would like to say that I got to know my therapist and have the highest respect for him. He is a warm, competent, and intelligent human being who treated me with the kind of concern that I needed. I'll always be grateful to him and will list him as a very special friend. He never attempted to overwhelm me with what he knew, and freely admitted what he didn't know, which to me is one of the highest virtues. It seems to me that he had a "touch of Zen" philosophy to him, calmly accepting the fact that there are some things we can never know and that some problems have no answers. A significant set of attitudes, because it gave him some gracious qualities, as he acknowledged his own humanness. He is not wise but shall be. He reminds me of the saying ,"Knowledge comes and wisdom follows."

He has his knowledge and his wisdom is coming. Suffice it to say that no one was comfortable on my first visits. But it is a privilege that we all understand this now, and have resolved it.

Things were beginning to move along at this point.

The reader will notice that priorities are changing. Where some verification of how I am coming across is still important, I seem to be more concerned with school and how to get money for surgery; emphases are changing and my world is beginning to solidify.

I feel embarrassed about what I said about camping in letter 9. During this period a concern was, gee what about my past and childhood. Experientially and internally there is a disjointed relationship between what I was expected to be as a child and what I am and who I am for that matter. During these months I became concerned about that. I can live with the disjuncture, but I was wondering how to communicate in a nonrevealing way about my past to other people. It was in this passage where I was reality testing and wanted to see the phrase, "when 1 was a little girl" in print in the letter. It didn't feel honest then, it doesn't feel honest now, and I've found that it isn't necessary for me to say things like that, so I don't. As far as I know this is the only example of such a reference that I've ever written. In conversation it's sufficient to say things like "when I was little" or "when I was young" the following things happened . . . .

On the whole my final letters are spent pondering professional and financial things. It's notable that gender transition is mentioned but only in terms of how to go about raising money for surgery and how to get rid of the company. Overall these are the kind of musings that all graduate students pondering the job market go through. In short it seem quite normal.

In conclusion, it seems to me that even with my tendencies toward abbreviation that after so many pages that there are still some loose ends left unanswered, so it seems creative for me to make up a list of questions that I would ask a transsexual and answer them myself. So I shall.

1. *Am I "happy"? If so, in what ways?*

A. I like myself more than I used to. I like my body and am pleased with the person I have become. It was an effort that took active striving and somehow through trial and error I have arrived at a place that seems to be fulfilling.

2. *Do you miss anything from your past?*

A. The question once again begs a dichotomy that there are highly differentiated realms belonging to males and females and that there are things or gender-related activities that I no longer participate in. It's not true. One reason I suppose might be because my past was sufficiently pan-sexual that I'm not doing different things, I'm doing things differently. It for me is a question of change of styles more than anything else. I think that people describing my behavior would pretty much agree.

3. *What difference do you see in the person that you are and the person that you expected to be going into the transition?*

A. I'm more alive and spontaneous. I'm surprised that people use the word sophisticated in describing me. I also don't see myself as being a "caricature" as I expected at the very onset. I'm more attractive than I thought I would be and more real.

4. *In terms of the "process" you went through, were there many surprises?*

A. Yes and no. There were no real surprises other than the fact that I perceive as much continuity as I do. I didn't leave the department at school or Houston, which in itself makes things seem very continuous.

5. *How different is your life?*

A. It's different and it's not different. As I said before, the changes are changes of style rather than areas.

I would say that I'm more maternal, more into human relations, perhaps more patient. But here it is also hard to separate the effects of the transition and plain maturation and growing up. It's really very hard to say what processes are responsible for what changes. Perhaps I'm underplaying the changes more than I want to.

I don't know that I have been at all successful, in putting the true width and depth of what I have felt as I have experienced these things. The reader will have to be the final judge. I'm too close to the topics at hand.

Postscript: Letter from Rachel, 1977, post-surgery

I am *very happy.* At times I wake up at night and remember that
everything has been taken care of and smile to myself and roll over,
not quite sure that I'm not faintly luminescent. . . . My doctor
required mammoplasty. Where I was a 32B I am now a 32C.
It's a little strange but I feel more adequate.

The worst time I had was with urination and defecation. It took
a lot of time to get me off the catheters. But now it seems like all
my imputs and outputs are working fine.

I've learned alot about my body and how to keep it going.

I've got several funny stories to tell. Herr Doctors lost several
debates. It was so much fun. They're not used to it.

For once I'll feel like I'm as good as you are.
(That's within me—nothing you've done).

Love,

Rachel

AN ANALYSIS OF
RACHEL'S LETTERS
AND COMMENTS

We have been in communication with Rachel from a period in
which she lived as a male through a "transition" period to the present when she is a female. During the first period of our correspondence, between our meeting her (as Paul) in the winter and her visit
with us (as Rachal) in the spring, we needed to make an effort to
think of her as female. We had never interacted with her as Rachel
and did not know whether the femaleness that she had been creating
in her letters would be enough, combined with a more deliberate
female physical appearance, to cause us to see her as female. The
"work" with which we approached her gender prior to her visit was,
for the most part, absent once we saw her. Although we slipped and
called her "Paul" a couple of times, there was, on the whole, little
difficulty in thinking of her and relating to her woman-to-woman
(whatever that means). In Rachel's later letters and visits the reality
of Paul dissolved. The salience of her femaleness in the letters
(heightened by such practices as closing "in sisterhood") reinforced
the femaleness of her presentation when we were together and vice
versa.

We included a full range of Rachel's writing in order to give the reader a broader sense of who she is and how she expresses herself. In particular, the reader, in seeing that what much of Rachel wrote could have been written by any woman, should gain some appreciation for how a sense of femaleness is accomplished by filtering material through a female gender attribution. The tone is experienced as "feminine" and the content is "made sense of" because the letters are seen as female authored.

There is a second and more important reason why we included material about all aspects of Rachel's life. What is most compelling about her letters and comments is that over time her preoccupation with transsexualism is replaced by other interests and concerns. Her gender has become an integrated feature of her life as it is for all women. No longer is she preoccupied with being seen as a woman, but she is concerned now with what kind of woman she should spend her life being. She has the kind of concerns we can readily associate with any construction of a "normal" female: What type of clothing will express her personal style and philosophy? What sexual orientation should she choose? What kind of work will make her happy? She gravitates from a plan to give up her technical work because it reflects an earlier (male) self to integrating those stereotypically "male" skills into a coherent female self. She now apparently enjoys that work.

Following her transition, as her gender became more natural, she made fewer and fewer references in her letters and phone calls to transsexualism. There are minimal references to her being a transsexual in the commentary she wrote for this book. Rachel's comments convey a strong sense that her past seems very remote to her and is difficult for her to identify with. While this is not an uncommon experience, even for those who do not have an extraordinary history, it is in this particular case suggestive. A distancing of herself from her past coupled with a new "rule" not to tell people about it, indicates that she is succeeding in constructing a sense of "natural" femaleness not only for others, but for herself as well.

Rachel has every reason to want to dissolve the salience of her transsexualism for us and others. To ask whether her preoccupation with transsexualism is as slight as her letters would lead us to believe, is legitimate, but is relevant only for concerns about psychodynamics, not for concerns about social construction. It cannot be denied, though, that the concerns that Rachel *does* verbalize are the kind that presume no doubt about what gender one is.

Like a good ethnomethodologist, Rachel understands that what people look for as discrediting or validating information (e.g., how feminine she is) are actually not what they use for deciding her gender, but instead constitute "good reasons" for the gender attribution.

In addition, there is evidence in her letters and commentary of how people construct gender to be invariant. There were a number of occasions where people were clearly trying to make sense out of Rachel as she changed from Paul. Making sense did not usually mean acknowledging her gender transformation. In fact, that was the last thing people did; their first method was to make sense out of contradictory information in any other possible way. She looked different because she had cancer or because she had lost a great deal of weight; she wanted her credit cards and driver's license changed because a clerical error had been made.

Unlike Agnes who was defensively adamant that Garfinkel see her as always having been female and not misunderstand the things she told him (not interpret her past as being the past of a male), Rachel allows us to see how she is constructing gender at the same time that she credibly displays it to us. She appears to know that her credibility is not dependent on hiding the construction, and is very clear in stating that she "had once been a male" and is now female. She can admit that to say "when I was a little girl" is dishonest, and unnecessary. The language she uses does not hedge the fact that she underwent a radical transformation: "(being) two people," "becoming me," "my change." Typical transsexual jargon like "I was always a woman" is absent from Rachel's letters. Although she would admit to always having felt like a woman, she differentiates gender identity from gender attribution and recognizes that a believable gender presentation does not depend on a denial of its evolution. She also is cognizant that it *is* an evolution. (Of course, the comparison between Agnes and Rachel is not really fair. Agnes made her transition during a more "conservative" era, and we are not physicians whom Rachel had to convince of always having been a woman in order to get surgery.)

Rachel is aware of the interaction between display and attribution in determining whether she is *really* (in a social sense) a woman or a man. There is no question that Rachel's surgery makes her feel more authentic, but all along she was able to see that genitals would also be important proof for others (particularly others who knew her as Paul) of her essential femaleness.

There are a number of examples in the letters which show the important role other people played in creating the legitimacy of the female gender for Rachel. The woman at the party who perceived

Rachel as a competitor for her man, the woman who asked to borrow a tampon, the woman who warned Rachel about tearing her nylons, the man in the hardware store who commented on her automotive interests—all of these people, knowing nothing about Rachel's past, helped create the reality of her gender by confirming its credibility through a gender attribution.

The behavior of those people who knew Rachel as Paul (and had to handle her change) illustrates another important point. What comes across in the letters is the relative ease with which they seemed to respond to Rachel as female. We only have Rachel's perception of their treatment of her, but this, in itself, is important since it seems clear that her perception of the positive feedback she got from both strangers and prior associates (even before she was deliberately presenting herself as Rachel) was crucial in instigating, maintaining, and even at points accelerating the rate of transition. It was the continual, pervasive *being* of Rachel in everyday interactions which created her femaleness, not just the concrete actions she had to take to change her legal identity: getting her credit cards and name changed, seeing doctors and preparing for surgery. There is much in Rachel's letters which reveals her understanding of this.

In looking over her past, Rachel is now able to discern that not every situation was conflict free, not everyone around her gave her unequivocal treatment as a "real" woman. She can see this now because she shares the natural attitude and for her as for all members who treat gender as a natural fact, constant reinforcement of one's "real" gender is not necessary (and is potentially insulting). Gender may now be taken for granted as something that exists independently of any concrete interaction.

BIBLIOGRAPHY _____

Amdur, N. E. German women's success stirs U.S. anger. *New York Times,* August 1, 1976, Section 5, p. 3.

Angelino, H., and Shedd, C. L. A note on berdache. *American Anthropologist,* 1955, **57**, 121–126.

Asch, S. E. Forming impressions of personality. *Journal of Abnormal and Social Psychology,* 1946, **41**, 258–290.

Bardwick, J. *The Psychology of Women.* New York: Harper and Row, 1971.

Barker-Benfield, B. The spermatic economy: A nineteenth century view of sexuality. *Feminist Studies,* 1972, **1**, 45–74.

Beck, F., Moffat, D. B., and Lloyd, J. B. *Human Embryology and Genetics.* Oxford: Blackwell Scientific Publications, 1973.

Bem, S. The measurement of psychological androgyny, *Journal of Consulting and Clinical Psychology,* 1974, **42**, 153–162.

Bem, S. Probing the promise of androgyny. *In* J. Sherman and F. Denmark (Eds.), *The Psychology of Women: Future Directions in Research.* New York: Psychological Dimensions, 1978.

Benedict, R. *Patterns of Culture.* Boston: Houghton-Mifflin, 1934.

Benjamin, H. *The Transsexual Phenomenon.* New York: Julian Press, 1966.

Birdwhistell, R. Masculinity and femininity as display. *In* R. Birdwhistell, *Kinesics and Context.* Philadelphia: University of Pennsylvania Press, 1970.

Block, J. Another look at sex differentiation in the socialization behaviors of mothers and fathers. *In* J. Sherman and F. Denmark (Eds.), *The Psychology of Women: Future Directions in Research.* New York: Psychological Dimensions, 1978.

Bogdan, R. (Ed.). *On Being Different: The Autobiography of Jane Fry.* New York: Wiley-Interscience, 1974.

Borgoras, W. *The Chukchee Religion.* Memoirs of the American Museum of Natural History. Vol. XI. Leiden: E. J. Brill (Ed. Franz Boas), 1907.

Botella Llusia, Jose. *Endocrinology of Women* (E. A. Moscovic, trans.). Philadelphia: Saunders, 1973.

Bronfenbrenner, U. The study of identification through interpersonal perception. *In* R. Tagiuri and L. Petrullo (Eds.), *Person Perception and Interpersonal Behavior.* Stanford, California: Stanford University Press, 1958.

217

Broverman, D. M., Klaiber, E. L., Kobayashi, Y., and Vogel, W. Roles of activation and inhibition in sex differences in cognitive abilities. *Psychological Review*, 1968, **75**, 23–50.

Broverman, I., Broverman, D., Clarkson, F., Rosenkrantz, P., and Vogel, S. Sex role stereotypes: A current appraisal. *Journal of Social Issues*, 1972, **28**, 59–78.

Castenada, C. *The Teachings of Don Juan*. Berkeley: University of California Press, 1968.

Churchill, L. *The Importance of Questioning*. Unpublished manuscript, 1969 (Graduate School and University Center, City University of New York).

Colley, T. The nature and origin of psychological sexual identity. *Psychological Review*, 1959, **66**, 165–177.

Crawly, E. *The Mystic Rose*. New York: Meridian Books, 1960.

Dalton, K. *The Premenstrual Syndrome*. Springfield, Ill.: Charles C. Thomas, 1964.

D'Andrade, R. G. Sex differences and cultural institutions: *In* E. Maccoby (Ed.), *The Development of Sex Differences*. Stanford: Stanford University Press, 1966.

Davenport, W. Sexual patterns and their regulation in a society of the Southwest Pacific. *In* F. Beach (Ed.), *Sex and Behavior*. New York: Wiley, 1965.

Deaux, K. *The Behavior of Women and Men*. Monterey: Brooks-Cole, 1976.

Deaux, K., and Enswiller, T. Explanations of successful performance on sex-linked tasks: What's skill for the male is luck for the female. *Journal of Personality and Social Psychology*, 1973, **29**, 80–85.

De Mause, L. (Ed.), *The History of Childhood*. New York: Harper Torchbooks, 1975.

Denig, E. T. Of the Crow nation. *In Five Indian Tribes of the Upper Missouri*. Norman: University of Oklahoma Press, 1961.

Devereux, G. Institutionalized homosexuality of the Mohave Indians. *General Biology*, 1937, **9**, 498–527.

Devereux, G. *From Anxiety to Method in the Behavioral Sciences*. New York: Humanities Press, 1967.

Dimen-Schein, M. *The Anthropological Imagination*. New York: McGraw-Hill, 1977.

Douglas, J. Understanding everyday life. *In* J. Douglas (Ed.), *Understanding Everyday Life*. Chicago: Aldine, 1970.

Dworkin, A. *Woman Hating*. New York: Dutton, 1974.

East German women's success stirs U.S. anger. *New York Times*, August 1, 1976, pp. 3, 5.

Edgerton, R. B. Pokot intersexuality: An East African example of the resolution of sexual incongruity. *American Anthropologist*, 1964, **66**, 1288–1299.

Ehrenreich, B., and English, D. *Complaints and Disorders: The Sexual Politics of Sickness.* Glass Mountain Pamphlet No. 2, The Feminist Press, Old Westbury, 1973.

Erikson Educational Foundation. *Guidelines for Transsexuals.* Baton Rouge, Louisiana, 1974.

Erikson Educational Foundation. *Counseling the Transsexual.* Baton Rouge, Louisiana, n.d.

Evans, G. "The older the sperm . . ." Ms., January 1976, **14**: 7, 48–49.

Feinbloom, D. *Transvestites and Transsexuals: Mixed Views.* New York: Delacorte, 1976.

Forgey, D. O. The institution of berdache among the North American Plains Indians. *Journal of Sex Research,* 1975, **11**, 1–15.

Frank, R. *The Female Sex Hormone.* Springfield, Ill.: Charles C. Thomas, 1929.

Freud, S. Some psychical consequences of the anatomical distinctions between the sexes. *Standard Edition,* London: Hogarth Press, 1925. Vol. 19.

Friedman, R., Richart, R., and Vande Wiele, R. (Eds.). *Sex Differences in Behavior.* New York: Wiley, 1974.

Frisch, R., and McArthur, J. Menstrual cycles: Fatness as a determinant of minimum body weight for height necessary for their maintenance or onset. *Science,* 1974, **185**, 949–951.

Garfinkel, H. *Studies in Ethnomethodology.* Englewood Cliffs, N.J.: Prentice-Hall, 1967.

Garfinkel, H. *In* R. C. Hill and K. S. Crittenden (Eds.), *The Purdue Symposium on Ethnomethodology.* Monograph 1, Institute for the study of social change, Purdue University, 1968.

Garfinkel, H. and Sacks, H. On formal structures of practical actions. *In* J. C. McKinney and E. Tiryakian (Eds.), *Theoretical Sociology: Perspectives and Developments.* New York: Appleton-Century-Crofts, 1970.

Goffman, E. *Stigma: Notes on the Management of Spoiled Identity.* Englewood Cliffs, N.J.: Prentice-Hall, 1963.

Goy, R., and Goldfoot, D. Neuroendocrinology: Animal models and problems of human sexuality. *Archives of Sexual Behavior,* 1975, **4**, 405–420.

Green, R. *Sexual Identity Conflict in Children and Adults.* New York: Basic, 1974.

Hanley, D. Personal communication, March 12, 1976.

Hassrick, R. B. *The Sioux.* Norman: University of Oklahoma Press, 1964.

Hastorf, A., and Cantril, H. They saw a game. *Journal of Abnormal and Social Psychology,* 1954, **49**, 129–134.

Haviland, J. M. *Sex-Related Pragmatics in Infants' Nonverbal Communication.* Paper presented at the annual meeting of the Eastern Psychological Association, New York, 1976.

Heilbrun, A. B. Parent identification and filial sex-role behavior: The importance of biological context. *In* J. Cole and R. Dienstbier (Eds.), *Nebraska Symposium on Motivation.* Lincoln: University of Nebraska Press, 1973.

Heiman, E. M., and Cao Van Lê. Transsexulism in Vietnam. *Archives of Sexual Behavior,* 1975, **4**, 89–95.

Herschberger, R. *Adam's Rib.* New York: Harper and Row, 1970.

Hill, W. W. The status of the hermaphrodite and transvestite in Navaho culture. *American Anthropologist,* 1935, **37**, 273–79.

Hill, W. W. Note on the Pima berdache. *American Anthropologist,* 1938, **40**, 338–340.

Hill, W. W. *Navaho Humor.* Menasha: Banta, 1943.

Hoebel, E. A. *The Cheyennes: Indians of the Western Plains.* New York: Holt, 1960.

Hollingworth, L. S. *Functional Periodicity: An Experimental Study of Mental and Motor Abilities of Women during Menstruation.* New York: Teachers College, 1914.

Honigmann, J. J. *The Kaska Indians: An Ethnographic Reconstruction.* New Haven: Yale University Press, 1954.

Horney, K. The flight from womanhood. *International Journal of Psychoanalysis,* 1926, **7**, 324–339.

Husserl, E. *Ideas.* New York: Humanities Press, 1931.

Hutt, C. *Males and Females.* Baltimore: Penguin, 1972.

Imperato-McGinley, J., Guerro, T., Gautier, T., and Peterson, R. Steroid 5 α-reductase deficiency in man: An inherited form of male pseudohermaphroditism. *Science,* 1974, **186**, 1213–1215.

Jones, E., Kanouse, A., Kelley, H., Nisbett, R., Valins, S., and Weiner, B. *Attribution: Perceiving the Causes of Behavior.* Morristown, New Jersey: General Learning Press, 1971.

Kando, T. *Sex Change: The Achievement of Gender Identity among Feminized Transsexuals.* Springfield, Ill.: Charles C. Thomas, 1973.

Karlen, A. *Sexuality and Homosexuality.* New York: Norton, 1971.

Katcher, A. The discrimination of sex differences by young children. *Journal of Genetic Psychology,* 1955, **87**, 131–143.

Key, M. R. *Male/Female Language.* Metuchen, N.J.: Scarecrow Press, 1975.

Kluckhohn, C. As an anthropologist views it. *In* A. Deutch (Ed.), *Sex Habits of American men: A Symposium on the Kinsey Report.* New York: Prentice-Hall, 1948.

Koeske, R. *"Premenstrual Tension"* as an Explanation of Female Hostility.

Paper delivered at the 83rd annual convention of the American Psychological Association, Chicago, 1975.

Koeske, R., and Koeske, G. An attributional approach to moods and the menstrual cycle. *Journal of Personality and Social Psychology*, 1975, **31**, 473–478.

Kohlberg, L. A cognitive-developmental analysis of children's sex-role concepts and attitudes. *In* E. Maccoby (Ed.), *The Development of Sex Differences*. Stanford: Stanford University, 1966.

Kohlberg, L. and Ullian, D. Stages in the development of psychosexual concepts and attitudes. *In* R. Friedman, R. Richart, and R. Vande Wiele (Eds.), *Sex Differences in Behavior*. New York: Wiley, 1974.

Kroeber, A. L. Psychosis or social sanction. *Character and Personality*, 1940, **8**, 204–215.

Kuhn, T. S. *The Structure of Scientific Revolutions*. Chicago: University of Chicago Press, 1970.

Lang, T. *The Difference between a Woman and a Man*. New York: Bantam, 1973.

LeGuin, U. Is gender necessary? *In* V. N. McIntyre and S. J. Anderson (Eds.), *Aurora: Beyond Equality*. Greenwich, Conn.: Fawcett, 1976, 130–139.

LeGuin, U. *The Left Hand of Darkness*. New York: Walker, 1969.

Lev-Ran, A. Gender-role differentiation in hermaphrodites. *Archives of Sexual Behavior*, 1974, **3**, 391–424.

Lewis, M. Early sex differences in the human: Studies of socioemotional development. *Archives of Sexual Behavior*, 1975, **4**, 329–336.

Lewis, M., and Weintraub, M. Sex of parent X Sex of child: Socioemotional development. In R. Friedman et al. (Eds.), *Sex Differences in Behavior*. New York: Wiley, 1974.

Lillie, F. R. Biological introduction. *In* E. Allen (Ed.), *Sex and Internal Secretions*. Baltimore: Williams and Wilkins, 1932.

Lopata, H. Z. Review Essay: Sociology. *Signs*, 1976, **2**, 165–176.

Lowie, R. H. *The Crow Indians*. New York: Farrar and Rhinehart, 1935.

Lyon, M. F. Sex chromatin and gene action in mammalian X-chromosome. *American Journal of Human Genetics*, 1962, **14**, 135.

Lurie, N. O. Winnebago berdache. *American Anthropologist*, 1953, **55**, 708–712.

Maccoby, E. (Ed.). *The Development of Sex Differences*. Stanford: Stanford University Press, 1966.

Maccoby, E., and Jacklin, C. *The Psychology of Sex Differences*. Stanford: Stanford University Press, 1974.

Malinowski, B. *The Sexual Life of Savages* (3rd ed.). London: George Routledge and Sons, 1932.

Martin, M. K., and Voorhies, B. *Female of the Species.* New York: Columbia University Press, 1975.

Matter of Fernandez, *New York Law Journal.* 3/15/76, p. 12, col. 2.

McClintock, M. Menstrual synchrony and suppression. *Nature,* 1971, **229,** 244–245.

McIlwraith, T. F. *The Bella Coola Indians.* Toronto: University of Toronto Press, 1948, Vol. 1.

McKenna, W. *The Menstrual Cycle, Motivation, and Performance.* Unpublished doctoral dissertation, City University of New York, 1974.

Mead, M. *Sex and Temperament in Three Primitive Societies.* New York: William Morrow, 1935.

Mead, M. Cultural determinants of sexual behavior. In W. C. Young (Ed.), *Sex and Internal Secretions.* Baltimore: Williams and Wilkins, 1961, Vol. 2.

Mehan, H., and Wood, H. *The Reality of Ethnomethodology.* New York: Wiley-Interscience, 1975.

Miller, J. B. (Ed.). *Psychoanalysis and Women.* Baltimore: Penguin, 1973.

Millet, K. *Sexual Politics.* New York: Doubleday, 1970.

Mischel, W. A social-learning view of sex differences in behavior. In E. Maccoby (Ed.), *The Development of Sex Differences.* Stanford: Stanford University Press, 1966.

Mischel, W. Sex-Typing and Socialization. In P. H. Mussen (Ed.), *Carmichael's Manual of Child Psychology.* New York: Wiley, 1970, Vol. 2.

Money, J. Letter to the editor. In Sagarin, E., 1975.

Money, J., and Brennan, J. G. Sexual dimorphism in the psychology of female transsexuals. *Journal of Nervous and Mental Disorders,* 1968, **147,** 487–499.

Money, J., and Ehrhardt, A. *Man and Woman/Boy and Girl.* Baltimore: Johns Hopkins Press, 1972.

Money, J., Hampson, J. L., and Hampson, J. G. An examination of some basic sexual concepts: The evidence of human hermaphroditism. *Bulletin of the Johns Hopkins Hospital,* 1955, **97,** 301–319.

Money, J., and Lewis, V. Q., genetics, and accelerated growth: Adrenogenital syndrome. *Bulletin of the Johns Hopkins Hospital,* 1966, **118,** 365–373.

Money, J., and Ogunro, C. Behavioral sexology: Ten cases of genetic male intersexuality with impaired prenatal and pubertal androgenization. *Archives of Sexual Behavior,* 1974, **3,** 181–206.

Money, J., and Tucker, P. *Sexual Signatures.* Boston: Little, Brown, 1975.

Morris, D. *The Naked Ape.* New York: McGraw-Hill, 1967.

Muensterberger, W. Perversion, cultural norm, and normality. In S. Lorand (Ed.), *Perversions: Psychodynamics and Therapy.* London: Ortolan Press, 1965.

Newton, E. *Mother Camp*. Englewood Cliffs, N.J.: Prentice-Hall, 1972.

Oakley, A. *Sex, Gender, and Society*. New York: Harper Colophon, 1972.

Opler, M. E. *An Apache Life Way*. New York: Cooper Square Pub., 1965.

Opler, M. E. Anthropological and cross-cultural aspects of homosexuality. In J. Marmor (Ed.), *Sexual Inversion: The Multiple Roots of Homosexuality*. New York: Basic Books, 1965.

Orne, M. On the social psychology of the psychological experiment: With particular reference to demand characteristics and their implications. *American Psychologist*, 1962, **17**, 776–783.

Ounstead, C., and Taylor, D. *Gender Differences: Their Ontogeny and Significance*. Edinburgh: Churchill Livingstone, 1972.

Paige, K. Women learn to sing the menstrual blues. *Psychology Today*, 1973, **7** (4), 41–46.

Parlee, M. B. *Diurnal, Weekly, and Monthly Mood Cycles in Women and Men*. Paper delivered at the 84th annual convention of the American Psychological Association, Washington, D.C., September 1976.

Parsons, E. C. The Zuni: Lá Mana. *American Anthropologist*, 1916, **18**, 521–528.

Pauly, I. B. The current status of the change of sex operation. *Journal of Nervous and Mental Disorders*, 1968, **147**, 460–471.

Pauley, I. B. Female transsexualism: Part I. *Archives of Sexual Behavior*, 1974, **3**, 487–507.

Pelto, P. J. *Anthropological Research: The Structure of Inquiry*. New York: Harper and Row, 1970.

Person, E. Some new observations on the origins of femininity. In J. Strouse (Ed.), *Women and Analysis*. New York: Grossman, 1974.

Piaget, J. *The Origins of Intelligence in Children*. New York: International Universities Press, 1952.

Prince, V. Sex vs. gender. In D. Laub and P. Gandy (Eds.), *Proceedings of the Second Interdisciplinary Symposium on Gender Dysphoria Syndrome*. Stanford: Stanford University Med. Center, 1973.

Raymond, J. Transsexualism: The ultimate homage to sex role power. *Chrysalis*, 1977, **1**(3), 11–23.

Rebecca, M., Hefner, R., and Oleshansky, B. A model of sex-role transcendence. *Journal of Social Issues*, 1976, **32**, 197–206.

Reichard, G. *Social Life of the Navajo Indians*. New York: Columbia University Press, 1928.

Reinisch, J. Fetal hormones, the brain, and human sex differences: A heuristic integrative review of the recent literature. *Archives of Sexual Behavior*, 1974, **3**, 51–90.

Reinisch, J., and Karow, W. Prenatal exposure to synthetic progestins and estrogens-Effects on human development. *Archives of Sexual Behavior*, 1977, **6**, 257–288.

Rekers, G. A., and Lovass, O. I. Behavioral treatment of deviant sex-role behavior in a male child. *Journal of Applied Behavior Analysis*, 1974, **7**, 173–190.

Rensberger, B. Jello test finds lifelike signal. *New York Times*, March 6, 1976, p. 50.

Rose, R. M., Gordon, T. P., and Bernstein, I. S. Plasma testosterone levels in the male rhesus: Influences of sexual and social stimuli. *Science*, 1972, **178**, 643–45.

Rosenberg, B., and Sutton-Smith, B. *Sex and Identity*. New York: Holt, Rinehart, and Winston, 1972.

Rosenthal, R. *Experimenter Effects in Behavioral Research*. New York: Appleton-Century-Crofts, 1966.

Rubin, G. The traffic in women: Notes on the "political economy" of sex. *In* R. Reiter (Ed.), *Toward an Anthropology of Women*. New York: Monthly Review Press, 1975, pp. 157–210.

Rubin, J. Z., Provenzano, F. J., and Luria, Z. The eye of the beholder: Parents' views on sex of newborns. *American Journal of Orthopsychiatry*, 1974, **4**, 512–519.

Sagarin, E. Sex rearing and sexual orientation: The reconciliation of apparently contradicting data. *Journal of Sex Research*, 1975, **11**, 329–334.

Schneider, D. M. *American Kinship: A Cultural Account*. Englewood Cliffs, N.J.: Prentice Hall, 1968.

Seavey, C. A., Katz, P. A., and Zalk, S. R. Baby X: The effect of gender labels on adult responses to infants. *Sex Roles*, **1**, 1975, 103–109.

Sherfey, M. J. *The Nature and Evolution of Female Sexuality*. New York: Vintage, 1972.

Sherman, J. Problem of sex difference in space perception and aspects of intellectual functioning. *Psychological Review*, 1967, **74**, 290–299.

Skinner, A. *The Mascoutensor Prairie Potawatoni Indians*. Bulletin of the Public Museum of the City of Milwaukee, 1924, **6**: 1, 1–262.

Stevenson, M. C. *The Zuni Indians, Their Mythology, Esoteric Fraternities, and Ceremonies*. U.S. Bureau of American Ethnology, Annual Report, (1901/1902), **23**, 1–634.

Stoller, R. J. *Sex and Gender* (Vol. I). New York: J. Aronson, 1968.

Stoller, R. J. Facts and fancies: An examination of Freud's concept of bisexuality. *In* J. Strouse (Ed.), *Women and Analysis*. New York: Grossman, 1974.

Stoller, R. J. *Sex and Gender* (Vol. II). New York: J. Aronson, 1975.

Strouse, J. (Ed.). *Women and Analysis*. New York: Grossman, 1974.

Sulcov, M. B. *Transsexualism: Its Social Reality*. Unpublished doctoral dissertation, University of Indiana, 1973.

Sverdrop, H. N. *Hostundrafolket (With the People of the Tundra)*. Oslo: Gyldendal Norsk Forlag, 1938.

Thompson, S. K. Gender labels and early sex role development. *Child Development*, 1975, **46**, 339–347.

Thompson, S. K., and Bentler, P. M. The priority of cues in sex discrimination by children and adults. *Developmental Psychology*, 1971, **5**, 181–185.

Thorne, B. Is our field misnamed? Toward a rethinking of the concept "sex roles." *Newsletter American Sociological Association, section on sex roles*, Summer, 1976. 4–5.

Thorne, B., and Henley, N. (Eds.). *Language and Sex: Difference and Dominance*. Rowley, Mass.: Newbury House, 1975.

Toulmin, S. *Foresight and Understanding*. New York: Harper Torchbooks, 1961.

Wachtel, S. S., Koo, G. C., Breg, W. R., et al. Serologic detection of a Y-linked gene in XX males and XX true hermaphrodites. *New England Journal of Medicine*, 1976, **295**, 750–754.

Walzer, S., and Gerard, P. Social class and frequency of XYY and XXY. *Science*, 1975, **190**, 1228–1229.

Waters, J., and Denmark, F. The beauty trap. *Journal of Clinical Issues*, 1974, **4**, 10–14.

Webster's New Collegiate Dictionary. Springfield, Mass.: G. & C. Merriam, 1973.

Weideger, P. *Menstruation and Menopause*. New York: Knopf, 1976.

West, D. J. *Homosexuality*. Chicago: Aldine, 1967.

Westermarck, E. *The Origin and Development of the Moral Ideas*. London: Macmillan, Vol. 2, 1917.

Westman, J., and Zarwell, D. Traumatic phallic amputation during infancy. *Archives of Sexual Behavior*, 1975, **4**, 53–64.

Whorf, B. L. *Language, Thought, and Reality*. New York: The Technology Press and John Wiley and Sons, 1956.

Winick, C. *The New People*. New York: Pegasus, 1968.

Wittgenstein, L. *Philosophical Investigations*. New York: Macmillan, 1953.

Yorburg, B. *Sexual Identity: Sex Roles and Social Change*. New York: Wiley-Interscience, 1974.

Zimmerman, D., and West, C. Sex roles, interruptions, and silences in conversation. In B. Thorne and N. Henley (Eds.), *Language and Sex: Difference and Dominance*. Rowley, Mass.: Newbury House, 1975.

Zuger, B. Comments on "gender role differentiation in hermaphrodites." *Archives of Sexual Behavior*, 1975, **4**, 579–581.

AUTHOR INDEX

SUBJECT INDEX

231